D1045498

Loneliness

Also by Gerald A. Arbuckle, SM

Strategies for Growth in Religious Life
*Out of Chaos**
*Earthing the Gospel**
Grieving for Change
*Refounding the Church**
From Chaos to Mission
*Healthcare Ministry**
Dealing with Bullies
Confronting the Demon
Violence, Society, and the Church
Crafting Catholic Identity in Postmodern Australia
A 'Preferential Option for the Poor'
Laughing with God
Culture, Inculturation, and Theologians
Humanizing Healthcare Reforms
*Catholic Identity or Identities?***
The Francis Factor and the People of God
Intentional Faith Communities in Catholic Education
Fundamentalism at Home and Abroad

*USA Catholic Press Award
**USA Association of Catholic Publishers Award, 2014

Loneliness

Insights for Healing in a Fragmented World

Gerald A. Arbuckle, SM

ORBIS BOOKS
Maryknoll, New York 10545

Founded in 1970, Orbis Books endeavors to publish works that enlighten the mind, nourish the spirit, and challenge the conscience. The publishing arm of the Maryknoll Fathers and Brothers, Orbis seeks to explore the global dimensions of the Christian faith and mission, to invite dialogue with diverse cultures and religious traditions, and to serve the cause of reconciliation and peace. The books published reflect the views of their authors and do not represent the official position of the Maryknoll Society. To learn more about Maryknoll and Orbis Books, please visit our website at www.maryknollsociety.org.

Copyright © 2018 Gerald A. Arbuckle.

Published by Orbis Books, Maryknoll, New York 10545-0302.

All rights reserved.

No part of this publication may be reproduced or transmitted in any form or by any means, electronic or mechanical, including photocopying, recording, or any information storage or retrieval system, without prior permission in writing from the publisher.

Scripture quotations are from the New Revised Standard Version of the Bible, copyright © 1989 by the National Council of the Churches of Christ in the USA. All rights reserved.

Queries regarding rights and permissions should be addressed to: Orbis Books, P.O. Box 302, Maryknoll, NY 10545-0302.

Manufactured in the United States of America
Manuscript editing and typesetting by Joan Weber Laflamme.

Library of Congress Cataloging-in-Publication Data

Names: Arbuckle, Gerald A., author.
Title: Loneliness : insights for healing in a fragmented world / by Gerald A.
    Arbuckle, SM.
Description: Maryknoll : Orbis Books, 2018. | Includes bibliographical
    references and index.
Identifiers: LCCN 2018008365 (print) | LCCN 2018021763 (ebook) | ISBN
    9781608337552 (e-book) | ISBN 9781626982895 (pbk.)
Subjects: LCSH: Loneliness—Religious aspects—Christianity.
Classification: LCC BV4911 (ebook) | LCC BV4911 .A73 2018 (print
    DDC 248.8/6—dc23
LC record available at https://lccn.loc.gov/2018008365

For Anthony Maher—
practical theologian par excellence

Contents

Acknowledgments

My particular thanks to Robert Ellsberg and Jill O'Brien for accepting on behalf of Orbis Books this book for publication; Maria Angelini, porduction coordinator; members of the community at Campion Hall, Oxford University, for providing me with a congenial atmosphere where the planning and research for this book took place; Suzanne Greenwood, CEO of Catholic Health Australia, for permission to use material previously published in my book *A "Preferential Option for the Poor": Application to Catholic Health and Aged Care Ministries in Australia* (pp. 22-34); and Thomas Ryan, SM, who patiently read and corrected my grammar, as well as at times offered wise comments on the text. These people, however, are in no way responsible for the book's inadequacies.

Introduction

Turn to me and be gracious to me, for I am lonely and afflicted.

—Psalm 25:16

The frequency and intensity of loneliness are not only underestimated but the lonely themselves tend to be disparaged.

—Robert S. Weiss, Loneliness

The hearts of many people are gripped by fear and desperation, even in the so-called rich countries.

—Pope Francis, *Evangelii Gaudium*

Loneliness is an inescapable and painful fact of human experience. St. Teresa of Calcutta believed that loneliness, often accompanied by despair and hopelessness, is *the* virulent affliction in the West.[1] In the United States, for example, it is estimated that "27–28 percent of the population feel lonely, an increase in the order of 3 to 7 percent over the last 20 years."[2] And among "middle-aged and older Americans, rates of loneliness have jumped from 14 percent in the 1970s to over

---

[1] See Mother Teresa of Calcutta, *A Simple Path* (London: Edbury Press, 1995), 83; see also Lori C. Bohm, "Introduction," in *Loneliness and Longing: Conscious and Unconscious Aspects*, ed. Brent Willcock, Lori C. Bohm, and Rebecca C. Curtis (New York: Routledge, 2012), 1–9.

[2] John T. Cacioppo, as interviewd by Olga Khazan, "How Loneliness Begets Loneliness," *The Atlantic* (April 6, 2017).

40 percent today."[3] In England loneliness is considered so serious that it has created an entire national Campaign to End Loneliness.[4] Loneliness is not only afflicting adults. It is on the rise among teenagers. As noted in *The Economist*, "Whether it is a consequence of phones, intrusive parenting, an obsessive focus on future job prospects or something else entirely, teenagers seem lonelier than in the past."[5]

Global Disease

Because of the impact of globally turbulent economic, social, and political forces, this disease is fast becoming entrenched in all parts of the world. It is now a worldwide pandemic affecting all age groups and cultures, some more than others.[6] Communities are fragmenting. Once-comforting personal and cultural identities are disintegrating as people lose their connectedness with each other and with their past.[7] Loneliness exists where it did not before.

Yet worse than fragmentation are the increasing polarizations in society that further increase loneliness, especially for those who feel powerless to act. Consider the enormous inequalities that widen the gulf between the rich and poor. Pope Francis writes:

> We fail to see that some are mired in desperate and degrading poverty, with no way out, while others have not the faintest idea of what to do with their possessions. In practice, we continue to tolerate that some consider themselves more human than others, as if they had been born with greater rights. (*Laudato Si'*, no. 90)

---

[3] Michael Harris, *Solitude: In Pursuit of a Singular Life in a Crowded World* (London: Random House, 2017), 32.

[4] Khazan, "How Loneliness Begets Loneliness."

[5] "The Youth of Today," *The Economist* (January 13, 2018), 52. The report further comments: "Some Western countries are beginning to look like Japan and South Korea, which struggle with a more extreme kind of social isolation in which young people become virtual hermits."

[6] See Khazan, "How Loneliness Begets Loneliness."

[7] See Thomas H. Eriksen and Elizabeth Schober, eds., *Identity Destabilised: Living in an Overheating World* (London: Pluto Press, 2016), 1–19.

And in *Evangelii Gaudium* he states:

> Today, everything comes under the laws of competition and the survival of the fittest, where the powerful feed upon the powerless. As a consequence, masses of people find themselves excluded and marginalized; without work, without possibilities, without any means of escape. (no. 53)

In a world of increasing fundamentalist movements of "wall-builders, door-slammers and drawbridge-raisers,"[8] huge groups of people are being pushed aside—unwanted, powerless, and lonely.

Increasingly, polarizing divisions based on differences in race or skin color are rising to the surface in some nations. The United States, for example, "has rarely undergone a period of racial regression as acute as that which accompanied Mr. Trump's assumption of the presidency."[9] Even as president-elect, Donald Trump intensified the loneliness of millions of unauthorized immigrants by insisting that they would be immediately deported.[10] Growing anxiety about global wars between the polarizing, great powers of the world is only adding to people's loneliness: "Conflict on a scale and intensity not seen since the second world war is once again plausible."[11] Then, there are the growing divides within the churches. Even in the once-united Roman Catholic Church there are hushed rumors of possible schisms. Fragmentation and polarization deepen feelings of loneliness in both individuals and societies.

Aims of This Book

This book is an exercise in practical theology. The first part of each chapter focuses on particular aspects of contemporary loneliness viewed mainly through the lens of cultural anthropology. The second

---

[8] "Liberty Moves North," *The Economist* (October 29, 2016), 11.

[9] "Workers Disunited," *The Economist* (August 19, 2017), 29.

[10] See "Trump's Plan to Purge the Nation," editorial, *Times Digest* (November 18, 2016), 1.

[11] "The Next War: The Growing Danger of Great-Power Conflict," *The Economist* (January, 25, 2018), 9.

part is a scriptural reflection on this material. The chapter ends with discussion questions to aid readers in pastorally responding to the issues raised in the two sections. By their responses, readers will hopefully contribute in small or not so minor ways to lessening debilitating loneliness within themselves and in the world around them. This work is written to assist a wide range of people in their various ministries, such as bishops, theologians, pastoral workers, educators, and college students.

Robert Weiss, a seminal sociological authority on loneliness, reported in 1975 that "research on the nature of ordinary loneliness is as yet fragmentary." There is a dearth of studies, he notes, into "the reasons for loneliness, the conditions under which loneliness occurs, or the subjective experience of loneliness."[12] Since this was written, research has of course progressed.[13] However, there has been little exploration into the cultural causes of loneliness. This book is a response to that missing area of study. The unique contribution of cultural anthropology is its ability to identify the cultural triggers that create loneliness. Anthropology's primary focus is the study of culture, the symbols, myths, and rituals that give meaning to people's lives, and the disheartening loneliness of people when culture breaks apart.[14]

Understanding Loneliness

Loneliness, a deeply emotional experience, involves painful feelings of not belonging and disconnectedness from and abandonment by others. It is an agonizing sense of emptiness or desolation that many of us have experienced at some time or other—when a loved one dies, for example, during a sudden illness, at the loss of employment, or upon the realization that we are aging and less mobile. "Loneliness," writes Jean Vanier, "is a feeling of being unworthy, of not being able to cope in the face of a universe that seeks to work against us."[15] The

---

[12] Robert S. Weiss, *Loneliness: The Experience of Emotional and Social Isolation* (Boston: MIT Press, 1975), 16.

[13] For contemporary references see Willcock, Bohm, and Curtis, *Loneliness and Longing*.

[14] See Gerald A. Arbuckle, *Culture, Inculturation, and Theologians: A Postmodern Critique* (Collegeville, MN: Liturgical Press, 2010).

[15] Jean Vanier, *Becoming Human* (New York: Paulist Press, 1998), 33.

lonely feel of little importance or value in other people's lives. Listen to the cry of the psalmist: "You have caused my companions to shun me" (Ps 88:8). Lonely people yearn for the intimacy of social connection that is denied them.

Yet loneliness is more than this emotion. The lonely person is more likely to become physically ill. Current multidisciplinary investigation has concluded that chronic loneliness is "a serious risk factor for illness and early death, right alongside smoking, obesity and lack of exercise."[16] It has been estimated that living with air pollution increases one's possibility of dying early by 5 percent; being obese, 20 percent; misuse of alcohol, 30 percent; but the impact of loneliness, 45 percent.[17] Researchers conclude that "loneliness not only alters behavior, but shows up in measurements of stress hormones, immune function, and cardiovascular function. Over time, these changes in physiology are compounded in ways that may be hastening millions of people to an early grave."[18] Peter Shmigel comments on an Australian national survey of loneliness: "Loneliness wears down your resilience to crisis. . . . When you are lonely . . . your resilience drops. As resilience drops, risk of suicide increases."[19]

Thus, in summary, there are two qualities that mark loneliness. People feel excluded and rejected. At the same time they yearn to be intimately accepted or included by others. As the psalmist pleads: "My whole being yearns and pines for Yahweh's courts" (Ps 84:2). But loneliness is not only an individual experience—it is a cultural one as well. Entire cultures can feel politically, economically, or socially oppressed and marginalized by more powerful groups. Such was the distressing experience of the Israelites in exile:

---

[16] John T. Cacioppo and William Patrick, *Loneliness: Human Nature and the Need for Social Connection* (New York: W. W. Norton, 2008), 108. See also Timothy B. Smith and Julianne Holt-Lunstad, "Social Relationships and Mortality Risk: A Meta-Analytic Review" *PLoS Med* 7/7 (July 27, 2010): 7.

[17] See J. Holt-Lunstad, M. Baker, T. Harris, D. Stephenson, and T. B. Smith, "Loneliness and Social Isolation as Risk Factors for Mortality: A Meta-Analytic Review," *Perspectives on Psychological Science* 10/2 (2015): 227–37; Smith and Holt-Lunstad, "Social Relationships and Mortality Risk."

[18] Cacioppo and Patrick, *Loneliness*, 5.

[19] Peter Shmigel, "Eighty-two percent of Australians Say Loneliness Is Increasing, Lifeline Survey Finds," *The Guardian* (September 27, 2016).

> By the waters of Babylon—
> there we sat down and there we wept
> when we remembered Zion. (Ps 137:1)

The exiled Israelites have had their symbols of cultural identity de-stroyed—the Temple, the kingship. Their resulting loneliness now slips into despair:

> Our tormenters asked us for mirth. . . .
> How could we sing the Lord's song
> in a foreign land? (Ps 137:3–4)

To belong, to be accepted, to share common values, to partici-pate—these are fundamental needs we all have as persons and cul-tures. To be denied these needs as individuals and cultures is to feel abandoned, lonely. When human dignity is overlooked and hope is in danger of becoming a forgotten word, people and cultures are thrown into loneliness. Such is the experience of many oppressed minority cultural groups today. Little wonder there is so much sadness and loneliness!

Loneliness and Solitude

> *I have never found a companion that was*
> *so companionable as solitude. . . . I went*
> *into the woods . . . to front only the essential*
> *facts of life.*
> —HENRY DAVID THOREAU

Loneliness is not the same as depression. They are "two distinct dimensions of experience. . . . [They] are in many ways opposites. . . . Depression makes us apathetic. Whereas loneliness urges us to move forward."[20] Hope is integral to loneliness (this apparent paradox will be addressed later in the book). Sadly, however, hope is absent

---

[20] Cacioppo and Patrick, *Loneliness*, 83.

in depression. Loneliness is also not the same as being alone. One can be alone without feeling loneliness. An ancient Christian hymn exquisitely articulates this; the traveler is alone but feels no loneliness because he is connected to God's abiding presence:

> Alone with none but thee, my God,
> I journey on my way:
> what need I fear when thou are near,
> O King of night and day?[21]

Nor is loneliness the same as solitude, but without the accompanying gift of solitude it can quickly turn into despair. Loneliness is an emotion that is mainly *imposed* on people by others and their cultures, but solitude is something people *choose*. Loneliness in intentional solitude has a kind of beautiful, bittersweet quality; loneliness in imposed aloneness is merely bitter.

The poet William Wordsworth explains the difference between loneliness and solitude in his legendary poem *I Wandered Lonely as a Cloud*. He describes his experience of walking in the beautiful scenery of the Lake District of northern England. He feels lonely, but his attention is suddenly drawn to "A host of Daffodils . . . fluttering and dancing in the breeze." With this his loneliness evaporates as he ponders within himself their inspiring beauty. It is not just the splendor of the flowers that inspires him to react positively; the beauty has its source in some higher power. He has hope that whenever he again feels lonely the memory of this experience will once more remove his sadness. He will reconnect with the beauty of nature, again evoking within himself great inner peace. Susan O. Weisser writes her impressions of the poem: "Wordsworth's metaphor of self as the wandering cloud . . . is a kind of alienation from humanity and the world, an inability to enter into it fully. The experience of the sublime beauty of the daffodils . . . allows the poet to recall his connection to a kind of community, the community of nature."[22]

---

[21] The hymn is attributed to the Irish monk St. Columba (521–97).

[22] Susan O. Weisser, "Loneliness, Emptiness, and Wordsworth's 'Bliss of Solitude' in Life and Literature," in Willcock, Bohm, and Curtis, *Loneliness and Longing,* 118.

Solitude is thus the ability to be alone, to be connected with one's inner self, without the emptiness and yearning of loneliness. Solitude provides the connection with what loneliness yearns for. Solitude is the entering into oneself to know oneself better and thus to learn how best to react positively to the loneliness that has been forced on one. Henri Nouwen describes it this way: "By slowly converting our loneliness into a deep solitude, we create the precious space where we can discover the voice telling us about our inner necessity—that is, our vocation."[23] Loneliness is the yearning to connect. Solitude is an act of connecting with oneself, thus fostering hope that one can connect with others in communion beyond oneself.

Consider the psalmist. He is in the depth of loneliness. He asks himself why this is the case and what he must do to relieve the loneliness:

> Why are you cast down, O my soul,
>   and why are you disquieted within me?

He answers the question:

> Hope in God; for I shall again praise him,
>   my help and my God. (Ps 42:5)

In the solitude hope restores meaning and energy to his loneliness. Once more the psalmist reflects on his loneliness:

> Even though I walk through the darkest valley,
>   I fear no evil;
> for you are with me;
>   your rod and your staff—
>   they comfort me. (Ps 23:4)

On a previous occasion the psalmist was in painful loneliness. But God came to his aid, and he is filled with hope that whatever loneliness lies ahead God again will be at his side to relieve it.

---

[23] Henri Nouwen, *Reaching Out* (New York: Doubleday, 1975), 27.

From Loneliness to Action

Ove is the central figure in a deeply moving yet humorous novel *A Man Called Ove*.[24] He is a grumpy fifty-nine-year-old who frequently attempts to kill himself following his beloved wife's death, but each time he fails because someone crosses his path who is in need of help. As he connects with his inner self and sees he must act, he responds creatively and with compassion. Eventually he dies, apparently in his sleep, leaving behind him people who have been touched and enlivened by his simple love and compassion. Surely this is at the very heart of the gospel message: love thy neighbor as thyself.

Dorothy Day, co-founder of the Catholic Worker Movement and leader for more than a half century in crusades of social justice, is right: "We have all known loneliness, and we have learned that the only solution is love that comes with community."[25]

As St. Teresa of Calcutta says: "The only cure for loneliness, despair, and hopelessness is love."[26] In fact, as Lori Bohm notes, "love is a mirror image of loneliness."[27]

Day teaches us yet another truth—to give to others in love and justice in order to pull down the walls of loneliness that exclude people demands in us a change of heart.

> The greatest challenge of the day is: how to bring about a revolution of the heart, a revolution which has to start with each one of us? When we begin to take the lowest place, to wash the feet of others, to love our brothers with that burning love, that passion, which led to the cross, then we can truly say, "Now I have begun."[28]

---

[24] Fredrik Backman, *A Man Called Ove* (New York: Washington Square Press, 2014).

[25] Dorothy Day, *The Long Loneliness: The Autobiography of the Legendary Catholic Social Activist* (New York: HarperOne, 1980), 286.

[26] Mother Teresa of Calcutta, *A Simple Path*, 83.

[27] Bohm, "Introduction," 8.

[28] Dorothy Day, *Loaves and Fishes* (Maryknoll, NY: Orbis Books, 1997), 215.

To change our heart ultimately requires that we be in touch with our inner selves in solitude. Pope Francis describes the challenge to connect with others through compassion and justice in this way. In light of the Good Samaritan parable, he calls for

> the revolution of tenderness. . . . Tenderness means to use our eyes to see the other, our ears to hear the other, to listen to the children, the poor, those who are afraid of the future. To listen also to the silent cry of our common home, the planet, of our sick and polluted earth. Tenderness means to use our hands and our heart to comfort the other, to take care of those in need. . . . A single individual is enough for hope to exist, and that individual can be you. And then there will be another "you," and another "you," and it turns into an "us." . . . When there is an "us" there begins a revolution [of tenderness].[29]

Overview of the Book

There are seven chapters in this book. Chapter 1, "Pondering the Meaning and Power of Loneliness," defines and initially explains the meaning of loneliness from a cultural anthropological perspective. However, since loneliness is a complex reality that can be viewed through many lenses, this anthropological explanation will be followed by a summary of other approaches to loneliness: psychoanalytical, philosophical, religious, and scriptural. Each discipline throws some additional light on the nature and power of loneliness.

Chapter 2, "Triggers of Exclusion and Mentors," describes various cultural actions that exclude people from society and the various kinds of loneliness that result.

Chapter 3, "Cultures of Inveterate Individualism," describes the founding mythology of the United States, its emphasis on individualism to the detriment of the common good, and its role in causing loneliness in individuals and groups.

Chapter 4, "Poverty as a Trigger of Loneliness," focuses on poverty as the catalyst for the social exclusion and loneliness of individu-

---

[29] Pope Francis, Address to TED (Technology, Entertainment, and Design), April 20, 2017.

als and cultures. Inaccurate assessments of and defective attitudes to poverty unvaryingly result in bad policies and practices that can intensify alienation and loneliness.

Chapter 5 is entitled "'You are Not Us!' The Loneliness of Strangers." There are abundant fundamentalist movements in the West, in the realms of economics, politics, nationalism, and religion. Rightwing, populist, anti-immigrant movements are on the rise in Europe, the United States, Australia, and elsewhere. One thing common to all fundamentalist movements is that they set up rigid inclusion/exclusion boundaries. Either one is *in* or *out*—that is, excluded and cast into the liminality of loneliness. However, rigid boundaries are not a characteristic of fundamentalist movements alone. On the contrary, any dominant society holds the power to exclude people unjustly from belonging and force them into loneliness.

Chapter 6, "Tribalism, Polarization, and Loneliness: Healing in Society and Church," examines tribalism and its resulting loneliness in two institutions—hospitals and the church—that are both mired in a culture of chaos that triggers loneliness for many of the people they serve and employ. Rivalries can become so entrenched that they lead to a bitter polarization that makes it difficult, and at times impossible, for institutions to realize their mission of helping people. Chapter 6 explores this dynamic of tribalism and its link to pervasive loneliness.

Chapter 7, "Authors in the Church: Triggers of Loneliness," is devoted to the loneliness inherent in an author's vocation in the church (that of a theologian and particularly a social scientist), whose task is to critique the church's culture from the perspective of various disciplines.

"Conclusion: Pastoral Responses" summarizes the basic theme of the book and refers to its relevant chapters while suggesting how readers can respond pastorally to the individual and cultural effects of loneliness.

1

Pondering the Meaning and Power of Loneliness

You have made us for yourself, O Lord, and
our heart is restless until it rests in you. . . . I
drew in my breath and now pant for you, and
I feel a hunger and thirst for you.
—St. Augustine, *Confessions*

This chapter explains:

- Loneliness from a cultural anthropological perspective.
- Types of loneliness; what loneliness is and is not.
- A psychoanalytical approach to loneliness.
- Philosophical theories of loneliness.
- The perspective of St. John of the Cross.
- Loneliness and solitude in the scriptures.

Loneliness from a Cultural Anthropological Perspective

Since loneliness is a *subjective* feeling it is hard to pin down or to define. It can be a feeling of isolation, of not belonging, emptiness, a feeling that no one cares, no one notices. Loneliness is a feeling of deprivation that painfully but hopefully turns outward for fulfillment.[1] When people struggle to describe loneliness, there is a common theme of *yearning* to belong, a *thirsting* to be connected, a *restlessness,* a *panting*—to use St. Augustine's expression—at last to belong, to build a satisfying relationship, to feel valued, to feel there is a pervading meaning in one's life, if only it could be found. Yearning or thirsting for a relationship is frequently and poignantly expressed by the psalmist:

> O God, you are my God, I seek you,
>   my soul thirsts for you; . . .
> as in a dry and weary land where there is no
>   water. (Ps 63:1)

This chapter's purpose is to define and initially explain the meaning of loneliness from an anthropological perspective, followed by a summary of other disciplinary approaches. I suggest that, as readers ponder these different explanations, they may need, at times, to pause. Some incident in their own lives may suddenly take on richer meanings in light of the material. Although loneliness is ubiquitous throughout all of life's various stages, there are particular moments and life circumstances that make it more prevalent and poignant.

Loneliness: An Anthropological Definition

Loneliness, whether experienced by individuals, cultures, or subcultures, has two intimately related qualities. First, as a consequence of some triggering action (such as racism, ethnicity, religion, poverty, age, gender, bereavement, inequalities, fundamentalism, or disabilities), people feel abandoned, disconnected, and excluded from belonging. Second, they have a hope-inspired yearning to belong to and to be connected with important others or desirable things. The intensity of the loneliness depends on personal circumstances and,

---

[1] Eric Ostrov and Daniel Offer, "Loneliness and the Adolescent," in *Anatomy of Loneliness*, ed. J. Hartog, J. R. Audy, and Y. A. Coen (New York: International Universities Press, 1980), 184.

more particularly, on changing cultural and historical realities. Hope, as noted earlier, is integral to keeping loneliness from slipping into depression or despair.

Charlotte Brontë, a Cultural Example

The life and writings of Charlotte Brontë (1816–54), the brilliant nineteenth-century novelist, offer initial insights into the nature of loneliness. With the exception of a short period prior to her death, she led a mainly lonely life.[2] At one particular point while living in Brussels in the early 1840s, when her personal loneliness felt especially intense, she describes her emotions: "If I could always keep up my spirits—and never feel lonely or long for companionship or friendship or whatever they call it, I should do very well."[3] Significantly, her loneliness was triggered by her contact with a markedly different culture that she caustically described as "the national character of the Belgians" as represented by the girls she was teaching; they were "singularly cold, selfish, animal and inferior. . . . Their principles are rotten to the core."[4] Again, writing to Ellen Nussey in England, she said: "I know you, living in the country can hardly believe it is possible life can be monotonous in the centre of a brilliant capital like Brussels, but so it is."[5] Her reactions are symptoms of what we today call culture shock. This feeling of loneliness, together with the yearning for relationship and a sense of belonging, infuses Charlotte's novels: "The distinctive atmosphere that pervades the lives of [her] heroines is loneliness, a loneliness almost intolerable."[6]

---

[2] See S. N. Singh, *Charlotte Brontë: A Thematic Study of Her Novels* (Delhi: Mittal Publications, 1987), 3; John Pfordresher, *The Secret History of Jane Eyre: How Charlotte Brontë Wrote Her Masterpiece* (New York: W. W. Norton, 2017).

[3] Charlotte Brontë, letter to Ellen Nussey (1817–97), Charlotte's lifelong friend, as quoted in Claire Harman, *Charlotte Brontë: A Life* (Falkirk: Penguin Books, 2016), 165.

[4] Ibid., 145.

[5] Ibid., 172.

[6] Walter Allen, *The English Novel* (Harmondsworth: Penguin Books, 1958), 192.

What, then, do the life and novels of Charlotte Brontë, and of other writers, teach us about the nature of loneliness?

Loneliness Seeks Connections with Others, Solitude with Oneself

Both loneliness and solitude are about yearning to make connections, but there is an important difference. Solitude is a yearning to connect with one's inner self in order to deepen self-knowledge; it prevents one from becoming emotionally and spiritually overwhelmed by the pressures and desires of others. So there must be a balance between the yearning to be connected to others and the inner journey that is solitude. Charlotte Brontë brilliantly used her novels' characters to decipher her own experiences of loneliness and solitude. For psychiatrist Anthony Storr, the yearning to connect with one's inner self "promotes self-understanding and contact with those inner depths of being which elude one in the hurly-burly of day-to-day life."[7] Solitude calls for courage to go against society's disdain of those who seek it, as they are often thought to be rather odd and antisocial. Yet solitude can be a frightening, even terrifying, experience. It means blocking off the noisy chattering world within and around oneself. Not easy! As Michael Harris writes, "The naked self . . . is a bogeyman. Yet facing up to it can eventually become a numinous encounter."[8] St. Augustine, at one point, describes how he avoided the rich experience of solitude by escaping into worldly pleasures: "And see, you were within and I was in the external world and sought you there, and in my unlovely state I plunged into those lovely created things which you made. . . . The lovely things kept me far from you."[9] Thomas Merton, when reflecting on the need for solitude in contemporary times, writes that "all men need enough solitude in their lives to enable the deep inner voice of their own true self to be heard. . . . If a man is constantly exiled from his own home, locked out of his own solitude, he ceases to be a true person."[10]

---

[7] Anthony Storr, *Solitude* (New York: Free Press, 2005), 34.

[8] Michael Harris, *Solitude: In Pursuit of a Singular Life in a Crowded World* (London: Random House, 2017), 37.

[9] St. Augustine, *Confessions*, Bk. 10, Ch. 27, v. 38.

[10] Thomas Merton, cited by Sara Maitland, *How to Be Alone* (London: Macmillan, 2014), 120.

Various Types of Loneliness

I explore the varieties of loneliness more fully in subsequent chapters; a summary of types as described by particular writers suffices for now. *Transient* loneliness is part of the human condition; it is caused, for example, by cultural changes, the death of a loved one, a change in one's job, or adjustment to aging or sickness. This type of loneliness will eventually disappear. *Chronic* loneliness, conversely, is constant, permanent, and beyond one's control.[11] However, despite the permanent quality of chronic loneliness, one still has hope that keeps the yearning for acceptance alive.

Brontë's loneliness tended to be more transient than chronic, though it lasted for considerable periods of time. However, in our contemporary postmodern cultures, with their rapid and complex changes, there is a constant danger that most people will suffer not just from temporary loneliness but risk becoming chronically and pathologically lonely—and such loneliness can lead to significant psychological stress, ill health, and social dysfunction. John Cacioppo and William Patrick wisely comment:

> We can all slip in and out of loneliness. Feeling lonely at any particular moment simply means that you are human. . . . The need for meaningful social connection, and the pain we feel without it, are defining characteristics of our species. Loneliness becomes an issue of serious concern only when it settles in long enough to create a persistent, self-reinforcing loop of negative thoughts, sensations, and behaviors.[12]

This type of negative loop is often indicative of *pathological* loneliness, an impairment that renders a person incapable of yearning for effective connectedness, due to its lasting and penetrating nature.

Closed loneliness sets rigid boundaries to prevent any possible connections with certain peoples or groups. True, contemplative solitude is feared lest it lead to a questioning of these inflexible frontiers.

---

[11] See Jeanne L. George, "Loneliness in the Priesthood," *Human Development* 10/4 (1989): 12.

[12] John T. Cacioppo and William Patrick, *Loneliness: Human Nature and the Need for Social Connection* (New York: W. W. Norton, 2008), 7.

Alternatively, *open* loneliness is an ongoing, enriching interaction between solitude and the desire to connect to people and new insights. In *parasocial* loneliness, unsuccessful attempts to build or maintain human relationships lead to a desire for connection with surrogates. John Cacioppo and William Patrick speak of "parasocial relationships," in which a lack of human connectedness causes people to seek substitutes in nonhuman objects, such as pets, television characters, or computers: "Pet owners project all sorts of human attributes onto their animal companions, and elderly people who have pets appear to be buffered somewhat from the negative impact of stressful life events."[13]

Loneliness is one of the four existential anxieties—together with death, fear, and meaninglessness. Irwin Yalom describes the unavoidable anxiety and estrangement of people who feel that they are all alone in the world and that no one really understands their distinctive difficulties or needs.[14]

Loneliness Is Not Synonymous with Being Alone or with Boredom

People can be alone and not experience loneliness simply because they know, despite their geographical isolation, that they are in significant relationships. Loneliness is the distressing experience of knowing that desired relationships do not exist. It is "the exceedingly unpleasant and driving experience connected with inadequate discharge of the need for human intimacy."[15] Robert S. Weiss describes the same point in his study of loneliness in more positive terms: "All loneliness syndromes would seem to give rise to yearning for the relationship—an intimacy, a friendship, a relationship with kin—that would provide whatever is at the moment insufficient. . . . And all may induce impatience or irritability with relationships that seem to impede access to the desired relationship."[16] Loneliness also is not the same as *boredom*, which is a feeling of weariness and restlessness that

---

[13] Ibid., 256–57.

[14] See Irwin D. Yalom, *Existential Psychotherapy* (New York: Basic Books, 1980).

[15] Harry Stack Sullivan, *The Interpersonal Theory of Psychiatry* (New York: W. W. Norton, 1953), 290.

[16] Robert S. Weiss, *The Experiences of Emotional and Social Isolation* (Cambridge, MA: MIT Press, 1975), 18.

arises when persons have no interest in making immediate connections with their environment. For example, people making long train journeys may become weary as the scenery becomes less and less interesting. This explains what the philosopher Arthur Schopenhauer means when he describes boredom as "a tame longing without any particular object."[17]

A Response to a Relational Lack

Along with a feeling of emptiness there is an impatient craving for supportive and intimate relationships that give a sense of meaning to life. "Loneliness," writes Robert Weiss, "is caused not by being alone but by being without some definite needed relationship or set of relationships. . . . It is a response to relational deficit."[18] Psychologist Carl Rogers defines loneliness as

> the lack of any relationship in which we communicate our real experiencing, and hence our real self, to another. When there is no relationship in which we are able to communicate both aspects of our divided self, our conscious facade and our deeper level of experiencing, then we feel the loneliness of not being in real touch with any other human being.[19]

As noted above, loneliness is not merely or even necessarily being alone.

Cultural Change Can Trigger Loneliness

Cultures provide us with identities and the consequent sense of belonging. Charlotte Brontë had become thoroughly inculturated into the English way of life, though she had not been so conscious of this before visiting Brussels. Culture change, or even contact with different cultures, can trigger loneliness (see Chapter 2). Moreover, Brontë's distressing description of the inferior role of women in English culture

---

[17] Arthur Schopenhauer, cited by Manoush Zomorodi, *Bored and Brilliant* (London: Macmillan, 2017), 16.

[18] Weiss, *The Experiences of Emotional and Social Isolation*, 17, 18.

[19] Carl Rogers, *A Way of Being* (Boston: Houghton Mifflin, 1980), 28.

illustrates that cultures, not just individuals, can collectively experience the isolation or marginalization that accompanies loneliness. Women in her time were culturally made to feel lonely, banished as they were from domestic, economic, social, and political power structures by the dominant patriarchal culture. Women were forced to feel lonely because they were denied the chance to integrate into society and to relate to men on an equal basis. For women, loneliness was culturally imposed.

Creative Potential Rather than Depression or Despair

Loneliness can be the catalyst for creativity; it is not synonymous with depression or despair. "In loneliness there is a drive to rid oneself of one's distress by integrating a new relationship or regaining a lost one; in depression there is instead a surrender to it."[20] Hope is lost. But people who are lonely are hope filled. They confidently and creatively yearn for new relationships, even though these relationships are still denied them. Loneliness is kept alive by hope, which is the ability to see an alternative and more confident future in any context and to discover the energy to initiate changes either now or later. "Whereas loneliness urges us to move forward, depression holds us back."[21]

Writer Olivia Laing recently published a book describing through examples the experience of loneliness in New York.[22] In today's world, she believes, loneliness is increasingly inadmissible, a taboo stage whose confession seems destined to cause others to turn and flee. People are more accepting of anger, envy, guilt, and greed. To be lonely is to have failed, according to the rules of a shrinking world.[23] Analyzing her own experience and that of other city-dwellers Laing makes a subtle case that loneliness, while inherently personal, is also collective. She argues that "loneliness is by no means a wholly worthless experience, but rather one that cuts right to the heart of what we value and what we need. Many marvelous things have emerged from the lonely city: things forged in loneliness, but also things that

---

[20] Weiss, *The Experiences of Emotional and Social Isolation*, 15.

[21] Cacioppo and Patrick, *Loneliness*, 83.

[22] See Olivia Laing, *The Lonely City: Adventures in the Art of Being Alone* (New York: Picador, 2016).

[23] See comments by Sara Maitland, *How to Be Alone* (London: Macmillan, 2014), 15–32.

function to redeem it."[24] In order to cure loneliness, she says, we need to learn how to befriend ourselves and understand that "many things that seem to afflict us as individuals are in fact a result of larger forces of stigma and exclusion, which can and should be resisted."[25]

Novelist Virginia Woolf also views loneliness positively as the chance to know oneself better, but she quickly acknowledges it also can be a painful experience: "Often down here I have entered into a sanctuary . . . of great agony and always some terror. . . . If I could catch the feeling, I would: the feeling of the singing of the real world, as one is driven by loneliness and silence from the habitable world."[26]

This positive view of loneliness is evident in Charlotte Brontë's heroines. Because in Victorian England women were still regarded as inferior to men and as a family liability, Brontë deliberately makes her lonely characters "poor, plain and parentless . . . both passionate and patient to make themselves as component and independent as their male counterparts."[27] Brontë used these heroines to protest the cultural and personal subservience of women. In other words, Brontë would not let her loneliness develop into depression. She used her loneliness constructively, by seeking justice for women.

Place: Potential Source of Belonging

Charlotte Brontë had a strong sense of belonging to a particular place—her village of Haworth, surrounded by moors. She pined for it whenever she was away from it.[28] Maori people in New Zealand speak of their *turangawaewae*, translated as "a place to put one's feet." No matter how big or small their piece of land may be, it remains a strong source of belonging because it has a special connection to the land handed down by their ancestors; the spirits of these ancestors remain there to this day. To be away from this land is to be lonely.[29]

---

[24] Laing, *The Lonely City,* 8.

[25] Ibid., 281.

[26] Virginia Woolf, *The Diary of Virginia Woolf, Vol. 3, 1925–30,* ed. Anne Oliver Bell (London: Hogarth Press, 1980), 260.

[27] Singh, *Charlotte Brontë,* 4.

[28] See Harman, *Charlotte Brontë,* 23–49.

[29] See Natacha Gagne, *Being Maori in the City: Indigenous Everyday Life in Auckland* (Toronto: University of Toronto Press, 2013), 77, 88–89.

David Goodhart, while researching the origins of Brexit (the British movement out of the European Union), distinguished between the "Somewheres" and the "Anywheres." The former, who supported Brexit, are the marginalized who feel desperately "at home" in parts of Britain that have been economically and politically left behind. Their deprived towns and cities paradoxically provide them with a feeling of belonging. They yearn to have these places restored, to be as they were in the past. Charlotte Brontë would have understood them. By contrast, the "Anywheres" are financially secure and mobile; hence, they are not wedded to a place for a feeling of belonging. Their education, secure income, and jobs allow for mobility and provide their source of belonging. They yearn to have symbols of success always available to them. A similar division is to be found in the United States, the "Somewheres" being significant supporters of Donald Trump.[30]

Loneliness: A Psychoanalytical Viewpoint

Psychoanalysts provide further insights into the nature and pains of loneliness. Some of the views expressed reinforce the anthropological definition of loneliness, while others diverge. However, Frieda Fromm-Reichmann (1889–1957), a widely known authority on the psychology of loneliness, has complained that psychiatrists have avoided researching and writing on loneliness. She proffers a reason: "Loneliness seems to be such a painful, frightening experience that people will do practically everything to avoid it. This avoidance seems to include a strange reluctance on the part of psychiatrists to seek scientific clarification on the subject."[31] Lori C. Bohm also notes: "Despite the familiarity and grave impact of loneliness, it is rarely explicitly addressed in the psychoanalytic literature."[32]

---

[30] See David Goodhart, *The Road to Somewhere: The Populist Revolt and the Future of Politics* (London: Hurst, 2017).

[31] Frieda Fromm-Reichmann, "Loneliness," *Psychiatry* 22 (1959): 1. She creatively writes of the loneliness caused by deafness, a disability that she herself progressively experienced. Despite the terrifying nature of loneliness that deafness can bring, she still hoped that ways could eventually be found to alleviate the resulting isolation. See Ann-Louise S. Silver, *International Forum of Psychoanalysis* 5 (1996): 39–46.

[32] Lori C. Bohm, "Introduction," *Loneliness and Longing: Conscious and Unconscious Aspects*, ed. Brent Willcock, Lori C. Bohm,, and Rebecca

Nonetheless, psychoanalysts generally agree that loneliness involves a longing for relationships, but they differ over the effectiveness of this longing.

American psychoanalyst Daniel Goldin identifies two major psychoanalytical schools of thought regarding the nature of loneliness: *pathological* loneliness, or loneliness as a mental disease; and *existential* loneliness.[33] He quotes from Fromm-Reichmann: "I think that Binswanger has come nearest to a philosophical and psychiatric definition of loneliness when he speaks of it as 'naked existence,' 'mere existence,' and 'naked horror,' and when he characterizes lonely people as being 'devoid of any interest in any goal.'"[34] People are left pathologically and emotionally paralyzed, powerless, and feeling utterly unable to communicate or relate to others.[35]

On the other hand, authors who emphasize the importance of existential loneliness, rather than pathological loneliness, conclude that loneliness does not solely result "from personal trauma or as an accident of culture" but "see it as an inevitable aspect of existence."[36] These authors belong to one of two groups: the optimistic camp or pessimistic camp. Authors who belong to the former camp assert that "acts of imagination at once *require* loneliness and *mitigate* its pain."[37] Thus, when Elizabeth Allured significantly emphasizes the creative relational potential of loneliness, she is equivalently describing the role of solitude:

Coleman Curtis (Hove: Routledge, 2012), 1. Nicky Hayes notes that loneliness was "not really studied by psychologists until relatively recently. During the 1970s and 1980s, however, psychologists made considerable headway in understanding some of the many aspects of loneliness." *Foundations of Psychology*, 3rd ed. (London: Thomson Learning, 2000), 459.

[33] See Daniel Goldin, "Review of *Loneliness and Longing: Conscious and Unconscious Aspects*" (Hove: Routledge, 2012), ed. Brent Willcock, Lori C. Bohm and Rebecca Coleman Curtis, in *International Journal of Psychoanalytic Self Psychology* 8 (2013): 231–42.

[34] Frieda Fromm-Reichmann, cited by Goldin in "Review of *Loneliness and Longing*," 234. Ludwig Binswanger (1881–1966) was an early Swiss psychiatrist and a pioneer in the field of existential psychology.

[35] See Roger Frie, "The Living Experience of Loneliness: An Existential-Phenomenological Perspective," in Willcock, Bohm, and Curtis, *Loneliness and Longing*, 34.

[36] Goldin, "Review of *Loneliness and Longing*," 236.

[37] Ibid., 239.

The capacity to be alone with one's self as an adolescent or adult depends upon an adequately internalized attachment relationship to the human caretaker. The ability to enjoy one's loneliness may also depend upon an adequately developed and internalized relationship with the nonhuman world. . . . Whether it is called the vision quest by Native peoples in the Americas, the Buddhist's seclusion in a meditation cave, the prophet Jeremiah's time in the wilderness, or St. Francis' deep communion with animal and plant life near Assisi, *something* is occurring across traditions and times. Perhaps this something includes developing a different kind of object relationship with the nonhuman world.[38]

Likewise, when Susan Ostrov Weisser describes loneliness "as a kind of challenge, and of being alone as a great privilege," she is at the same time insisting on the importance of solitude. Once she had been frightened of loneliness, the feeling of being abandoned— but now, she has come to appreciate the transformative value of solitude. The sting of loneliness is under control.[39] Weisser quotes Eric Ostrov and Daniel Offer: "Loneliness is a feeling of deprivation that painfully, *but hopefully,* turns outward for fulfilment."[40]

Melanie Klein on Loneliness

Authors who belong to the pessimistic school of loneliness, however, claim that loneliness is the yearning for an unachievable object. Melanie Klein sees internal loneliness as "the result of a ubiquitous yearning for an unattainable perfect internal state. Such loneliness, which is experienced to some extent by everyone, springs from paranoid and depressive anxieties which are derivatives of the infant's

---

[38] Elizabeth Allured, "Lonely for the Other Mother: Nature and the Relational Fourth," in Willcock, Bohm, and Curtis, *Loneliness and Longing*, 253, 254–55.

[39] See Susan Ostrov Weisser, "Loneliness, Emptiness, and Wordsworth's 'Bliss of Solitude' in Life and Literature," in Goldin, "Review of *Loneliness and Longing*," 117, 118.

[40] Ibid., 113. Psychoanalyst Carl Winnicott claimed that loneliness and anxiety do not occur in healthy individuals because they are able to recall the parental, caregiving experience of childhood. See Harris, *Solitude,* 38.

psychotic anxieties."[41] Loneliness for Klein embraces a yearning for a romanticized relationship between an infant and its mother, but such a relationship of wholeness can never be achieved because "the infantile ego is dominated by splitting mechanisms, dividing its impulses into good and bad and projecting them outward into the world, separating it too into good and bad objects."[42] On the one hand there is the yearning for security and on the other the desire to protect the good ego from harmful urges. The weakened ego cannot integrate these desires because there is the constant fear that the destructive impulses within and external to oneself will overwhelm what is good. Integration of these opposing forces is highly problematic. Klein argues that "full and permanent integration is never possible for some polarity between life and death instincts always persists and remains the deepest source of conflict. Since full integration is never achieved . . . this continues as an important factor in loneliness."[43] Klein continues:

> It is generally supposed . . . that loneliness can derive from the conviction that there is no person or group to which one belongs. This not belonging can be seen to have a much deeper meaning. However much integration proceeds, it cannot do away with the feeling that certain components of the self are not available because they are split off and cannot be regained. Some of these split-off parts . . . are projected into other people, contributing to the feeling that one is not in full possession of one's self, that one does not fully belong to oneself or, therefore, to anyone else. The lost parts too, are felt to be lonely.[44]

In brief, the ultimate source of loneliness, for Klein, is the lifelong battle between love-giving relationships and violence.[45] The desire for full acceptance and for personal and social integration remains even though such realities are impossible. Klein makes the significant point that "when feelings of loneliness are strongly experienced there is a

---

[41] Melanie Klein, "On the Sense of Loneliness," *Writings of Melanie Klein: 1946–1963* (New York: The New Library of Psychoanalysis, 1984), 300.

[42] Laing, *The Lonely City,* 174.

[43] Klein, "On the Sense of Loneliness," 302.

[44] Ibid.

[45] See Meira Likierman, *Melanie Klein: Her Work in Context* (London: Bloomsbury, 2002), 196.

great need to turn to external objects, since loneliness is partially allayed by external relations."[46] The external objects may be people or things.

Klein also offers reflections on the tensions of old age. The best way to tolerate it is "gratitude for past pleasures without too much resentment because they are no longer available."[47] As death approaches, human persons need to cherish the good in order to prevent a primeval disdain of an unjust world overwhelming them. She notes pragmatically that sometimes "preoccupation with the past" is a defense adopted "in order to avoid the frustrations of the present."[48] Sometimes longing for the past connotes the desire to hold onto good memories, but at other times, tedious ponderings about the past represent a defense against accepting present problems. Klein's writing thus concludes that human beings are, by their very nature, destined to be lonely. "Although loneliness can be diminished or increased by external influences, it can never be completely eliminated, because the urge towards integration, as well as the pain experienced in the process of integration, spring from internal sources which remain powerful throughout life."[49]

Loneliness:
Philosophers' Views

Significant philosophers have explored the purpose of loneliness, and they conclude that experiences of loneliness are necessary "for self-awareness and for coming to terms with one's essential aloneness in the world."[50] Some philosophers, however, are not so positive about loneliness. Loneliness and alienation have been proposed as "the pathologic reciprocals of freedom and individualism by a series of western writers."[51] The influence of Friedrich Nietzsche (1844–1900)

---

[46] Klein, "On the Sense of Loneliness," 312.

[47] Melanie Klein, *Envy and Gratitude* (London: Hogarth Press, 1975), 311.

[48] Ibid.

[49] Ibid., 313.

[50] George, "Loneliness in the Priesthood," 12.

[51] Frank Johnson, "The Western Concept of Self," *Culture and Self: Asian and Western Perspectives*, ed. Anthony J. Marsella, George DeVos, and Francis L. Hsu (New York: Tavistock, 1985), 120.

on the development of self-centered individualism in postmodernity is profound. As an anti-Christian philosopher, he revolted against the dominant morality in the Western world that had its roots in the Judeo-Christian tradition. For him, the world has no intrinsic meaning and individuals can either accept this—which he would see as a mark of weakness—or create their own meaning and impose it on others. The more one creates meaning for oneself by dominating others, the more one is able to develop a sense of identity. But the cost of this individualism and drive to dominate is intense personal loneliness. The struggle must never cease. The Christian ideal of loving one's neighbor is a mark of mediocrity; those who are too weak to dominate others hide their timidity behind proclamations of love and justice for others.[52] The sign of progress for an individual is the ability to dominate others for one's own benefit: "To see others suffer does one good, to make others suffer even more . . . is a . . . principle to which even the apes might subscribe. . . . Without cruelty there is no festival."[53]

Søren Kierkegaard (1813–55), a poet and philosopher, has had a profound impact on the history of last century's theology and philosophy. Despite the immense density of his writings, Kierkegaard simply wanted to awaken in his readers an experience similar to his own, which had revealed the meaning of life. He wanted to plumb "the depths of what it is to be a human being; one who lives with anxiety and aspiration, and who trusts and rejoices in God, finding in that relationship the resources that make for wholeness."[54] In order to articulate his own experience of loneliness he lived alone and in increasing poverty; marriage, he believed, would distract him from fully experiencing the richness of loneliness.[55] He wrote that "the greater the degree of consciousness [of oneself] the more intensive the

---

[52] See Jonathan Glover, *Humanity: A Moral History of the Twentieth Century* (London: Jonathan Cape, 1999), 11–17; and Gerald A. Arbuckle, *Violence, Society, and the Church: A Cultural Approach* (Collegeville, MN: Liturgical Press, 2004), 165.

[53] Friedrich Nietzsche, quoted by Jonathan Glover, *Humanity: A Moral History*, 16–17.

[54] Quoted in Daphne Hampson, *Kierkegaard: Exposition and Critique* (Oxford: Oxford University Press, 2013), 1.

[55] Ibid., 303–4.

despair."[56] Patricia Huntingdon explains this text: "The more aware we become, the more intensive our responsibility to live well; but the more we refuse a potentially new order of awareness, the deeper we fall into a sickness of spirit. Loneliness is such a disease."[57] Authentic self-consciousness should lead to one's need of God. Then the disease of loneliness is removed.

Martin Heidegger (1889–1976), a particularly complex philosopher, asserted that loneliness is the most authentic experience because it permits human persons to contemplate Being, thus allowing them to escape the "herd-like" atmosphere around them. Interactions with others, what Heidegger calls the "they," tempt us to a dishonest predicament in which we have become alienated.[58] Loneliness can relate us to the world, forming the connection more robustly, but at the same time it can make the world more remote, leaving us feeling totally abandoned.

Gabriel Marcel (1889–1973), also an existentialist and follower of Kierkegaard, avoided the emphasis on despair in loneliness made evident in Heidegger by asserting that the first choice that is constitutive of our personality is the acceptance of the self as created by God, in whom it will find its rest and joy. The basic free act, in his opinion, is to say yes to grace. The weakness of our freedom fills this yes with humble and fearful anguish but also with confident hope. The aim of life, therefore, is to render testimony to God by faithfulness to one's interior yearning.

More recent philosophers, such as atheistic existentialists Jean-Paul Sartre (1905–80) and Albert Camus (1913–60), were deeply influenced by the traumatic events of the Second World War and the growing fears of nuclear disaster. For these existentialists every person in our contemporary world is confronted with the "naked concerns of human existence—suffering and death, loneliness and

---

[56] Søren Kierkegaard, *The Sickness unto Death: A Christian Psychological Exposition for Upbuilding and Awakening*, ed. Howard V. Hong and Edna H. Hong (Princeton, NJ: Princeton University Press, 1980), 42.

[57] Patricia Huntington, "Loneliness and Innocence: A Kierkegaardian Reflection on the Paradox of Self-Realization," *Continental Philosophy Review* 39 (2006): 416.

[58] See Martin Heidegger, *Being and Time,* trans. John Macquarrie and Edward Robinson (San Francisco: Harper & Row, 1962).

dread, guilt, conflict, spiritual emptiness and ontological insecurity, the void of absolute values or universal contexts, the sense of cosmic absurdity, the frailty of human reason, the tragic impasse of the human condition."[59] It is an intensely bleak world that logically ends in despair. Sartre famously declared "'existence comes before essence,'[60] namely, that there is no predetermined or God-given blueprint for human existence; human beings create themselves by choosing the self each wishes to become."[61] An authentic life is impossible by following the collective "herd" and its beliefs and concerns, but only by living out of a profoundly personal self—that is, out of the recognized and accepted loneliness of an individuality that finds itself in a murky and meaningless world. We are destined to search for meaning as intensely lonely individuals, yet that meaning can never be attained because our powers of reasoning are inherently faulty. As Richard Tarnas writes, for philosophers like Sartre and Camus, "to be authentic one had to admit, and choose freely to encounter, the stark reality of life's meaninglessness. Struggle alone gave meaning."[62] We cannot trust anyone to relieve our loneliness. For Sartre, we must in our hopeless search for meaning accept the fact that bleak loneliness is our destiny in life.

Loneliness and Solitude:
St. John of the Cross

Religious writers frequently concentrate their reflections on loneliness and claim that "periods of loneliness are necessary for self-awareness and for coming to terms with one's essential aloneness in the world."[63] That is, *loneliness for the most part is something imposed on a person by others. Solitude is a personal choice.* Without hope-inspiring solitude, loneliness cannot be sustained and creative. The finest exponent

---

[59] Richard Tarnas, *The Passion of the Western Mind* (New York: Ballantine Books, 1991), 389.

[60] Jean-Paul Sartre, *Existentialism and Humanism* (London: Methuen), 26.

[61] David Law, "Existentialism," *The Oxford Companion to Christian Thought,* ed. Adrian Hastings, Alistair Mason, and Hugh Pyper (Oxford: Oxford University Press, 2000), 227.

[62] Tarnas, *The Passion of the Western Mind,* 389.

[63] George, "Loneliness of the Priesthood," 12.

of this insight is St. John of the Cross.[64] John's fearful loneliness was triggered by his horrible experience of being kidnapped and imprisoned at the age of thirty-nine by members of his own congregation because they feared his calls for their radical reform.[65] Then, thirteen years later, he was also falsely charged by them for libel. Having been rejected by people who should have been his friends, John embraces solitude in faith. He begins to write about his experiences.

He views life as a pilgrimage in which the pilgrim begins to feel joy in God's presence and in prayer. Then suddenly the soul is cast into intense loneliness, a darkness in which there is no pleasure to be found in God or the world and human friendship. The soul is at an impasse. No merely human effort, says St. John, no matter how logically prepared it may be, can break this impasse. It must be God focused, where only *desire* matters. The person yearns in solitude for a "genuine and thoroughly intimate partnership with God."[66]

Dedicated persons will be confronted with two impasses or periods of inner darkness in which they are called by God: first, for the purification of their senses; and then, for the purification of their spirit. Speaking of the first phase of darkness, St. John writes: "This small gate is the dark night of sense, in which the soul is despoiled and denuded . . . that it may be capable of walking along the narrow road which is the night of the spirit."[67] These bleak transitional periods, in which the soul is called to forsake attachments that hold it back from receiving the transforming presence of God's love, are called by St. John the dark nights of the soul.

They are times of intense loneliness. People feel they are at an impasse. And the usual human solutions to problems of this nature—for example, connecting with friends—no longer work. These difficult experiences paradoxically have the potential to be catalysts for unimagined new life—but the constant danger is that people will reject

---

[64] See Gerald A. Arbuckle, *The Francis Factor and the People of God: New Life for the Church* (Maryknoll, NY: Orbis Books, 2015), 154–59.

[65] See Richard P. Hardy, *The Life of St. John of the Cross* (London: Darton, Longman, and Todd, 1987), 61–98.

[66] Gillian T. W. Ahlgren, *Enkindling Love: The Legacy of Teresa of Avila and John of the Cross* (Minneapolis: Fortress Press, 2016), 71.

[67] John of the Cross, "The Dark Night," trans. Kieran Kavanaugh and Otilio Rodriguez, in *The Collected Works of St. John of the Cross* (Washington, DC: ICS Publications, 1979), 320.

these opportunities by engaging in distracting activities and may even take refuge in despair and cynicism.[68] People must be patient while in the darkness of solitude.

The second phase, the dark night of the spirit, is more excruciating than that of the senses. It is noted for its particularly agonizing experience of loneliness, alienation, and isolation, in which the participant finds it very difficult to pray and fulfill everyday tasks.[69] In this darkness, where faith alone supports us, we cry out to God for help as we struggle to abandon every attachment that holds us back from continuing our pilgrim vocation.

Yet there is consolation. St. John writes:

> It should be known that if a person is seeking God, his Beloved is seeking him much more. . . . God is the principal agent in this matter, and that He acts as the blind man's guide who must lead it by the hand to the place it does not know how to reach (to supernatural things of which neither its intellect, nor will, nor memory can know the nature).[70]

The person must say yes to the experience and let God create the empty space. There is a choice point: flee back to a familiar past, be paralyzed by the chaos, or move forward in hope by letting go attachments to what has gone before. To attempt to escape back to the past, or to be held captive by the chaos, only leads to increased frustration.[71] It is the gift of hope that will keep the soul focused and striving to be open to the loving presence of God. "Hope," writes John, "empties and withdraws the memory from all creature possessions . . . and fixes it on that for which it hopes."[72] Only hope can release the soul from its attachments to the past. God leads us by the hand "to discover in ourselves a purely passive power, a pure capacity

---

[68] See Constance Fitzgerald, "Impasse and the Dark Night," in *Living with Apocalypse: Resources for Social Compassion*, ed. Tilden H. Edwards (San Francisco: Harper & Row, 1984), 94.

[69] John of the Cross, "The Dark Night," 335.

[70] John of the Cross, "The Living Flame of Love," in *The Collected Works of St. John of the Cross*, 620–21.

[71] See John of the Cross, "The Ascent of Mount Carmel," in *The Collected Works of St. John of the Cross*, 70.

[72] John of the Cross, "The Dark Night," 381.

to be attracted, a desire for God which, being no longer grounded in the desire to possess, to dominate, and to destroy, can be the desire for God himself."[73] Only then can God "find" us, creating *our true self* and an even deeper solitude.

Theological Reflection: Loneliness and Solitude in the Scriptures

> I think, dear child, the trouble and the long loneliness you hear me speak of is not far from me. . . . The pain is great, but very endurable, because He who lays on the burden also carries it.[74]

Recall that loneliness is frequently caused by culture, but solitude—the way to enrich experiences of loneliness—is a personal choice. Solitude, for the Christian, is the time and space wherein to be alone for the purpose of realizing a closer union with God. Below are four New Testament readings that illustrate how loneliness and solitude interact.

The Storm: Disciples React to Loneliness

The incident in which the disciples are caught in a life-threatening storm aptly illustrates their need to stop grappling with their loneliness in mere human terms but rather through the eyes of faith in Jesus Christ and his mission. To achieve this shift, the disciples must choose solitude, even when their instincts are to call out for Jesus to save their lives.[75]

In the story Jesus climbs into the boat and is followed by his disciples (Matt 8:23) and the journey begins, but suddenly the boat is "swamped by the waves" (Matt 8:24). Then the paradox—Jesus, like

---

[73] Denys Turner, *The Darkness of God: Negativity in Christian Mysticism* (Cambridge: Cambridge University Press, 1999), 236.

[74] Mary Ward, cited in Dorothy Day, *The Long Loneliness* (New York: HarperCollins, 1952), frontispiece. Mary Ward (1585–1645) was an English nun.

[75] This section is adapted from Gerald A. Arbuckle, *Laughing with God: Humor, Culture, and Transformation* (Collegeville, MN: Liturgical Press, 2008), 76.

Jonah in a similar situation, is asleep despite the noise, water, and tossing of the boat. Jesus is awakened by the desperate cries of the disciples, for they are perishing (Matt 8:25). The disciples not only doubt the promise of Jesus, but they rebuke him for what they see as his failure to care for them (Mark 4:38). Jesus then uses the occasion to teach them a fundamental lesson: if they truly have faith they will not doubt his concern (Matt 8:26). And they must desire to be connected with Jesus through hope and faith. They must remember that Jesus is man *and* God. And to prove his point, he calms the storm.

Implicit in the account are the different reactions of two biblical figures—Jonah and Jesus. The first handles sudden loneliness in purely human terms. Jonah is sent by Yahweh to warn Nineveh of the consequences of its great evil and its consequences, but he boards a ship to escape the task. He sees the task as too lonely and frightening. The storm hits the boat and he is thrown overboard by the crew because they believe he has caused their misfortune. Jonah eventually accomplishes his mission but remains reluctant to the end. He is everything that a true believer should not be, demonstrating the failure to contemplate the challenges of loneliness in faith and hope; self-centered, nasty, and relishing the destruction of Nineveh. Jesus, however, is willing to carry out God's wishes without reluctance, for "something greater than Jonah is here" (Luke 11:32).

Gethsemane: Jesus Confronts Loneliness and Solitude

In the Garden of Gethsemane, Jesus is forced to confront his future. This triggers a short but painful period of loneliness and solitude as he reacts with fear, anxiety, and numbness.[76] Following the example of the lament psalms, Jesus does not camouflage or deny the sufferings he is to experience. Thus the evangelist Mark writes that as Jesus begins to pray he began "to be distressed and agitated" (Mark 14:33), but the English translation simply cannot convey the power of the Greek text. Words such as *horrified, shocked,* and *devastated* are still too weak to grasp what Mark is trying to say. The evangelist Luke also highlights the intensity of the loneliness of Jesus when he describes him praying

---

[76] This section adapted from Gerald A. Arbuckle, *The Francis Factor and the People of God: New Life for the Church* (Maryknoll, NY: Orbis Books, 2015), 204–5. See also David M. Stanley, *Jesus in Gethsemane: The Early Church Reflects on the Suffering of Jesus* (New York: Paulist Press, 1979).

with such earnestness that "his sweat became like great drops of blood falling down on the ground" (Luke 22:44). A little later Jesus describes it as "the power of darkness" overwhelming him (Luke 22:53).

The dramatic nature of his emotional reaction to this anticipated grief is further accentuated by the fact that when Jesus foretold his death previously, only the disciples had expressed anxiety and desolation. Peter rebuked Jesus for thinking of his coming death. Peter fears the loneliness that would result for him. The response of Jesus is filled with self-confidence, no hint of sadness: "Get behind me, Satan! For you are setting your mind not on divine things but on human things" (Mark 8:33). But now, in Gethsemane, Jesus confronts the harsh reality of his imminent scourging and death. This evokes in him the strong emotions of horror and fear, and the temptation to escape this shattering loneliness. Jesus experiences the absolute loneliness of a grief like that which was so poignantly described by the psalmist:

> There is no one who takes notice of me;
>   no refuge remains to me;
>   no one cares for me. (Ps 142:4)

An additional cause of his despondency is the failure of the disciples to remain empathetically alert and at prayer with him in his time of need. Three times he goes to them for the support of their friendship, to be again connected to people who love him. But they fail him. They remain asleep, uninterested in the pain of his journey and grieving. Finally, failing to reconnect with his companions, Jesus embraces his solitude and cries out to the Father with a vigorous hope that he will intervene to help him. The spirit of detachment remains throughout the text: "Father, if you are willing, remove this cup from me; yet, not my will but yours be done" (Luke 22:42). Turning to his Father in solitude, he recommits himself to his vocation and moves from holding back and hesitation to a position of surrender as he embraces his destiny. Having prayed and freed himself from clinging to the old security of companionship, Jesus is strengthened with new life to accept his death for the sins of the world in a fully conscious way.

Now Jesus encounters a freshness and vitality in his actions that contrast markedly with his earlier dreads. In hope, he now fully embraces the mission of the Father. He knows what the Father wishes of him, and he now has the inner strength to do it, so he commands his sleeping followers to wake up and come with him to face his betrayal. Energized, Jesus, on his own initiative, informs his captors-to-be that he is the one they want: "Then Jesus, knowing all that was to happen to him, came forward and asked them: 'Whom are you looking for?' They answered, 'Jesus of Nazareth.' Jesus replied, 'I am he'" (John 18:4–5). Loneliness remains, but it is now controlled by hope.

Road to Emmaus: Inner Conversion Calls for Solitude

As the two disciples meet the unrecognized Jesus on the road to Emmaus, they mirror the sadness of the wider community of disciples (Luke 24:13–25). When asked what is troubling them, the disciples freely and breathlessly express their grief to Jesus with anger and bewilderment because things have not turned out as they had desired: Jesus, their hoped-for political and revolutionary leader against the Roman oppressors, is dead. In their loneliness they yearn for something that cannot exist. Jesus, by his empathetic listening, wins their trust, recounts the founding story of their salvation, and challenges them to recognize and accept their loss and view the world from the perspective of his mission. They must now yearn in hope not for a worldly kingdom but for "a new heaven and a new earth" where "God himself will be with them. . . . Death will be no more . . . for the first things have passed away" (Rev 21:1, 3, 4). For this to happen, they must embrace solitude. Faith in Christ will open them to a community and a personal newness beyond human imagination as a result of Jesus's death and resurrection (Luke 24:25–32).

As they digest this message their loneliness is transformed and despair disappears: "Were not our hearts burning within us?" (Luke 24:32). Immediately they want to share their joy with others. "That same hour they got up and returned to Jerusalem" where "they told what had happened on the road" (Luke 24:33, 35).[77]

St. Paul: Cosmic Loneliness

The evangelist Paul in so many places directly or indirectly articulates what loneliness in this world means for himself personally as well as for all creation. In Romans 8 the entire cosmos is in loneliness;

---

[77] See Arbuckle, *Laughing with God*, 86–87.

the whole creation is yearning or groaning to be renewed through the death and resurrection of Christ. And hope is what keeps this loneliness focused and vibrant:

> For the creation waits with eager longing for the revealing of the children of God. . . . We know that the whole creation has been groaning in labor pains until now; and not only the creation, but we ourselves . . . groan inwardly while we wait for adoption, the redemption of our bodies. For in hope we were saved. (Rom 8:19–24)

This is part of a pattern in which the Trinity acts through the "three witnesses" of divine desire: the Holy Spirit yearning in creation; humanity; and each person of faith crying out, "Abba! Father!" These are all embraced in the Spirit's "alluring and comforting" into the life of the Son, such that "prayer, at its deepest, is God's, not ours."[78] "So if anyone is in Christ, there is a new creation: everything has passed away; see, everything has become new!" (2 Cor 5:17).

Summary

- Loneliness, from a cultural anthropological perspective, is the yearning for acceptance and connectedness when important others or desirable things are missing. Hope prevents loneliness from turning into despair.
- The faith-based quality of loneliness is splendidly expressed by the psalmist: "As a deer yearns for running streams, so I yearn/ for you, my God. I thirst for God, the living God;/ when shall I go to see the face of God?" (Ps 42:1–2, NJB).
- There are several types of loneliness, such as *closed* and *open*. The former sets rigid boundaries to prevent any possible connections with certain people or groups, and the latter is an ongoing enriching interaction between solitude and the desire to connect to people.

---

[78] Sarah Coakley, *God, Sexuality, and the Self: An Essay on the Trinity* (Cambridge: Cambridge University Press, 2013), 112–13.

- Loneliness is often caused by cultural changes, but solitude is a person's deliberate choice to deal positively with loneliness.

Reflection Questions

In the midst of the constant hurry and noise of contemporary society, the human spirit yearns for moments of stillness, quiet, and solitude. Find some moments today, however brief, when you are able to block out noise and distractions in order to be in touch with your inner self. While you do this, ponder these questions:

- What are you feeling in these moments?
- What do you fear in your loneliness?
- Which of the scripture readings mentioned above particularly appeals to you? Why?
- As you ponder your chosen scripture reading, what do you learn about how to respond positively to loneliness?
- After reading this chapter is there anything you need to do to change your life?

2

Triggers of Exclusion
and Mentors

*Both Brexit and Trump's election were un-
expected victories given a decisive tilt by
unhappy white working-class voters—motivated, it seems, more by cultural loss, related
to immigration and ethnic change, than economic calculations.*
  —David Goodhart, *The Road to Somewhere*

*Turn to me and be gracious to me,
I am lonely and afflicted.*
  —Psalm 25:16

This chapter explains:

- How culture provides people with a comforting sense of belonging.
- That when a culture breaks down, people are thrown into chaotic confusion.
- That people in chaotic experiences either seek to escape, become socially paralyzed, or embrace loneliness.
- How rituals of exclusion trigger phases of loneliness.

- That in loneliness, individuals and cultural groups need supportive mentors.
- Examples of loneliness and mentoring in the Old Testament.

The above observation by David Goodhart is particularly relevant. For several years over half of British people have approved of the following statement: "Britain has changed in recent times beyond recognition; it sometimes feels like a foreign country and this makes me feel uncomfortable."[1] People feel excluded from their own country; they have a sense of no longer belonging there, a feeling of cultural and individual loneliness. Why do they feel this way? Rollo May offers a vital clue: "*The loneliness of mythlessness is the deepest and least assuageable of all.* Unrelated to the past, unconnected with the future, we hang as if in mid-air."[2]

To appreciate the importance of this statement we need to clarify the meaning of culture because myths are at the heart of all cultures.[3] Myths give meaning to life. Without them we lose all sense of belonging and connectedness. We no longer have identities. We become culturally lonely. The British in question feel "uncomfortable" in their own country because their familiar myths no longer seem to be working. Their experience is a common one. This chapter looks closely at what triggers cultural loneliness and why mentors are important for guiding people back to a sense of belonging.

Example of Culturally Triggered Loneliness

In 1990 I was traveling back to Sydney in a commuter train. I was seated in the front coach reading a good novel while surrounded by strangers. As the train was climbing a steep hill we crashed into a stationary train with immediate tragic consequences causing several fatalities and multiple injuries to many passengers. I and those immediately beside me suffered minor injuries. Without any formal

---

[1] David Goodhart, *The Road to Somewhere: The Future of Revolt and the Future of Politics* (London: Hurst, 2017), 2.

[2] Rollo May, *The Cry for Myth* (New York: Delta, 1991), 99.

[3] See Gerald A. Arbuckle, *Culture, Inculturation, and Theologians: A Postmodern Critique* (Collegeville, MN: Liturgical Press, 2010), xix, 2.

introductions, we all began to converse with one another. Names were unimportant. Our different and set roles and statuses in society ceased to mean a thing. Faced with such a powerful force of nature, we had become conscious of our common fragile humanity. We shared some common fears: Would the coach catch fire? Would we roll over the cliff? As a fellow passenger said: "Suddenly I feel I am in a situation I cannot control. I am feeling a desperate sense of loneliness. Our orderly lives have been destroyed. I feel a yearning for safety from the perils that threaten us." It was a fear-evoking experience—a physical, psychological, spiritual shock. We had become powerless, vulnerable to forces beyond our control. Our comforting cultural symbols, myths, and rituals no longer gave us a sense of belonging. We had been thrown into a state of chaos. All predictability had evaporated. As individuals, and now as a group, we felt dreadfully lonely. This is what Rollo May means when he writes: "*The loneliness of mythlessness is the deepest and least assuageable of all.* Unrelated to the past, unconnected with the future, we hang as if in mid-air."[4]

Defining Culture

We need to unravel further the meaning and power of culture. Anthropologist Roger Keesing describes culture as a "system of shared ideas, a system of concepts and rules and meanings that underlie and are expressed in the way that humans live, not what they do and make."[5] Clifford Geertz in a similar way refers to culture as "the fabric of meaning in terms of which human beings interpret their experience and guide their actions."[6] For him, "Human behavior is seen as symbolic action," that is, action that is generated and interpreted according to "the fabric of meanings."[7] In this definition a culture is not primarily an entity but a process or a journey that is actively or pervasively at work, particularly in the unconscious of the group

---

[4] May, *The Cry for Myth,* 99.

[5] Roger M. Keesing, *Cultural Anthropology* (New York: Holt, 1981), 68–69.

[6] Clifford Geertz, "Ritual and Social Change: A Javanese Example," *American Anthropologist* 59/1 (1959): 33.

[7] Clifford Geertz, *The Interpretation of Cultures* (London: Hutchinson, 1973), 10.

and of individuals. It is a pattern of shared assumptions or values, expressed in its constituent parts—symbols, myths, and rituals—that have been invented, discovered or developed by a group as it relentlessly struggles to cope with problems of external adaptation and internal cohesion. Its primary function is to provide *felt meaning* or a sense of order in the process of living, because what we most fear as humans is chaos or disorder. In brief, a culture provides people with a sense of belonging.

Because a culture is essentially a living construct of meanings—encased primarily in symbols, myths, and rituals—the feelings of belonging to it are basically inaccessible to outsiders. For example, the experience of being culturally different or of confronting a history of prejudice and discrimination produces in a people a set of memories or feelings that are not easily shared with outsiders. A nonmember of a culture may gain some understanding from participation in the visible activities of the group, such as dances or food rituals, but the inner experiences and feelings of a cultural group are still difficult, if not impossible, to comprehend fully. In fact, these feelings are so deep within a culture that people find it difficult to identify and name them in their *own* culture. Often all they can say is: "We just feel we belong together," or, "We feel different from the people of another culture." Anthropologist Edward Hall aptly comments:

> Deep cultural undercurrents structure life in subtle but highly consistent ways that are not consciously formulated. Like the invisible jet streams in the skies that determine the course of a storm, these hidden currents shape our lives; yet their influence is only beginning to be identified.[8]

People are inescapably shaped by the culture and subcultures in which they live, work, and worship. Hall notes, "It is a mold in which we are all cast, and it controls our daily lives in many unsuspected ways."[9] Hall entitles his book on culture *The Silent Language*. Culture is so soundless that we do not know we are encased in it until suddenly we become aware that it no longer exists.

---

[8] Edward Hall, quoted in Philip R. Harris and Robert T. Moran, *Managing Cultural Differences* (Houston: Gulf Publisher, 1993), 264.

[9] See Edward Hall, *The Silent Language* (New York: Doubleday, 1959), 30.

A Definition of Culture

Culture may be defined as a pattern of meanings, encased in a network of symbols, myths, narratives and rituals, created by individuals and subdivisions, as they struggle to achieve their identities in the midst of the competitive pressures of power and limited resources in a rapidly globalizing and fragmenting postmodern world that instructs its adherents about what is considered to be the correct and orderly way to *feel*, *think*, and *behave*.[10]

This definition[11] has several advantages. First, a people's identity is so shaped by its culture that each individual can say: "When I meet a person from another culture, that person is meeting not just me but my culture also, though I may be unconscious of the fact." Second, it stresses that cultures are not static entities frozen in time, without internal conflict, closed to outside forces, but processes or journeys in which people strive to discover meaning in an ever-changing and often threatening milieu of limited resources. Third, it emphasizes that a culture shapes people's *emotional* responses to the world around them. It infuses the deepest recesses of the human group, and of

---

[10] Arbuckle, *Culture, Inculturation, and Theologians*, 17. This book extensively explains the nature and power of culture. Donald Palmer and Gemma McKibbin note that the Australian Royal Commission into Institutional Responses to Child Sexual Abuse uses a different definition of culture: "The conception understands culture to consist of content and form. Cultural content includes assumptions (most importantly, presumptions of fact regarding people's attitudes and behaviours), values and beliefs (most importantly, understandings regarding the virtue of alternative ways to think and act) and norms (expectations regarding how people should think and behave). Forms include artefacts and practices that symbolically convey cultural content." *Final Report: The Role of Organisational Culture in Child Sexual Abuse in Institutional Contexts* (December 2016), 6. The weakness of the definition is that it overlooks the *affective* aspects of a culture. An appreciation of these aspects is essential for understanding the power of grief that can haunt the lonely. See Arbuckle, *Culture, Inculturation, and Theologians*, 1–98.

[11] There is considerable confusion in theological and managerial literature about the definition of *culture*. This is unfortunate because inaccurate perceptions of and defective attitudes to cultures invariably result in bad theology and faulty managerial decisions and practices.

individuals, especially their feelings. Through a culture people feel an affective sense of belonging. That sense of belonging temporarily disintegrated for me at the moment of the train crash. The comment by psychoanalyst Erich Fromm, therefore, is particularly incisive. The "fact that ideas have an emotional matrix" is "of the utmost importance" as this is "the key to the understanding . . . the spirit of a culture."[12] Fourth, the definition emphasizes the struggle people have in negotiating personal and institutional identities. Cultures give us our identities; to lose our culture is to lose our identities. Nothing can be more emotionally demoralizing.

As an anthropological axiom, we can say that the interference with or destruction of the inner mythological framework of cultures, even when there is conscious and intellectual assent to what is happening, destroys the stable, deep-rooted sense of people's felt belonging; cultural and personal loneliness result.

Summary

- Culture is the hidden language that influences how we feel, think, and act; its constituent elements are symbols, myths and rituals. Symbols are felt meanings; myths are narrative symbols, emotionally charged stories that articulate in imaginative ways basic values and truths for those who accept them; rituals are the visible expression of symbols and myths in actions.
- Culture provides people with a sense of order and predictability in a world of threatening chaos; when people's expectations of order are significantly disrupted, there is fear and anxiety. Sociologist Emile Durkheim long ago invented the term *anomie* to describe the abrupt breakdown of meaning in life. But *cultural* anomie, more specifically, is the crushing grief over the loss of the familiar, the radical disintegration of normative order and its accompanying emotional bonding.[13] This grief expresses itself

---

[12] Erich Fromm, *The Fear of Freedom* (London: Routledge & Kegan Paul, 1960), 240.

[13] See Emile Durkheim, *Suicide*, trans. J. A. Spaulding and G. Simpson, ed. G. Simpson (London: Routledge and Kegan Paul, 1952), 258. Other sociologists, following Durkheim, also fail to focus on the *cultural trauma* quality of anomie. Robert K. Merton equates *anomie* with instability and refers to its connection to "demoralization" in *Social Theory and Social Structure*

in collective sadness, sorrow, anger, loneliness, anguish, confusion, shame, guilt, and fear.[14] There is a mythological vacuum. People are no longer able to find an adequate mythological response to the stresses they are undergoing, and loneliness results. Not only are myths able to inculcate a sense of pride, energy, direction, or simply an *esprit de corps,* but they are also reservoirs of memory and identity that people can draw on to face the challenges of life. President Trump complained that the removal of Confederate monuments was "so foolish!" He saw them purely from an artistic perspective, saying that "the beauty that is being taken out of our cities, towns, and parks will be greatly missed and never able to be comparably replaced!"[15] He failed to realize that the monuments are, for the protestors, "reservoirs of memory"—reminders of years of bitter oppression of marginalized peoples.

- Rollo May writes, "Myths are like the beams in a house: not exposed to outside view, they are the structure which holds the house together so people can live in it."[16] Myths can also be likened to the information concealed in the DNA of a cell or the programmed technology of a computer. A myth is the cultural DNA, the unconscious information, the software program that controls the way we picture and then react to the world around us.

Triggering Inclusion/Exclusion: Ritual Power

A *ritual* is a repetitive, prescribed, or spontaneous symbolic use of bodily movement and gesture to express and articulate meaning within

---

(Glencoe: The Free Press, 1957), 136. Talcott Parsons sees *anomie* as "the polar antithesis of full institutionalization," as "the absence of structured complementarity of the interaction process or, what is the same thing, the complete breakdown of normative order." *The Social System* (Glencoe: The Free Press, 1951), 136.

[14] See Gerald A. Arbuckle, *The Francis Factor and the People of God: New Life for the Church* (Maryknoll, NY: Orbis Books, 2015), 61–84.

[15] Jeremy Diamond, "Trump Calls Removal of Confederate Monuments 'So Foolish,'" CNN, August 17, 2017.

[16] May, *The Cry for Myth,* 15.

a social context in which there is possible or real tension/conflict and a need to resolve or hide it.[17] A ritual follows a set pattern expressing a public or shared meaning through symbols.

Prescribed rituals vary from simple gestures—shaking hands, greeting a person, or bowing—to elaborate dramas such as a British royal coronation or the inauguration of an American president. Thus, the expression "How do you do?" or "How are you?" as a routine method of starting conversations is a simple prescribed ritual of everyday interaction in many cultures. The ritual hides tensions that could exist.

Consider, for example, the Western custom of shaking hands. This is a stylized gesture of set form that outwardly, at least, conveys the meaning that peace, not chaos, prevails. Many rituals demand the use of bodily movement that symbolically articulates meaning in situations that are potentially capable of unleashing conflict or chaos.[18] Rituals can also be spontaneous. For example, after terrorist attacks total strangers gather to place flowers at the site. People unknown to the families of the deceased want to express symbolically to the bereaved their deep human sympathy for the enormity of the loss they have experienced.

It is the capacity of rituals to transform people and their environment, to resolve, prevent, and even to *cause* conflicts, that gives them their positive or negative power. Rituals have the power to evoke significant positive emotional reactions, such as the joy of a birthday party.[19] Yet rituals also can arouse a whole range of negative emotions, even violent ones. The annual summer parades of the Protestant Orangemen through Catholic suburbs in Northern Ireland's towns and cities can be ritual acts of symbolic warfare to Catholics, reminding them that their minority status will continue to be enforced.[20] It is common in many sports for opposing team members to shake hands at the end of a game. The gesture is saying that no matter which team

---

[17] See Arbuckle, *Culture, Inculturation, and Theologians,* 83.

[18] See Gerald A. Arbuckle, *Earthing the Gospel: An Inculturation Handbook for Pastoral Workers* (Maryknoll, NY: Orbis Books, 1990), 96–97.

[19] See Roy A. Rappaport, *Ritual and Religion in the Making of Humanity* (Cambridge: Cambridge University Press, 1999), 258–59.

[20] See Catherine Bell, *Ritual Theory—Ritual Practice* (New York: Oxford University Press, 1992), 197–223.

has won or lost it is of no importance. What is important is the game. However, if members actually refuse to shake hands, this is insulting and could possibly provoke a riot. Rituals thus may create a well-behaved school pupil or a brutal terrorist, a devoted employee or a dictator. Such is their power.[21]

Hiding Tension and Conflict

On June 14, 2017, President Trump, on a visit to Paris to join the Bastille celebrations, sealed his visit with a handshake with President Macron that lasted an uncomfortably long time, almost twenty-five seconds. President Trump had excluded himself from the Paris climate accords, an act that had deeply offended the French people. The hand-shake concealed this tension-evoking fact, along with other tensions. Uri Friedman comments: "It was a final act full of symbolism: Two men who have starkly different views of the world—an international-ist and a nationalist, an environmentalist and a climate-change skeptic, a centrist and a populist—gradually acknowledging that they have no choice but to work together. A true moment of truth. And a painfully awkward moment for the rest of us."[22]

Rituals of Inclusion and Exclusion

Among the many types of ritual two are especially relevant here: rituals of *inclusion* and *exclusion*. Every time I renew my passport, I participate in a ritual of inclusion— the government is saying to all that I officially belong to my country with all the appropriate rights and privileges. But the ritual has a flip side. It is excluding from officially belonging to Australia everyone who has no right to an Australian passport. Rituals define boundaries, classifying who belongs and who does not. Thus, my passport sets boundaries, and the law will enforce these boundaries whenever anyone threatens to break them by illegally entering the country. Many rituals of exclu-sion send an unequivocal message to outsiders—keep out, you do

---

[21] For a fuller explanation of ritual power, see Arbuckle, *Culture, Incultura-tion, and Theologians*, 81–98.

[22] Uri Friedman, "The Trump-Macron Handshake: A Play in Four Parts," *The Atlantic* (July 15, 2017).

not belong here, if you try to belong you will be punished. *Rituals of exclusion, therefore, are any symbolic actions that aim to marginalize individuals or cultures by preventing them from belonging to the dominant power on the basis of socially defined markers.* For example, during Christ's time Jewish society socially excluded the disfigured and sick because the Jews believed them to be ritually impure. This was in vivid contrast to the inclusivity that Jesus taught: "But when you give a banquet, invite the poor, the crippled, the lame, and the blind. And you will be blessed, because they cannot repay you" (Luke 14:13–14). Marcus Borg emphasizes the radical nature of this inclusivity: "The simple act of sharing a meal had exceptional religious and social significance in the social world of Jesus. It became a vehicle of cultural protest, challenging the ethos and politics of holiness."[23]

In brief, *rituals of inclusion and exclusion are symbolic triggers that evoke feelings of belonging or not belonging.* When the exclusion is total and irrevocable, then the resulting loneliness becomes "the deepest and least assuageable of all," as the earlier Rollo May quotation has noted. This feeling of "assuageable loneliness" is powerfully evident, for example, in the biblical myth of the Fall—when Adam and Eve are tempted by the serpent, they are excluded by God from the garden. All three are punished, and division thus replaces relationship (Gen 3:17–19). In place of the unspoiled simplicity of Eden, Adam, Eve, and their descendants must suffer unremitting loneliness. Similarly, when Cain murders his brother Abel, he is excluded from the comforting support of his family and condemned to the lonely life of a nomad: "And now you are cursed from the ground, . . . When you till the ground, it will no longer yield to you its strength; you will be a fugitive and a wanderer on the earth" (Gen 4:11–12). Cain is doomed to be a nonperson. What loneliness!

Ritual Exclusion Triggers: Examples

Exclusion triggers or rituals take many forms. In South Africa in 1950 the government introduced the Population Registration Act, the law that first triggered the apartheid system of race classification that led

---

[23] Marcus J. Borg, *Jesus, a New Vision: Spirit, Culture, and the Life of Discipleship* (London: SPCK, 1993), 133.

to the forced removal of over three million people and the deaths of thousands through brutal police action.[24]

When I was a boy in New Zealand, it was not uncommon for jobs to be advertised with this added statement: "Catholics Not Accepted." This was an unequivocal public exclusion on the basis of religion. Sometimes an exclusion trigger could be quite subtly applied—for example, Catholics, once employed in certain jobs, could find themselves quietly overlooked for promotion on the basis of their religion.

In analyzing the rise of Brexit in Britain, David Goodhart concludes that its major support came from the "'left behind'—mainly older, white, working-class men with little education." He writes: "They have lost economically with the decline of well-paid jobs for people without qualifications and culturally, too, with the disappearance of a distinct working-class culture and the marginalization of their views in the public conversation."[25] That is, the economic, cultural, and political changes have become for these people cumulative ritual triggers of exclusion. The pattern has been very similar in the United States. Donald Trump also drew significant support for his election to the presidency from voters who had come to feel excluded from mainstream society.[26]

As Jenny Sinclair writes in her examination of Brexit and the election of Donald Trump, "For too long, a 'progressive' agenda has held people with traditional views and interests in contempt. This has touched many groups, not least communities from the old industrial heartlands who have been ignored and culturally sidelined. They felt patronised and insulted."[27] The triggers in their case have been the speedy development of automation, globalization, and the failure of politicians to tackle the consequent problems.

Other examples of triggers for collective exclusion are the sudden decision in January 2017 by newly elected President Trump to bar most people traveling with passports from seven Muslim-majority nations from entering the United States and his promise to eject millions of illegal immigrants from the United States.

---

[24] See Robin Renwick, *The End of Apartheid: Diary of a Revolution* (London: Biteback, 2015), 132, 136.

[25] David Goodhart, *The Road to Somewhere: The Future of Revolt and the Future of Politics* (London: Hurst, 2017), 3.

[26] See ibid., 2.

[27] Jenny Sinclair, "Rebuilding the Broken Body," *The Tablet* (8 April, 2017), 4.

Triggering Loneliness through Exclusion: A Model

In the train crash described above, my fellow passengers and I were left in cultural chaos. Our sense of mythological order and belonging had dramatically and painfully evaporated. Anthropologist Victor Turner calls this chaos state *liminality* or a *liminal* experience.[28] For Turner, life is a process or journey whereby persons move regularly through two dialogical and cultural interacting processes: *societas* and *liminality.*[29] In *societas* we all know our status and role in daily living. For example, everyone has a status of some kind: father, mother, doctor, head teacher, student, and so forth. With each title there is an expected form of behavior, or role, that gives us a much-needed sense of security and predictability. However, in *liminality*, status and role are totally unimportant. We cross over from a world of status into a period of chaos or "cultural nakedness." The liminal stage is sometimes referred to as the chaos phase simply because chaos is the breakdown of the predictable order of living. Turner describes the creation of chaos and its impact: "Liminality . . . breaks, as it were, the cake of custom and enfranchises speculation."[30] Or put in another way, "Liminality may be partly described as a stage of reflection."[31] The anti-structure symbols provide the physical, psychological, moral, and spiritual shocks necessary to evoke this reflection. Liminality is "likened to being in the womb, to invisibility, to darkness . . . to the wilderness,"[32] without "status, property, insignia . . . kinship position."[33] Liminality begets cultural chaos. It can beget escapist denial of what is happening, but also paralyzing depression or loneliness.

Liminality culture is of two kinds: *spontaneous* and *normative.* The train incident was an example of *spontaneous* liminality. When I boarded the coach, I had clearly identifiable status and role: a religious minister and an anthropologist. But when the train crashed, *societas,*

---

[28] Turner was building upon a concept originally developed by ethnographer and folklorist Arnold van Gennep.

[29] See Victor Turner, *The Ritual Process: Structure and Anti-Structure* (Ithaca, NY: Cornell University Press, 1977), 94–120.

[30] Ibid., 106.

[31] Victor Turner, *The Forest of Symbols: Aspects of Ndembu Ritual* (Ithaca, NY: Cornell University Press, 1967), 105.

[32] Turner, *The Ritual Process*, 95.

[33] Turner, *The Forest of Symbols*, 99.

with its neatly defined statuses, roles, and comforting myths, disappeared. The fears and darkness of *liminality* took its place. "Liminality," writes Turner, "may be partly described as a stage of reflection."[34] We survivors shared a common chaos, faced with the options of loneliness, denial, or paralyzing depression. And the immediacy and gravity of our situation shocked us awake and challenged us, perhaps more in our unconscious than our conscious minds at first, to confront the primary questions of human life: *Who am I? What is the purpose of life? What should I change?*

Alternatively, a *normative* liminality occurs when an event is so structured that it is expected that people will experience the chaos of uncertainty. The Trump attempt to ban Muslims from entering the United States is an example, for these people, of normative liminality. And would-be Marines, in training for the army in the United States, are deliberately thrown into liminality, without roles or statuses—it is as though, in relation to the society from which they have come or to the society into which they are to be incorporated later, they are anonymous, nonpersons, deprived of all social roles other than that of initiates. As mentioned above, their state is often compared to being in the womb.[35] "They have no status, insignia, secular clothing, rank, kinship position, nothing to demarcate them structurally from their fellows."[36] In the midst of all *liminal* experiences, people are confronted with a choice point: ignore the challenge and seek escape or solace in past securities, for example in fundamentalist movements;[37] become paralyzed in depression by the experience; or yearn for an as-yet unattained feeling of belonging (and that yearning is loneliness).[38]

Cultural Triggers of Liminality

Every liminal experience begins with a cultural trigger, that is, some action that threatens the orderliness and security of *societas*. The

---

[34] Ibid., 105.

[35] Turner, *The Ritual Process,* 95.

[36] Turner, *The Forest of Symbols*, 99.

[37] See Gerald A. Arbuckle, *Fundamentalism at Home and Abroad: Analysis and Pastoral Responses* (Collegeville, MN: Liturgical Press, 2017), 1–29.

[38] See Gerald A. Arbuckle, *Healthcare Ministries: Refounding the Mission in Tumultuous Times* (Collegeville, MN: Liturgical Press, 2000), 132.

trigger can be the catalyst for individual or collective liminality. Triggers for individual liminality can be such events as the death of a loved one, retirement, or loss of a job. The liminality trigger in my case was the actual train crash. For Charlotte Brontë, it was an experience of meeting a culture that was unfamiliar to her: "the national character of the Belgiums."[39] However, Emile Durkheim (1858–1917), one of the founding figures of sociology, skillfully reminded academics that even supposedly personal decisions are conditioned by cultural realities. Put another way, what seems at first to be an *individual* incident requiring a psychological clarification is often, when seen in a larger *cultural* context, a *societal* fact that requires a cultural explanation. Thus, how people mourn is deeply influenced by the culture to which they belong. The distinction between the two types of triggers (cultural and individual) is not a precise one; for example, the 9/11 disaster was aimed directly at the American nation, but it naturally affected individuals at the same time.

Steps toward Loneliness

There are four steps in the journey toward loneliness, each of which will be explained and illustrated in this and subsequent chapters:

Step 1: Ritual exclusion
Step 2: Liminality/chaos
Step 3: Reactions
Step 4: Mentor accompaniment

In Step 1, people are ritually excluded from belonging; once excluded, they experience the "cultural nakedness" of liminality or chaos (Step 2). In Step 3, people react in one of three ways: denial, depression-despair, or loneliness. People who embrace loneliness, as defined, may then be helped to maintain their focus by skilled guides (Step 4).

---

[39] Quotation from Claire Harman, *Charlotte Brontë: A Life* (Falkirk: Penguin Books, 2016), 172.

An Example from Premodern Cultures

Premodern cultures commonly emphasize group harmony, cohesiveness, togetherness, interdependence, stability.[40] Therefore, an experience of liminality that threatens these order-emphasized values can result in very painful loneliness for groups and individuals. For example, the trigger that begins the initiation ritual of boys into adulthood in Bougainville, Papua New Guinea, is very brief and dramatic. The men of the village forcefully take the boys from their mothers amid much crying and hide them in the jungle. Not only the boys but also their mothers are compelled to experience unnerving loneliness.[41]

Mentoring through Liminality

As a reaction to liminality, mentors may emerge to support people in their loneliness by offering them hope that a new belonging will eventually emerge. Charlotte Brontë sought to relieve her loneliness by seeking to develop an intimate relationship with her Belgian teacher Constantin Heger, an older man with a wife and children, but as a good mentor, Heger rejected her advances.[42] In my case a young and total stranger assumed the comforting role of mentor. He gently said to fellow passengers: "Keep calm, we will find a way out of this disaster. Let us support one another." While waiting for help he invited us to sing softly a popular Australian song.

A mentor is an experienced and trusted adviser. Liminality mentorship, therefore, is a relationship in which a more informed person guides a less experienced and less knowledgeable person or group through the cultural loneliness of liminality. To do this successfully, mentors must themselves have experienced the fears and dangers of loneliness. In the Emmaus story Jesus is able to act as the perfect mentor of the two lost disciples because he had himself suffered through

---

[40] See Gerald A. Arbuckle, *Violence, Society, and the Church: A Cultural Approach* (Collegeville, MN: Liturgical Press, 2004), 34–54.

[41] See Gilbert H. Herdt, ed., *Rituals of Manhood: Male Initiation Rites in Papua New Guinea* (Berkeley and Los Angeles: University of California Press, 1981).

[42] See Harman, *Charlotte Brontë*, 202–6.

the relentless fears of loneliness in Gethsemane and on Golgotha: "For we do not have a high priest who is unable to sympathize with our weaknesses, but we have one who in every respect has been tested as we are, yet without sin" (Heb 4:15).

By their inner conversion and conviction, mentors thus make concrete the idea that a new world of personal and cultural integration is possible. They hold out hope and inspire the lonely to remain focused. Myth specialist Joseph Campbell describes the mentor as a "hero" who "ventures forth from the world of common day into a region of supernatural wonder; fabulous forces are encountered and a decisive victory is won. The hero comes back from this mysterious adventure with the power to bestow boons on his fellow man."[43] The mentor is a hero who has visited and been converted to the vision of a new world of integration; the mentor's behavior mirrors this interior transformation. The lonely in their journey, recognizing that their leader carries an internal vision of their journey's end, are drawn to experience the same action-oriented conversion.

Example: Dante Alighieri Seeks a Mentor

Ponder the example of Dante Alighieri (c. 1265–1321), who was exiled from his beloved Florence in 1302 because of a trumped-up conviction for graft. Not only did he lose his wife and property, but he was threatened with death if he attempted to return to the city-state. For the next impoverished twenty years he was forced to wander throughout Europe, from one patron to the next. Haunted by loneliness, he wrote his famous allegory, the *Divine Comedy*, in which he describes his journey through Hell (*Inferno*), Purgatory, and Paradise. While traveling in Hell, Dante becomes lost and is overcome with fear-evoking loneliness.

> Midway upon the journey of our life
> I found myself within a forest dark,
> For the straightforward pathway had been lost.
> Ah me! how hard a thing it is to say

---

[43] Joseph Campbell, *The Hero with a Thousand Faces* (Princeton, NJ: Princeton University Press, 1949), 30.

What was this forest savage, rough, and stern
Which in the very thought renew the fear.[44]

He feels the urgent need for a mentor and chooses Virgil, the great poet of the Classical Roman Empire, because he had masterfully explored the political, ethical, and religious questions of his time:

When I beheld him in the desert vast,
"Have pity on me," unto him I cried,
"Whiche'er thou art, or shade or real man!"[45]

Virgil describes his role:

Therefore, I think and judge it for thy best
Thou follow me, and I will be thy guide,
And lead thee hence through the eternal place.[46]

Virgil is the right leader because he has shown by his actions, Rollo May observes, "especially in the *Aeneid*, a thorough familiarity with the dangerous moral landscape they will now traverse."[47] When Dante becomes hesitant and fearful during the liminal journey, Virgil, a true mentor, vigorously challenges him to stay on task:

"If I have well thy language understood,"
Replied that shade of the Magnanimous,
"Thy soul attainted is with cowardice,
Which many times a man encumbers so,
It turns him back from honoured enterprise,
As false sight doth a beast, when he is shy."[48]

Later Dante again begs Virgil for help:

---

[44] Dante Alighieri, *Inferno* (London: Harper Press, 2011), 9.
[45] Ibid., 5.
[46] Ibid., 7.
[47] May, *The Cry for Myth*, 156.
[48] Dante, *Inferno,* 11.

> "O my dear Guide . . .
> Do not desert me," said I, "thus undone."

Virgil reassures Dante:

> And the Lord, who had led me thitherward,
> Said unto me: "Fear not. . . .
> For in this nether world I will not leave thee."[49]

Virgil thus mentors Dante through liminality, accompanying him on his journey.

Populist Leaders as Mentors?

It is possible that charismatic populist leaders can be mentors of their lonely followers, but history is not very encouraging. Populist leaders arise when a nation, in whole or in part, falls into a liminal state. For example, economic and social depressions create high levels of anxiety and uncertainty. Conditions become particularly conducive for people who are seeking to assuage their fear and loneliness to search for existing charismatic leaders and "to perceive charisma"[50] in would-be leaders. To a significant extent, "it is followers who bestow charisma on leaders, when that person seems to embody the qualities they are looking for."[51]

The problem is that it is "easy to be seduced by superheroes who could come and 'rescue' us, but who possibly then plunge us into greater peril."[52] Therefore, populist charismatic leaders, as mentors, "may, indeed, do either appalling harm or great good. . . . How such leaders are ultimately assessed depends, in large part, on how

---

[49] Ibid., 49.

[50] Margarita Mayo, "If Humble People Make the Best Leaders, Why Do We Fall for Charismatic Narcissists?" *Harvard Business Review* (April 7, 2017).

[51] Archie Brown, *The Myth of the Strong Leader: Political Leadership in the Modern Age* (London: Bodley Head, 2014), 4.

[52] Mayo, "If Humble People Make the Best Leaders, Why Do We Fall for Charismatic Narcissists?"

we judge the causes that their inspirational speeches and example serve."[53] Consider Adolf Hitler. Three totally inaccurate propaganda statements acted as triggers for the rise of populist Adolf Hitler in the 1930s in Germany, during the Great Depression. The first erroneous claim was that the German military command had failed to win the Great War (1914–18) because it was inept; the second was that the Versailles Treaty had unjustly humiliated Germany; and the third was that Jews were to blame for the existing economic chaos. In consequence, Hitler promised to relieve Germany of its international shame and feeling of national loneliness. Hitler, with the assent of many Germans at that time, manipulated the nation's liminality in favor of Nazi ideology. We know the horrendous consequences.

Consider Donald Trump, who campaigned with the slogan "Make America Great Again" and promised to help lonely blue-collar workers, who were feeling economically and culturally dispossessed and excluded. How could we ever speak of Trump making America great again when he freely used racist rhetoric: in his fostering of the birther falsehood;[54] in his claim that Mexicans are "rapists and criminals"; and in his insistence that Muslims must be banned? Behind him was his chief strategist, Steve Bannon, whose vision was euphemistically called "economic nationalism."[55]

It combines white supremacy; the Leninist "deconstruction" of the New Deal/cold war administrative state; Islamophobia (especially in seeing a titanic and irreconcilable clash of civilizations between Islam and the West); the dismantling of the current international order . . . in favor of a return to unfettered and self-assertive, ethnically homogeneous nation-states.[56]

---

[53] Brown, *The Myth of the Strong Leader,* 4.

[54] In 2011 Donald Trump started spreading a story that President Obama was an "illegitimate president" because, Trump claimed, he was not born in the United States. The White House published the long-form version of Obama's Hawaii birth certificate, but it took five years for Trump to retract his conspiracy theory (in a news conference during his own 2016 presidential campaign).

[55] See Joshua Green, *Devil's Bargain* (New York: Penguin Press, 2017), 222.

[56] Christopher R. Browning, "Lessons from Hitler's Rise," *The New York Review of Books* (April 20, 2017) (PDF).

However, there are examples where populist leaders have been able to lead their nations in a constructive way through major liminal periods of great uncertainty and loneliness. Winston Churchill and Franklin D. Roosevelt immediately come to mind. Also, there are the stories of populist leaders in countries such as Britain, New Zealand, Australia, and Canada[57] who, in order to overcome widespread poverty among their peoples, were able to establish welfare systems deeply influenced by the residual myth of the Good Samaritan. The social democratic founders may not have been conscious of this, but they certainly drew on the values inherent in the myth, such as solidarity, equity, compassion, and justice. Just as the wounded Jew in the parable had a right to receive care from the Samaritan, so also everyone today has the right to healthcare. It is not a commodity to be bought only by those who can afford it. Aneurin Bevan in Britain often emphasized this fundamental right:

> Society becomes more wholesome, more serene and spiritually healthier, if it knows that its citizens have at the back of their consciousness the knowledge that not only themselves, but all their fellows have access, when ill, to the best that medical skill can provide.[58]

In 1946, Bevan had even more forcefully declared that "it is repugnant to a civilized community for hospitals to have to rely upon charity."[59] Michael Savage (1872–1940), the New Zealand prime minister from 1935 to 1940 and the founder of the nation's welfare state, was of the same mind: "I want to see that people have security. . . . I want to see humanity secure against poverty, secure in illness in old age. . . . What is more valuable in our Christianity than to be our brother's keepers

---

[57] For example, Tommy Douglas (1904–86), architect of universal healthcare in Canada, was deeply influenced by the Social Gospel movement, which combined Christian principles with social reform.

[58] Aneurin Bevan, cited in Margaret Whitehead, "Is It Fair? Evaluating the Equity Implications of the NHS Reforms," in *Evaluating the NHS Reforms*, ed. Ray Robinson and Julian Le Grand (London: King's Fund Institute, 1993), 210.

[59] Aneurin Bevan, quoted by Andrew O'Hagan, *London Review of Books* (March 3, 2011), 34.

in reality."[60] Savage also called Social Security Act 1938 "applied Christianity."[61] There is no denying the explicit and implicit influence of Christian thinking on the original formation of the philosophy of the welfare state.[62]

In more recent times there are the examples of Martin Luther King, Jr., and Nelson Mandela. The latter, having spent years in prison as a political prisoner, could, once released, have led his followers to a violent and revengeful overthrow of the existing government, despite the fact that his people had suffered decades of humiliating cultural and political loneliness. Why did he not do this? Because in the solitude of prison he had gradually wrestled with his own inner loneliness. "I was angry. And I was afraid, because I had not been free in so long. But as I got closer to the car that would take me away, I realized that when I went through the gate, if I still hated them, they would still have me. I wanted to be free. And so I let it go."[63] As a result of his inner conversion of heart, "he did not believe in the supremacy of the party (ANC) over the institutions of the country, including the judiciary and the press. . . . The least power-hungry of political leaders, he flatly refused to serve more than one term as President."[64]

Theological Reflection: Mentoring in Loneliness

> Let your steadfast love come to me, O Lord,
> your salvation according to your promise.
> Then I shall have an answer for those who taunt me,
> for I trust in your word . . . for my hope is in your
>   word. (Ps 119:41–42)

---

[60] Michael Savage, cited by the Department of Social Security, *The Growth and Development of Social Security in New Zealand* (Wellington: Government Printer, 1950), 17.

[61] Savage, quoted in ibid.

[62] See Francis Davis, Elizabeth Paulhus, and Andrew Bradstock, *Moral, But No Compass: Government, Church, and the Future of the Welfare State* (Chemsford: Mathew James, 2008), 29.

[63] Nelson Mandela, *Long Walk to Freedom: The Autobiography of Nelson Mandela* (Boston: Little Brown and Co., 1994), foreword.

[64] Robin Renwick, *The End of Apartheid* (London: Biteback Publishing, 2015), 3.

The Old Testament books are filled with the stories of liminal experiences triggered by all kinds of incidents. People respond by denying the liminal challenges or by attempting to seek escape in aberrant ways such as false gods or by accepting hope-filled loneliness. David, when his own son had risen against him, had to flee for his life, leaving Jerusalem and his family. Utterly isolated and lonely, he turns in hope to God:

> Turn to me and be gracious to me,
>   for I am lonely and afflicted.
> Relieve the troubles of my heart
>   and bring me out of my distress. . . .
> Consider how many are my foes,
>   and with what violent hatred they hate me. (Ps
>   25:16–17, 19)

God became David's mentor:

> The Lord is my light and my salvation;
>   whom shall I fear? . . .
> Though an army encamp against me,
>   my heart shall not fear;
> though war rise up against me,
>   yet I will be confident. (Ps 27:1, 3)

This psalm significantly illustrates that in faith-based loneliness, trust is an alternative to fear and anxiety in the face of opposition. But this trust must be nurtured in prayer, otherwise fear and anxiety will once again grip the wary traveler.[65]

The exodus from Egypt is the core liminal religious journey for the Israelites, and it forms the creation myth of how they were initiated as a people. Moses is appointed by God as the mentor[66] of Israelites in this experience. "The exodus is remembered in Israelite literature and liturgy as the initiating, defining event in biblical faith . . . so that other

---

[65] See Walter Brueggemann and William H. Bellinger, *Psalms* (Cambridge: Cambridge University Press, 2014), 141–42.

[66] See Gerald A. Arbuckle, *The Francis Factor and the People of God: New Life for the Church* (Maryknoll, NY: Orbis Books, 2015), 201–3.

occurrences are presented as replications of the exodus event."[67] The exile to Babylon is the second major liminal journey in which God's prophets are the people's mentors, as is now explained.

Loneliness of the Exile: Prophets as Mentors

As a consequence of their successful campaigns against Judah and Jerusalem, in 597–582 BCE the Babylonians deported to Babylon the leading Jews from Jerusalem (2 Kings 24:14; 25:11; Jer 52:28–30). Jerusalem itself was destroyed—and with its destruction, Judah's identity as a political institution ceased to exist.[68] Thus began the long and lonely exile. Evicted from their sacred land, deprived of their Temple and worship, the exiles, now deeply discouraged, felt that they had been totally abandoned by God (Ezek 11:15; 37:11; Isa 49:14). Their intense loneliness and pain of loss are expressed in Psalm 74:

> O God, why do you cast us off forever? . . .
> Direct your steps to the perpetual ruins;
>> the enemy has destroyed everything in the sanc-
>>> tuary. . . .
> At the upper entrance they hacked
> the wooden trellis with axes. (Ps 74:1, 3, 5)

And there is guilt:

> Jerusalem sinned grievously,
>> so she has become a mockery; . . .
> Her uncleanness was in her skirts;
>> she took no thought of her future;
> her downfall was appalling,
>> with none to comfort her. (Lam 1:8–9)

Yet despite the depression of the people in their liminal exile, God remained with them and prophets became God's spokespeople, their

---

[67] Walter Brueggemann, *Reverberations of Faith* (Louisville, KY: Westminster/John Knox Press, 2012), 72.

[68] See ibid., 70.

mentors, offering them hope. The more they embraced hope the more the exiles discovered the enriching rewards of loneliness:

> As a deer longs for flowing streams,
>   so my soul longs for you, O God.
> My soul thirsts for God,
>   for the living God;
> when shall I come and behold
> the face of God? (Ps 42:1–2)

The hopeful message of the prophets is clear (e.g. Is 43:16–21; Jer 31:31–34; Ezek 37:1–14): while God is punishing the people, God desires nothing so much as that the first tenderness should blossom anew:

> Therefore, I will now allure her,
>   and bring her into the wilderness,
>   and speak tenderly to her.
> From there I will . . .
>   make the Valley of A'chor a door of hope.
> There she will respond as in the days of her youth,
>   as at the time when she came out of the land of
>   Egypt. (Hos 2:14–15)

There were times in the exile, however, when the people forgot the enriching power of hope in their loneliness. They turned to Babylonian gods and worship for consolation. Then the anger of their prophetic mentors condemned them and called them back to their pilgrimage journey:

> All who make idols are nothing, and the things they delight in do not profit; their witnesses neither see nor know. And so they will be put to shame. . . . Look, all its devotees shall be put to shame; the artisans too are merely human. Let them all assemble, . . . they shall be put to shame. (Isa 44:9, 11).

For Elijah, a ninth-century BCE prophet, the contract on his life by the scheming Jezebel (1 Kings 19:2) triggered the beginning of a sorrowful liminal phase of loneliness. But he fears that loneliness is too threatening, and he opts to escape: "Then he was afraid; he got up and fled for his life" (19:3).[69] Exhausted from his prophet's work, overwhelmed by the turmoil around him, he pleads with God that his life might end: "He asked that he might die rather than face the challenge to journey in hope-filled loneliness: 'It is enough; now, O Lord, take away my life, for I am no better than my ancestors'" (19:4). Not only does God refuse his prayer, but God encourages Elijah to begin a lengthy lonely pilgrimage to regain his strength. All the while God is his mentor, accompanying and sustaining Elijah in his loneliness. Eventually God drew Elijah to Mount Horeb: "Go out and stand on the mountain before the Lord, for the Lord is about to pass by" (19:11). On Mount Horeb, where Moses received the law from God, and one of the founding sites in the life of the nation, Elijah, inwardly stilled by his long reflective journey, is at last able to come face to face with God. How did this happen? Did God pass by in "a great wind . . . an earthquake . . . a fire"? No, but in "a sound of sheer silence" (19:12). The message is clear: As in the time of Elijah and the other prophets, mentors need to discover God in times of prayerful "sheer silence."

The prophet Ezekiel is particularly interesting; he was one of the exiles from Jerusalem in 597 BCE. His God-given task as mentor was twofold: First, to help the despondent exiles and the people left behind in Jerusalem recognize that the devastation of the city is God's judgment on the nation. Second, to be a prophet of hope, creating a vision of new life, a refounding of the nation. For a quarter of a century he has been an exile and he "has stared desolation in the face and contemplated the grace and wonder of Almighty God."[70] It is a vision of the "mobility" of God, whose glory is not contained solely in the temple (Ezek 1) and whose presence is a covert sanctuary for the exiles (Ezek 11:16). God will seek out the exiles, as a shepherd: "I myself will search for my sheep, and will seek them out" (Ezek 34:11). God will purify them of all their defilements and give them a new heart: "A new heart I will give you, and a new spirit I will put within you" (Ezek 36:26). Hope was to sustain the exiles in their journey of loneliness. The prophets are optimistic people, full of hope,

---

[69] See Steven Croft, *The Gift of Leadership: According to the Scriptures* (Norwich: Canterbury Press, 2016), 27–35.

[70] Ibid., 20.

and for this reason they are so imaginatively creative about how the people are to keep to their pilgrim road in the presence of God. No matter how dark and chaotic the world may be, God still loves us.

Prophets Themselves Marginalized

The hardworking prophets are often marginalized, verbally and physically abused, and at times even murdered, because their message describing the conditions necessary for maintaining hope in the midst of loneliness sounds too hard to people. And it is not just evil people who reject their message, but also those who feel affronted and annoyed that they should be told to be better:

> "Let us lie in wait for the righteous man,
> because he is inconvenient to us and opposes our
>   actions;
> he reproaches us for sins against the law, . . .
> He became to us a reproof of our thoughts;
> the very sight of him is a burden to us, . . .
> Let us test him with insult and torture." (Wis 2:12,
>   14–15, 19)

Of Hosea, an eighth-century BCE prophet who foretold the exile, the people cry: "The prophet is a fool, the man of the spirit is mad" (Hos 9:7). God's special heroes suffer intensely at times for their "madness"; in fact, suffering is a mark of their authenticity as messengers of God. Take Jeremiah, a prophet from the sixth century BCE, who testifies to his faithfulness to God not only in his private spiritual journey of loneliness, but also publicly through a life of ostracism and persecution. He is rejected by his family and friends (Jer 11:18), and he cannot marry and enjoy the comfort of family life. He knows the loneliness of being separated from what is dear and familiar to him:

> But I was like a gentle lamb
>   led to the slaughter.
> And I did not know it was against me
>   that they devised schemes, saying,

"Let us destroy the tree with its fruit,
    let us cut him off from the land of the living,
so that his name will no longer be remembered!"
    (Jer 11:19)

There are times when the prophets are tempted to run away from their burdensome tasks (Jer 2:9), and they even fall victim to the people's desire to be flattered with fake news to avoid having to tell the hard truth:

"Do not prophesy to us what is right;
speak to us smooth things,
    prophesy illusions,
leave the way, turn aside from the path,
    let us hear no more about the Holy One of Is-
    rael." (Isa 30:10–11).

Yet as faithful mentors they do not fail the Lord, because they themselves are radically converted to God and to his service in faith and love. They are "overpowered" (Jer 20:7) by the friendship they share with God:

The friendship of the Lord is for those who fear
    him,
and he makes his covenant known to them. (Ps
    25:14)

Summary

- Cultures, with their symbols, myths, and rituals, give people a sense of meaning and belonging; when cultures are disrupted, people are thrown into loneliness.
- Rituals define boundaries that classify who belongs and who does not. Rituals of exclusion are events that marginalize people from involvement in the dominant culture; people are made to feel abandoned.

- When abandoned, people can despair, deny what is happening, or embrace hope-inspired loneliness. In order to maintain hope, people need trustworthy mentors or guides. Biblical prophets are models for all would-be mentors.

Reflection Questions

- When have I felt excluded from belonging to a gathering? What did it feel like?
- What were the events, or triggers, that led to this exclusion?
- How did I cope with this marginalization?
- Of the scriptural examples of mentoring, which one most appeals to me? Why?

3

Cultures
of Inveterate Individualism

The risks of individualism have been debated since America's earliest days. Alexis de Tocqueville worried about frontiersmen withdrawing from society and believing that they "owe nothing to any man." Despots love to stoke selfishness among their subjects, he went on, because it usefully divides the masses.

—"Normalizing Narcissism,"
The Economist, August 20, 2016

Lack of hope and faith in the future . . . is reflected in real-world outcomes. . . . The recent increase in mortality rates for middle-aged, uneducated whites is a stark marker of this ill-being and lack of hope. . . . This is a depressing picture, and the American Dream is clearly tattered.

—Carol Graham, *Happiness for All?*

A new politics of the common good isn't only about finding more scrupulous politicians. . . . It requires a more robust public discourse—one that engages more directly with moral and even spiritual values.

—Michael Sandel,
2009 Reith Lecture Series

This chapter explains:

- Cultures of individualism foster individual and group loneliness.
- The constituent qualities of cultures of individualism.
- Myths can hide historical facts so that people are socially and economically marginalized.
- The myth of the "American Dream" thwarts the common good.
- The encyclical *Laudato Si'* critiques cultures of individualism.

Loneliness is a yearning—or in Augustine's words, a panting—for belonging through interconnectedness with others. It can be creative for the common good. However, individuals and cultures that cultivate habitual individualism attempt to escape this creativity and to flounder instead in a fruitless loneliness. They lack a desire for connectedness with others for the sake of the common good; they use other people and cultures only to satisfy their self-centered desires.[1] Pope Francis describes this in *Laudato Si'*:

> Men and women of our postmodern world run the risk of rampant individualism, and many problems of society are connected with today's self-centered culture of instant gratification. . . . Furthermore, our inability to think seriously about future generations is linked to our inability to broaden the scope of our present interests and to give consideration to those who remain excluded from development. (no. 162)

A culture of inveterate individualism becomes a culture of loneliness and the ephemeral.

> [It is noted for] the speed with which people move from one affective relationship to another. . . . I think too of the fears associated with permanent commitment, the obsession with free time, and those relationships that weigh costs and benefits

---

[1] My thanks to Andrew Nee for his comments on this chapter.

for the sake of remedying loneliness, providing protection, or offering some service. We treat affective relationships the way we treat material objects and the environment: everything is disposable. . . . Then, goodbye. (no. 39)

The more this culture of the ephemeral motivates the social, economic and political behavior of the powerful, the more the poor and powerless are stigmatized and excluded from society. This chapter describes the founding mythology of the United States, its emphasis on individualism[2] to the detriment of the common good, and its role in triggering loneliness among individuals who imbibe its values.

The "American Dream" and Loneliness

In his numerous nineteenth-century novels Horatio Alger helped to popularize the American Dream, which is inherent in the founding mythology of the United States—the rags-to-riches myth, namely, that anyone could work hard and become rich, a "self-made American."[3] If people did not succeed, it was their own fault. Alger did stress the importance of moral behavior in his heroes, but this emphasis was quickly forgotten by his readers. Success became the dominant quality for readers, no matter how it was achieved. Though an emphasis on individualism characterizes many other cultures in places like Western Europe, Australia, and New Zealand, there is something unique in American individualism: its extreme quality. Other countries

---

[2] Sociologist Ernst Troeltsch argues that the Reformation in the realm of ideas and mentalities pushed the "autonomy," "individualism," and "this-worldliness" that is characteristic of "modern culture." See Christian Joppke, *The Secular State under Siege: Religion and Politics in Europe and America* (Cambridge: Polity, 2015), 63.

[3] See Carol Graham, *Happiness for All? Unequal Hopes and Lives in Pursuit of the American Dream* (Princeton, NJ: Princeton University Press, 2017), 22. Robert Putman, writing on the roots of the expression "American Dream," says: "In 1843, *McGuffey's Reader*—in effect, our first national school textbook—told students, 'The road to wealth, to honor, to usefulness, and happiness, is open to all, and all who will, may enter upon it with the almost certain prospect of success.'" *Our Kids: The American Dream in Crisis* (New York: Simon and Schuster, 2015), 33.

balance their individualism with their concern for the common good. That sharp observer, Alexis de Tocqueville, noted decades ago the ever-emerging problems of growing individualism, loneliness, and alienation: "Selfishness blights the germ of all virtues; individualism, at first, only saps the virtues of public life; but in the long run it attacks and destroys all others and is at length absorbed in downright selfishness."[4] Such individualism fosters deep-seated loneliness in the culture. As Philip Slater notes, "The competitive life is a lonely one and its satisfactions short-lived, for each race leads only to a new one."[5]

Robert Bellah, reflecting on the impact of individualism in the United States, concluded that morality is so focused "exclusively on individual self-improvement that the larger social context hardly comes into view. . . . Marriage, friendship, job . . . church are dispensable, if these don't meet my needs."[6] Yet this emphasis on the potential of individuals to achieve anything they wish in the United States results in intense loneliness: "The individual . . . when picking himself or herself up after a failure, has nowhere to turn except to a very small and frail unit indeed: the self."[7] In 1984, Christopher Lasch observed of US culture:

> The concern with the self, which seems so characteristic of our time, takes the form of a concern with its psychic survival. . . . Faced with an escalating arms race, an increase in crime and terrorism, environmental deterioration, and the prospect of long-term economic decline, they have begun to prepare for the worst, sometimes by building fallout shelters and laying in provisions, more commonly by executing a kind of emotional retreat from the long-term commitments that presuppose a stable, secure, and orderly world.[8]

---

[4] Alexis de Tocqueville, *Democracy in America by Alexis de Tocqueville,* ed. Phillips Bradley (New York: Alfred A. Knopf, 1953), 2:98.

[5] Philip Slater, *Pursuit of Loneliness: American Culture at the Breaking Point* (Boston: Beacon Press, 1990), 9.

[6] Robert Bellah, *Habits of the Heart* (Berkeley and Los Angeles: University of California Press, 1985), 33, 354.

[7] Rollo May, *The Cry for Myth* (New York: Delta, 1991), 122.

[8] Christopher Lasch, *The Minimal Self: Psychic Survival in Troubled Times* (New York: W. W. Norton, 1984), 16.

Again, it is important to note other "critical voices" within the United States: Michael Harrington on poverty in the 1960s; the United States Bishops' pastoral letter on the economy and the common good (1986); Michael Sandel's more communitarian approach to justice as he engaged John Rawls's theory of distributive justice.[9]

Shortly before her death, psychoanalyst Frieda Fromm-Reichmann described the American mythological emphasis on individualism and success in this way:

> I feel so strongly that the Americans are different from Europeans in that for them there is no [tragedy] and no fate. You *are* a success and you *are* a failure and it's your fault if you are a failure and if you try hard you can be a success, including [being] the President of the United States. And there isn't such a thing as fate or energies outside yourself [influencing things]. . . . Therefore, Americans say, "I *am* a success," and "I *am* a failure." In every other language, it is "I have success" or "I have failure."[10]

The mythological assumption is that, in the United States, anyone can achieve anything on his or her own—particularly wealth and material things. President Ronald Reagan articulated this rags-to-riches mythology when he said: "What I want to see above all is that this country remains a country where someone can always get rich."[11] Whatever works is to be encouraged *unless* the person's wrongdoing is discovered. Little wonder that there was opposition to the New Deal of President Franklin D. Roosevelt, which sought to relieve poverty following the Great Depression. For example, the American Liberty

---

[9] See Michael Harrington, *The Other America: Poverty in the United States* (New York: Macmillan, 1962); USCCB, *Economic Justice for All* (1986); Michael Sandel, *Liberalism and the Limits of Justice* (New York: Cambridge University Press, 1998).

[10] Ann-Louise S. Silver, "Frieda Fromm-Reichmann, Loneliness and Deafness," *International Forum of Psychoanalysis* 5/1 (1996): 39–46, 40.

[11] Ronald Reagan, quoted in *The New York Times* (June 29, 1983). Robert Putman comments: "On balance most Americans have believed (at least until recently) that equality of opportunity characterizes our society—that the American Dream, in other words, endures." Putnam, *Our Kids*, 34.

League was formed in 1934 primarily by wealthy business elites and prominent political figures to oppose the New Deal but also to uphold the individualistic mythology of the American Dream.[12] The contemporary move to destroy the Affordable Care Act (Obamacare), as described below, is another example.

American Dream: Contradictory Values

The American myth emphasizes two contradictory values—competitive utilitarian individualism *and* egalitarianism—but while other Western countries struggle to develop a balance between the two, the United States emphasizes individualism to the detriment of egalitarianism. Governments, particularly Republican ones, deliberately favor the first value to the neglect of the second. Those people who cannot compete are apt to fall into chronic loneliness. The difference in emphasis has its roots in the unique nature of the creation myth of the United States.

In the mythology of democracy there are two complementary poles: the rights of the individual and the common good. A third quality, fraternity, is the balance between these two mythological poles. When the rights of the individual are overemphasized by governments, many of their more vulnerable citizens suffer ever-increasing social and personal loneliness. Appropriate welfare and health services are denied them. For example, in most Western countries outside of the United States, governments—such as those in Norway, Britain, Australia, France, and New Zealand—actively emphasize the rights of the common good when it comes to safeguarding the health of citizens, even those who have limited resources.[13] According to the American Dream mythology, however, individualism means that the rights of the individual are to be respected even though the common

---

[12] See Oliver Stone and Peter Kuznick, *The Untold History of the United States Volume 1* (New York: Simon and Schuster, 2014), 138–40.

[13] In their study of eleven national healthcare models, researchers at the New York–based Commonwealth Fund ranked their own country's system the worst. The United States came in last on performance overall, and last or near last in the access, administrative efficiency, equity, and healthcare outcomes domains. See Eric C. Schneider, Dana O. Sarnak, David Squires, Amav Shah, Michelle M. Doty, "Mirror, Mirror 2017: International Comparison Reflects Flaws and Opportunities for Better US Health Care" (July 14, 2017).

good may suffer. In 2013, there were 33,169 deaths relating to firearms, yet the National Rifle Association (NRA), supported by a powerful political lobby, continues to uphold its interpretation of the Second Amendment. The NRA is firmly committed to upholding the Second Amendment despite the risks and costs to people's lives.[14]

The basic assumption, according to this mythology, is that the poor are poor through their own fault. Success is possible if only an individual tries hard enough. Yet the reality is so different. The American founding mythology has been so romanticized and sanitized over centuries that millions of people have been, and continue to be, trapped in cultures of poverty and low socioeconomic classes. Award-winning author and historian Nancy Isenberg has uncovered the crucial legacy of the ever-present, poor "white trash" and the deeply entrenched class system that dates back to America's colonial roots, where a disposable white underclass was the price of succeeding in business. Racial injustice has long been an ugly stain on the nation's history, but the truth about the enduring, malevolent nature of class has been long ignored.[15]

Example: Healthcare Reforms

An excellent example of the overemphasis on individualism, with its consequent loneliness for individuals and groups in America, was the effort by President Obama to reform the American healthcare system. It aimed to allow millions of uninsured poor people lifelong healthcare security. Without this security these people would continue to face incredible social and personal loneliness due to the constant fears of indebtedness resulting from poor health. In March 2010, despite massive opposition, President Obama signed into law a sweeping set of healthcare reforms under the title of the Patient Protection and Affordable Care Act. The act had two main aims: first, to improve access to necessary healthcare for millions of uninsured and under-insured Americans, and second, to control healthcare costs more successfully so that access to necessary healthcare would be more affordable for all citizens. The act mandated coverage for 96 percent

---

[14] See Gerald A. Arbuckle, *Fundamentalism at Home and Abroad: Analysis and Pastoral Responses* (Collegeville, MN: Liturgical Press, 2017), 72.

[15] See Nancy Isenberg, *White Trash: The 400–Year Untold History of Class in America* (New York: Penguin, 2016), 1–14.

of American citizens, including thirty-six million of those who were then uninsured; approved federal subsidies to help people with low incomes afford the premiums; mandated employers to provide health insurance for workers with an exemption for small businesses; and set limitations on insurers, so that they could only sell policies that met government requirements and could no longer refuse coverage to people with preexisting conditions or drop policyholders who become seriously ill. The opposition to the law has been, and continues to be, intense. Many Republicans consider it unconstitutional and have vowed to repeal it. They claim that Congress does not have the authority to command that citizens purchase healthcare insurance.[16]

Evangelical Religion Reinforces Individualism

Evangelical Christianity's emphasis on individual salvation and its lack of concern for social conversion powerfully reinforce individualism.[17] White evangelicals constitute about one-fifth of the population in the United States; they include a wide range of religious groups such as Southern Baptist, Mennonite, Holiness groups, Pentecostal, and Dutch Reformed. The entire evangelical movement could perhaps be summed up according to this slogan: "the do-it-yourself church." It is "a bottom-up religiosity" because it "prefers the improvised over the prescribed, spontaneity over tradition, experience over expertise, emotion over slower religious reasonings. . . . It is a revival religion, that of emotional contagion."[18] George W. Bush became their much-praised president, but Bill and Hillary Clinton were heartily condemned along with Barack Obama because of their support of such issues as government-backed healthcare reform, which is considered to be contrary to the teachings of the Bible.[19]

A survey in 2015 revealed that 53 percent of white American evangelical Protestants believe that "immigrants threaten traditional

---

[16] See David Cole, "Health Care Reform Unconstitutional?" *The New York Review of Books* (February 24, 2011), 9–11.

[17] See Arbuckle, *Fundamentalism at Home and Abroad,* 83–96.

[18] Garry Wills, "Where Evangelicals Came From," *The New York Review of Books* (April 20, 2017), 29, 26.

[19] See Frances Fitzgerald, *The Evangelicals: The Struggle to Shape America* (New York: Simon and Schuster, 2017), 599, 625–36.

American customs and values."[20] In the early 2000s, televangelist Jerry Falwell[21] said the prophet Muhammad was a terrorist, Pat Robertson declared Muslims "worse than the Nazis," and the leader of the moderate National Association of Evangelicals feared that Muslims were becoming "the modern day equivalent of the Evil Empire."[22]

The Great Gatsby and Loneliness: Critique of the American Dream

In 1925, F. Scott Fitzgerald published *The Great Gatsby*[23]—a brilliant description and ultimately a scathing critique of the American Dream with its cult of individualism, materialism and inherent hollowness, all of which beget a chronic culture of loneliness. The main character, Jay Gatsby, a wealthy New Yorker, lives the American Dream of the individual's rise from rags to riches. He and the other characters are thoroughly individualistic, obsessed with gaining and maintaining money, no matter how it is obtained. There is cheating, lying, physical abuse, crime eventually including murder, but no one is confronted with the legal consequences. Gatsby is locally famous for his lavish weekly parties attended by various social-status seekers and ambitious financial opportunists.

A pivotal theme of the novel is loneliness.[24] The weekly party guests never really communicate with one another, ultimately

---

[20] Public Research Institute poll cited by Leonardo Blair, "Majority of White Evangelicals Believe Immigrants Threaten American Values, Study Finds," *Christian Post Reporter* (March 29, 2016).

[21] See Arbuckle, *Fundamentalism at Home and Abroad*, 92.

[22] Colin Woodard, "How Trump Breathed New Life into the Cultural War Waged by Evangelicals," *The Washington Post* (April 14, 2017).

[23] See F. Scott Fitzgerald, *The Great Gatsby* (London: Penguin, 2000). Others have critiqued the American Dream mythology. For example, the American writer Ta-Nehisi Coates published in 2015 a book in the form of a letter to his son about racism in the United States: *Between the World and Me*. The American Dream, he writes, is a lie, made up by historians and Hollywood. "It is not a dream of America. It is a dream of *white* America, built on the sweat and bones of African slaves, and made to control, exploit, and break black bodies."

[24] See May, *The Cry for Myth,* 135.

remaining strangers to one another, not even knowing their names. Nick Carraway, the book's narrator, also senses this pervading loneliness when he wanders around the streets of New York: "I felt a haunting loneliness sometimes, and felt it in others—poor young clerks who loitered in front of windows waiting until it was time for a solitary restaurant dinner . . . wasting the most poignant moments of night and life."[25] Despite his wealth and manipulative skills, Gatsby is the loneliest of all. The loneliness is stark, even at his own funeral, to which "nobody came."[26] The loneliness caused by individualism is also emphasized in the book by the author's frequent reference to people who do not *care*. For example, Nick recounts a dream: "Gravely the men turn in at a house—the wrong house. But no one knows the woman's name, and no one cares."[27] The word *careless* is used by Fitzgerald on almost every page, but it is not an idle word; the author uses the word *care* in "its literal meaning: the ability of people to have compassion, to communicate on deeper levels and to love each other."[28] The book's characters do not relate to one another as human persons; they relate instead to nonhuman realities such as money and social class. A soulless loneliness is inevitable.

The American Dream: A Strong Grid/Weak Group Culture Model

Anthropologist Mary Douglas has developed a system of classifying culture types or models based on two variables, namely *group* and *grid* (more fully explained in Chapter 6).[29] *Group* denotes the power of the boundary around a social group, while *grid* is concerned with

---

[25] Fitzgerald, *The Great Gatsby*, 57.

[26] Ibid., 137.

[27] Ibid., 178.

[28] See May, *The Cry for Myth*, 134.

[29] A culture model aims to illuminate reality by highlighting emphases and downplaying details or nuances that might interfere with the clarifying process. A model is modified or put aside in the light of the data being reviewed. A model is simply a way of helping us explore very complex processes, and we should expect no more from it. See Giovanni Bennardo and Victor C. De Munck, *Cultural Models: Genesis, Methods, and Experiences* (New York: Oxford University Press, 2014), 3–5.

the degree of hierarchy and social differentiation within it.[30] For example, cultures that are *strong grid/strong group*, such as an army or police force, emphasize formal rules and power. Disobedience is not acceptable. On the other hand, *strong grid/weak group* cultures are highly individualistic and competitive. Such is the culture model of the American Dream as depicted in *The Great Gatsby* and elsewhere.

The purpose of this section is to apply the insights of Douglas's *strong grid/weak group* culture model to the analysis of the American Dream as described in *The Great Gatsby*. It will be shown that once individualism becomes the dominant symbol, other qualities logically follow. Entrepreneurial capitalists, with little commitment to collective identity, flourish in this model. People are sturdily egalitarian oriented, individualistic, utilitarian, and competitive, but they have a very weak sense of belonging or of having obligations to the group. People obtain their personal identity from submitting to, and interiorizing, the clearly stated norms and goals of their culture's inner structure. Individuals form alliances with one another to provide better opportunities for competitive successes, but such alliances are very fragile.

Strong Grid/Weak Group Model Explained: Qualities

Extreme Individualism

This is the culture's liminality trigger. The mythology of extreme individualism influences every aspect of this culture. People have a very weak sense of belonging, or of having obligations, to any group. It is a highly utilitarian and competitive culture. Individuals form alliances with one another to provide better opportunities for the all-important competitive successes, but such alliances are very fragile, since they are held together only for the self-interest of the

---

[30] See Mary Douglas, *Natural Symbols: Explorations in Cosmology* (New York: Pantheon Books, 1970); and idem, *Cultural Bias* (London: Royal Anthropological Institute, 1978). These models are explained and applied in Gerald A. Arbuckle, *Refounding the Church: Dissent for Leadership* (Maryknoll, NY: Orbis Books, 1993), 80–97; and idem, *Culture, Inculturation, and Theologians: A Postmodern Critique* (Collegeville, MN: Liturgical Press, 2010), 42–48.

individuals themselves. These alliances break apart once more profitable interrelationships appear. The culture is patriarchal, because it is assumed that only men can develop sufficient aggression to be effectively competitive.

Narcissism

Narcissists are focused only on themselves as individuals. Narcissism is self-admiration taken to an extreme. Consequently, narcissists "lack emotionally warm, caring, and loving relationships with other people . . . manipulate and cheat to get ahead, surround themselves with people who look up to them . . . exploiting people and viewing others as tools to make themselves look and feel good."[31] Commitments of all kinds are highly fragile, for every relationship, even marriage, is dispensable if it fails to serve the self-fulfillment aspirations of the narcissist.[32] Inevitably, the ongoing search by narcissistic individuals for sustained personal economic success in a rapidly changing world produces many fragile, insecure, and depressed people.

Business: Neo-capitalism

Neo-capitalism (market capitalism, neoclassical capitalism, or market liberalism) believes that profit is the sole measure of value; the economics profession serves as its priesthood.[33] The assumptions of laissez-faire economics are (1) sustained economic growth is the best way to distribute wealth; (2) free markets, unrestrained by government interference, result in the most efficient use of resources; (3) lower taxation and reduced government spending are desirable; (4) governments must privatize services; and (5) the government's primary task is to support individual initiatives in commerce. Thus the pursuit of business profits is far more important than the workings of governments.[34] Economic rationalists also aim to change public institutions

---

[31] Jean M. Twenge and W. Keith Campbell, *The Narcissism Epidemic* (New York: ATRIA, 2013), 19.

[32] See Christopher Lasch, *The Culture of Narcissism* (New York: Warner, 1991); May, *The Cry for Myth*, 110–24.

[33] See David C. Korten, *When Corporations Rule the World* (London: Earthscan, 1996), 69.

[34] Ibid., 70.

into pseudo businesses;[35] for example, healthcare is considered an economic commodity and must be subject to the principles of supply and demand of the marketplace.[36] When people are poor, it is their own fault. To provide welfare services will only make people's poverty worse.

Morality

Wrongdoing (or sin) is just negligence or the making of mistakes through one's own fault in the personal mission to succeed or achieve one's destiny; it is the failure to take advantage of this or that relationship that will guarantee one an economic, social, or political advantage. Such morality might be termed Watergate morality: One does everything to get ahead, including lying and bullying, without any concern for the common good, provided one is not found out. The end justifies any means. Truth is highly relative. What serves the welfare of the individual is truth. A *strong grid/weak group* culture so encourages individualism and self-fulfillment, no matter what the costs to the group, that people will turn to any fad or magic (such as astrology) that offers them the secret to and promise of instant success.

When people speak of justice they primarily mean the commutative or contractual type between equals, for example, between individual and individual, or between individual and group; a culture that fosters a "my rights first" approach provides lawyers with a flourishing income from litigations in which people are constantly suing or threatening to sue one another for supposed personal injuries. In this culture model the task of governments at any level is to facilitate the success of individuals, not to concern themselves with the welfare of the common good.

Populism and Conspiracy Theories

The term *populism* is applied to a variety of political movements—the main quality they share is an appeal to the people as a whole, with an

---

[35] See Chris Shore and Susan Wright, "Coercive Accountability," *Audit Cultures,* ed. Marilyn Strathern (London: Routledge, 2000), 63–85.

[36] See Gerald A. Arbuckle, *Violence, Society, and the Church: A Cultural Critique* (Collegeville, MN: Liturgical Press, 2004), 170–71.

emphasis on the ordinary citizens who have been ignored or swept aside by neo-capitalists and their supporting government.[37] The political and business elites are described as trampling in an unlawful manner upon the rights, values, and voices of the legitimate people.[38] Populist leaders use extremist language and behavior to assert that innocent citizens are "beset by remote, powerful and malign enemies" that must be named and marginalized, or silenced.[39] "Populism is a reactionary movement that seeks to turn back the dominant developments of contemporary times and return to an unreal utopian past. Moisés Naím writes that populists suffer from 'ideological necrophilia': a blind fixation with dead ideas. Populists keep demanding social, economic, and political changes that have failed in the past and will collapse also in the future. Naím argues that there are many reasons why bad ideas endure, but perhaps the most important is people's need to believe in a leader amid rapid change and its resulting cultural trauma."[40] Not surprisingly, conspiracy theories flourish when people feel that others are secretly working together to prevent them from succeeding or to destroy whatever success they have achieved.

Religion

Religion within this cultural model reflects the basic stress on individualism. Religion's primary purpose is to support individuals in

---

[37] See Arbuckle, *Fundamentalism at Home and Abroad*, 11–12, 78.

[38] An early example in the United States was the Populist Party in the 1880s and 1890s—a grassroots, politically oriented alliance of agrarian reformers who were unhappy because of crop failures, falling prices, poor credit services, and assumed neglect by politicians in Washington, DC. See Chris Lehmann, *The Money Cult: Capitalism, Christianity, and the Unmaking of the American Dream* (Brooklyn: First Melville House, 2016), 210–12.

[39] Michael Mann, ed., *Macmillan Student Encyclopedia of Sociology* (London: Macmillan Press, 1983), 298; see also Margaret Canovan, "Populism," in *The Social Science Encyclopedia*, ed. Adam Kuper and Jessica Kuper (London: Routledge and Kegan Paul, 1985), 629–31; John B. Judis, *The Populist Explosion: How the Great Recession Transformed American and European Politics* (New York: Columbia Global Reports, 2016); Jan-Werner Muller, *What Is Populism?* (Philadelphia: University of Pennsylvania Press, 2016).

[40] Arbuckle, *Fundamentalism at Home and Abroad*, 78; see Moisés Naím, "What Is Ideological Necrophilia?" *The Atlantic* (February 24, 2016).

their efforts to succeed economically and politically. Religion is not to be concerned with aspects or components of the common good, such as welfare services for people who are poor or disadvantaged. "Since cosmic forces in whatever form do not appear to intrude into people's lives, so secularization flourishes. If gods or spirits do exist, they are befriended for the benefit of individuals in pursuit of success." The society has the potential for millenarian or fundamentalist movements, that is, for enthusiastic crazes under the direction of charismatic and populist leaders, offering quick and "miraculous" shortcuts "to the desired goals of the individual. Traditional rituals are critically assessed according to the utility principle: Will they advance one's position in society? If they feel right and useful, then let's accept them and see what happens. Gods and spirits are therefore seen as 'enablers in my journey of success.'"[41]

Age Discrimination

Certain groups, such as elderly and disabled populations, are sidelined whenever they are judged to be a drag on the country's financial resources. For example, *ageism* describes the negative stereotyping of and/or discrimination against people by reason of their age. The victims may be young or old. Where youth is exalted, because of its economic potential, the mass media encourage images of older people that are outdated, discourteous, and often ludicrous. Older people are stereotyped as being unable to learn, having poor health, and being dependent on others.[42] They are expected to behave according to these images and commonly suffer work discrimination in consequence.[43]

---

[41] See Arbuckle, *Refounding the Church,* 88–89.

[42] See Christina Victor, *The Social Context of Ageing* (London: Routledge, 2005).

[43] In Britain, "60 percent of older people agree that age discrimination exists in the daily lives of older people; 53 percent of adults agree that once you reach very old age, people tend to treat you as a child." See *Later Life in the United Kingdom: January 2018*, AgeUK website, 4. John Paul II, in his 1981 apostolic exhortation *Familiaris Consortia* (On the Role of the Christian Family), writes of the social exclusion of elderly people. See no. 41.

Trumpism: Triggering More Loneliness

Mr. Trump harnessed . . . popular anger brilliantly. Those who could not bring themselves to vote for him may wonder how half of their compatriots were willing to overlook his treatment of women, his pandering to xenophobes and his rank disregard for the facts. . . . He threatens to deprive over 20 million hard-up Americans of health insurance.[44]

He purports to "refound" the nation. . . . He governs through confrontation and polarization.[45]

No person can be elected president of the United States unless that person is able to relate his or her political rhetoric to the founding myths of the nation. Trump is no exception. The dominant founding myth of the United States, with its heavy emphasis on individualism, *strong grid/weak group* culture as described above, reminds Americans that God, or some extraordinary destiny, calls them to participate in a new Exodus, a new journey from the poverty and oppression of other nations, in order to join in the building of a new promised land. This is assumed to be the nation's DNA, its binding glue (see Chapter 2). However, political commentator George Packer believes this myth no longer unifies.[46] He claims that other conflicting and rival residual myths, with their roots in American history, have effectively arisen in recent times. When this happens the Exodus myth becomes only a public myth, the myth that is openly pronounced on important ritual occasions such as ceremonies for the Fourth of July (Independence Day). But as an operative myth it is seriously weakened. All residual myths can become operative myths, and can also coexist, but one may be dominant. Before proceeding, it is important to distinguish among several types of myths—public, operative, and residual—and their relationship to history.

---

[44] "The Trump Era," *The Economist* (November 12, 2016), 9.

[45] "A Peronist on the Potomac," *The Economist* (February 18, 2017), 42.

[46] See George Packer, quoted in David Brooks, op-ed, "The Four American Narratives," *The New York Times* (May 26, 2017).

Myths, Types, and History: Clarifications

Recall that "myths are value-impregnated beliefs or stories that bind people together at the deepest level of their group life, and which they live by and for (see Chapter 2). A myth is a story or tradition that claims to reveal in an imaginative or symbolic way a fundamental truth about the world and human life. The truth is encased in a story simply because it is so powerful for those who accept it that it cannot be contained in any strictly technical or rational statement. In this sense myths are closer to poetry than any other form of speech. Myths can be a mixture of remembering, forgetting, interpreting, and inventing historical happenings."[47] That is, myths can blot out historical facts, particularly if they may be detrimental to the dominant society in power. For example, the founding mythology of the United States seriously conflicts with history and with other mythologies on two points: the exclusion of a white underclass and of Native Americans and African Americans. To understand this, recall that the Revolutionary War was immensely bloody and violent on both sides—yet the victors "scrubbed their own . . . record, which they celebrated as 'untarnished with a single blood-speck of inhumanity.'"[48] This is historical amnesia.

A *public* myth is a set of stated ideals that people openly claim binds them together, for example, the mission statement of a hospital. In practice these ideals may have little or no cohesive force. For example, Tyler Cowen argues that the public myth that America is a land of opportunity, in which its citizens revel in their innovative dynamism and diversity, lacks credibility, giving way to stagnation.[49] With regard to diversity, for example, a report by the Civil Rights Project of UCLA indicated that while desegregation orders in the South made

---

[47] Gerald A. Arbuckle, Cultu*re, Inculturation, and Theologians: A Postmodern Critique* (Collegeville, MN: Liturgical Press, 2010), 30. For a fuller explanation of this section on types of myths, see Arbuckle, *Violence, Society, and the Church,* 7–13.

[48] Holger Hoock, *Scars of Independence: America's Violent Birth* (New York: Crown, 2017), 391.

[49] See Tyler Cowen, *The Complacent Class: The Self-Defeating Quest for the American Dream* (New York: St. Martin's Press, 2017), 47–70.

a clear difference between 1968 and 1988, the proportion of black students in majority-white schools peaked at 44 percent in 1988, and has been declining since. In 2011, only 23 percent of black students attended a majority-white school—the same percentage as in 1968.[50]

An *operative* myth is what actually gives people their felt sense of identity; the operative myth of a group can and often does differ dramatically from the public myth.

A *residual* myth is one with little or no daily impact on a group's life, but which, at times, can become a very powerful operative myth. For example, St. Vincent's is a world-class public hospital in the heart of Sydney; it was founded in 1857 by three Irish religious sisters who braved enormous difficulties primarily to serve the poor. In the 1990s, when the state government threatened to close it, this residual myth of serving the poor surfaced in the public discourse. It so galvanized local support that the government was forced to rescind its decision.

The purposes of myth and history differ; myth is concerned not so much with a succession of events as with the moral significance of these happenings. A myth is a "religious" commentary on the beliefs and values of a culture. Rollo May describes it this way: "The myth is a drama which begins as a historical event and takes on its special character as a way of orienting people to reality."[51] Thus, George Washington can be viewed in historical or mythological terms. As seen from the historical perspective, he is depicted as fitting into a definite time period, influencing and being influenced by events around him. If, however, he is evaluated as a person who exemplifies the virtues of honesty, hard work, and inventiveness in the face of difficulties, then we are measuring him by the founding mythology of the nation. Ultimately, a story that becomes a myth can be true or false, historical or not historical—what is important is not the story itself but the purpose it serves in the life of an individual, a group, or a whole society. Myths allow people of different societies and subcultures to understand themselves and their world.[52]

---

[50] Gary Orfield and Erica Frankenberg, with Jongyeon Ee and John Kuscera, "Brown at 60: Great Progress, a Long Retreat and an Uncertain Future," Civil Rights Project/Proyecto Derechos Civiles (May 15, 2014).

[51] May, *The Cry for Myth*, 26.

[52] Arbuckle, *Culture, Inculturation, and Theologians*, 29–30.

The Land of the Free?

Let us return to George Packer. The *first* myth he describes, which is strongly linked to the Exodus myth, claims that America is a land of free individuals responsible for their own fate. It is a nation that fundamentally values freedom and the dynamism of the free-market economy. In a speech quoted by David Brooks, Packer states: "The libertarian idea in its current shape regards Americans as consumers, entrepreneurs, workers, taxpayers—indeed everything except citizens."[53] But as noted earlier, Packer argues that there are three other narratives vying for position as the dominant myth in America today. The *second* myth, he says, is of globalized America, emphasizing the egalitarian quality of the original founding mythology. The myth "comes with an exhilarating ideology of flattening hierarchies, disrupting systems, discarding old elites and empowering individuals."[54]

The *third* myth is that of multicultural America.

It sees Americans as members of groups, whose status is largely determined by the sins of the past and present. . . . It makes the products of these educations [America's classrooms, from elementary school through university]—the students—less able or less willing to think in terms larger than their own identity group—a kind of intellectual narcissism—which means they can't find common ground or effective arguments that can reach people of different backgrounds and views.[55]

It is a myth that highlights individual groups that do not connect with one another, many of whom are excluded from the American Dream.

The *fourth* myth is the one that effectively united Donald Trump with his supporters: the America First myth. It describes a nation that has lost its identity due to the polluting effect of immigration and the allegiance of the elite to global interests rather than to local needs. Packer writes:

---

[53] Packer, quoted in Brooks, "The Four American Narratives."
[54] Ibid.
[55] Ibid.

America First is the conviction that the country has lost its traditional identity because of contamination and weakness—the contamination of others, foreigners, immigrants, Muslims; the weakness of elites who have no allegiance to the country because they've been globalized. . . . This narrative has contempt for democratic norms and liberal values, and it has an autocratic character. It personalizes power, routinizes corruption and destabilizes the very idea of objective truth.[56]

Implicit in this myth is the promotion of conspiracy theories that blame other people and events for perceived contemporary crises. As with the first myth, this one insists on less federal government. I also observe a violent quality in this myth, with its penchant for wildly denigrating and destroying the past in order to allow a secular nirvana to emerge. I would add a *fifth* residual myth, namely, the racial narrative as spoken by Trump, which was particularly evident in the last presidential campaign.

Residual Xenophobic Mythology

The fourth and fifth residual myths are certainly operative now.[57] Donald Trump was elected president in late 2016 despite his well-publicized "fear-mongering and narcissism and cheerleading for torture . . . racism, misogyny, and xenophobia."[58] His campaign slogans and his behavior during and since the election mirror qualities of the *strong grid/weak group* culture model described above. As David Cay Johnston described the pre-election Trump, "He dismisses those who do not see as he sees himself. In this he is a world-class narcissist."[59] An article in *The Economist* describes his "paranoia and vanity: the press lies about him; the intelligence services are disloyal; his predecessor tapped his phones. It's neither pretty nor

---

[56] Ibid.

[57] See Cowen, *The Complacent Class*, 182.

[58] Mark Danner, "On the Election II," *The New York Review of Books* (November 10, 2016), 19; Carol Anderson, *White Rage: The Unspoken Truth of Our Racial Divide* (New York: Bloomsbury, 2017), 161–80.

[59] David Cay Johnston, *The Making of Donald Trump* (London: Hardie Grant, 2016), 207.

presidential."[60] Later, *The Economist* declared in its lead article that Trump "is politically inept, morally barren and temperamentally unfit for office."[61]

In his campaigning Trump had skillfully articulated the fears of his followers by calling for less government control and intervention, a border ban on Muslims, murdering families of suspected terrorists, and using nuclear arms as a tactical weapon. He expressed hatred of the "other" by describing illegal immigrants as rapists and murderers; claiming that the Mexicans and Chinese and others had "stolen our jobs"; and insisting that allies in Europe and Asia were calculating freeloaders usurping the protections of American power. This is a populist creating fear in order to legitimize the politics of exclusion.[62] His technique was to warn Americans that they are the victims of financial and political conspiracies that he will quickly break apart. In this, *The Economist* notes, he "is tapping into a political tradition with deep roots. . . . The 'America First' movement of the early 1940s accused decadent Europeans and well connected Jews of conspiring to drag America into a new world war. In the 1960s the John Birch Society saw communist cunning at every turn."[63] By his failure to condemn outright the white nationalists actively expressing their hate in Charlottesville in August 2017, Trump seemed to confirm his xenophobic preferences. He has brought white nationalists and fascist sympathizers "into mainstream politics for the first time in living memory."[64] In brief, Trump revived the residual racist myth that the following quotation from historian Robert Parkinson describes, namely, that African

---

[60] "Frustration," *The Economist* April 1, 2017), 11.

[61] "Unfit," *The Economist* (August 19, 2017), 7.

[62] See Ruth Wodak, *The Politics of Fear: What Right-Wing Populist Discourses Mean* (London: SAGE, 2015), 4–6.

[63] "Conspiracy Thinking," *The Economist* (July 15, 2015), 31.

[64] "Workers, Disunited," *The Economist* (August 19, 2017), 29. Among the groups present were The League of the South, a group seeking a southern republic that would reject non-white culture and people; Vanguard America, one of several white supremacist organizations established after the presidential election of 2016; Radical Agenda, a fascist group that helped organize the march; Loyal White Knights of the Ku Klux Klan; and the National Policy Institute, a group known for its use of the Nazi salute.

Americans and Native Americans were excluded from the nation's founding story—a myth that still haunts the present:[65]

> "Good" blacks and Indians were all but invisible in patriot newspapers throughout the conflict (Revolution of Independence). Rather, they were lumped together, as Jefferson would in the Declaration, as "domestic insurrectionists" and "merciless savages." The totality of these printed stories created a convincing interpretation: . . . they were not eligible for any of the benefits of American independence.[66]

Racist rhetoric by Trump, a populist,[67] also immediately appealed to white working-class Americans who felt their cultural and religious securities were under threat from migrants and neglected by the politicians in Washington. They had begun to feel like strangers in their own land.[68] They believed that the nation's emphasis on multiculturalism must cease. Responding to their nostalgia for the securities of the 1950s, Trump promised his followers that America would be great again. Trump shrewdly grasps that the them-against-us fury is

---

[65] See Bryan Stevenson, "The Presumption of Guilt," *The New York Review of Books* (July 13, 2017). E. J. Dionne writes: "We fought the Civil War over the question of who was included in the phrase 'all men are created equal.' And we still have not come to terms with that fact." "There's a Right Way to Judge America's Past," *The Washington Post* (July 2, 2017).

[66] Robert G. Parkinson, *The Common Cause: Creating Race and Nation in the American Revolution* (Chapel Hill: University of North Carolina, 2016), 22.

[67] David Goodhart comments: "In the US and Latin America the term (i.e. populist) has generally been associated with the left and in Europe with the right. Actually there has been a left-wing anti-corporate elite strand to US populism and a right-wing strand that is also nativist and anti-immigrant. . . . Donald Trump combines aspects of both left and right populism." *The Road to Somewhere: The Populist Revolt and the Future of Politics* (London: Hurst, 2017), 54.

[68] See Emma Green, "It Was Cultural Anxiety that Drove White, Working Class Voters to Trump," *The Atlantic* (May 9, 2017); Arlie R. Hochschild, *Strangers in Their Own Land: Anger and Mourning on the American Right* (New York: Free Press, 2016).

deeply imbedded in American history. And white evangelicals loved what they were hearing—81 percent voted for Trump.[69]

Many titles bestowed on Donald Trump—from president to commander-in-chief—are hard for non-supporters to digest. But the honorific that most puzzles the world, perhaps, is that bestowed by American conservatives who praise the swaggering, thrice-married tycoon as a man of God. . . . Mr. Trump's language is filled with echoes of a much-mocked but potent American religious movement with millions of followers, known by such labels as "positive thinking" or the "prosperity gospel," . . . In an address to graduating students at Liberty University on May 13th, Mr. Trump promised his audience a "totally brilliant future", and said that his presidency is "going along very, very well." He ascribed both happy observations to "major help from God." Lots of believers credit God for success, but Mr. Trump went further. He described an America in which winners make their own dreams come true. . . . Like the Trump family, megachurch pastors and their immaculately groomed wives and children are held up as models of divine favour: winners who have found the rungs of an invisible ladder to success.[70]

Political "Cargoism"

Anthropologically, millenarian movements are noted for their declarations of the end of one age or form of life and the coming or dawning of another more perfect one. In Christianity, the term *millennial* refers to a specific type of millenarianism that describes a wide variety "of social movements that have in common an aspiration to reform or to overturn the social order with supernatural assistance."[71] These move-

---

[69] See John Haldane, "The End of 'Coercive Liberalism,'" *The Tablet* (November 19, 2016), 4.

[70] "Why Evangelicals Love Donald Trump," *The Economist* (May 20, 2017): 33.

[71] L. Lindstrom, "Millennial Movements," in *Encyclopedia of Social and Cultural Anthropology,* ed. Alan Barnard and Jonathan Spencer (London: Routledge, 1996), 372.

ments flourish during periods of social, economic and political disruption. Visions of the Nazi new world order or the Marxist classless society are particularly tragic examples of millenarian movements. Less well known are the past and present "cargo cult" movements in Melanesia in the South Pacific.[72] It is claimed that specified ritual actions and bizarre practices will *suddenly* and *spectacularly* bring their adherents a better, even paradisiacal, and plentiful supply of Western goods (called cargo) under messianic leadership. The "cargo" message of leaders is: Repudiate the past by dramatically destroying crops and other goods as the pre-condition for the coming of the "new heaven" of prosperity.[73]

Trump's attempted reforms often follow a millenarian cargo-cult pattern. In his campaign for presidency, Trump promised to "make America great again," claiming that he would demolish Obamacare and much of the work of the previous administration. This would, he claimed, lead to the new promised land—many more jobs, international trade agreements, the best health system, and American prestige in the eyes of the world. Those who were disloyal, who failed to support his destructive methods, would hold back the "cargo." Once in power he immediately demonized his predecessor and began to raze as much of the previous administration's policies as he could. His targets included Obamacare, international trade agreements, and immigration: "For Trump, the mark of a successful president is the degree to which he can expunge Obama's presidency."[74]

When Trump made xenophobic comments about Hispanics and Muslims during his presidential campaign, he tapped into the residual racist aspects of the nation's founding story.[75] Historian Nicholas

---

[72] For an example, see Peter Lawrence, *Road Belong Cargo: A Study of the Cargo Movement in the Southern Madang District, New Guinea* (Manchester: Manchester University Press, 1964).

[73] See Kenelm Burridge, *New Heaven, New Earth: A Study of Millenarian Activities* (Oxford: Basil Blackwell, 1969), 47–74.

[74] Charles M. Blow, "Trump's Obama Obsession," *The New York Times* (June 29, 2017).

[75] Joshua Green argues that ideas about race are not fixed beliefs but a tactic to tap into the American residual mythology. He also pointed out that Trump's contentions that Obama was possibly a Muslim and had not been born in the United States were another political tactic to win votes. *Devil's Bargain: Steve Bannon, Donald Trump, and the Storming of the Presidency* (New York: Penguin Press, 2017), 39–40.

Guyatt has shown "the degree to which some of the early founders—among the finest political minds of their time—were deeply bigoted about race."[76] Historian Robert Parkinson writes:

> Though thousands of Indians and African Americans did support the patriot side [in the revolution], they were never part of the common cause appeal [of the founding story]. Because that narrative lived at the heart of the republic . . . it continued to prevent their inclusion as Americans. . . . [All] those nonwhite faces had evaporated, vanished in a mythology of American patriotism that coded heroic freedom fighters as unquestionably white people. . . . The founders wanted Americans to remember only a certain segment of the fight for independence. . . . In so doing, they distorted our understanding of the Revolution . . . delineating merciless savages and domestic insurrectionists as American enemies and thereby disqualifying them from pursuing happiness inside the new American republic.[77]

Exclusion Trigger for Loneliness

Trump's election has acted as a massive trigger for further excluding a wide variety of individuals and groups from ever being able to participate in the American Dream, and thus assigning them to individual and cultural loneliness. As president, Mark Danner writes, Trump "uses chaos to shock his opponents into varying crouches of outrage and contempt and then lunges forward amid the tumult wherever he sees an opportunity presenting itself."[78] Significantly, Trump appointed as his chief strategist and senior adviser Stephen Bannon, the former head of the right-wing *Breitbart News*, "the crusading, racially charged, hard-right populist website";[79] and Jeff Sessions as attorney general, who has echoed Trump's emphasis on immigration as a danger to national security.

---

[76] David S. Reynolds, "Our Ruinous Betrayal of Indians and Black Americans," *New York Review of Books* (December 22, 2016), 90.

[77] Parkinson, *The Common Cause*, 666, 673.

[78] Mark Danner, "What He Could Do," *The New York Review of Books* (March 23, 2017).

[79] Green, *Devil's Bargain*, 4. Trump dismissed Bannon in August 2017.

Within days and weeks of his inauguration, Trump had repudiated the Trans-Pacific Partnership; ordered the construction of the wall with Mexico; decreed an absolute prohibition on immigration from seven Islamic countries; and warned American "sanctuary cities" that they would lose federal funding if they refused to cooperate with his plans to detain and expel undocumented immigrants. The process of dismantling Obamacare began. All reference to climate change was removed from the White House and State Department websites. David Bromwich warned in early 2017 that "we are not yet close to anarchy or despotism, but the checks and limitations will require constant guarding and frequent use in the months to come."[80] *The Economist* warned in early 2016 that "Mr. Trump has prospered by inciting hatred and violence. He is so unpredictable that the thought of him anywhere near high office is terrifying."[81] His unpredictable behavior is affecting people beyond America. His "politics of deliberate uncertainty is terrifying America's friends and partners: no trade treaty, international institution or alliance is sacrosanct."[82]

The fear and loneliness among vulnerable groups and individuals that has particularly been evoked by Trump's behavior can only be imagined. In early 2017 he gave "immigration officials greater discretion to deport otherwise law-abiding undocumented immigrants and to harass travellers with valid papers."[83] Millions of people in America have been made "justifiably frightened by the tide of racism, anti-Semitism and xenophobia that has swept the country" since the election of Trump.[84]

For example, in September 2017, Trump ended an amnesty for 800,000 people brought illegally into the country as minors—many were Hispanics now in their twenties. Obama's 2012 executive order (Deferred Action for Childhood Arrivals) had granted them the security of work permits. As a result of Trump's action, thousands

---

[80] David Bromwich, "Act One, Scene One," *London Review of Books* (February 16, 2017), 3.

[81] "Time to Fire Him," *The Economist* (February 27, 2016), 9.

[82] Ibid.

[83] Editorial, "Who Belongs to Trump's America?" *Times Digest* (February 26, 2017), 8.

[84] Editorial, "Donald Trump Rages, at the Wrong Target," *Times Digest* (November 22, 2016), 8.

are now left feeling abused, disrespected, fearful for their future—and lonely![85]

Trump's relentless plan to repeal the Affordable Care Act (Obamacare) will mean that millions of Americans will lose their health coverage—many of these are poor people currently covered by the Affordable Care Act's Medicaid expansion. The plan's "underlying and increasingly obvious purpose [is] to reduce taxes for the wealthy by cutting benefits for the needy."[86] Sister Carol Keehan, the president and chief executive officer of the Catholic Health Association USA, noted in an interview with *Crux* that since the ACA was signed into law in 2010, an estimated 22 million Americans gained health insurance coverage for the first time. "To see that go away, and know what that means in their lives is heartbreaking," she stated. "Think about these 22 million people, if they are pregnant, getting treatment for cancer, have diabetes, or if their child has cystic fibrosis, suddenly the security they had is gone. Think how frightening that is. These are people who work very hard. They wait on us in restaurants. They drive taxis. They clean our rooms in hotels. They work one or two jobs, but they can't (otherwise) afford to go to the doctor."[87] Trump's proposed reductions in individual and business income tax rates would "significantly benefit the wealthy."[88] In brief, "vulnerable populations are under relentless attack by this administration."[89] And relentless attacks beget fear and loneliness.

Shortly after Trump's presidential election, teachers in the United States faced "a difficult task of fostering respectful dialogue in classrooms where some children come from Trump-loving families and others from families terrified the president-elect will bring them harm."[90] It was reported that children at a school in Sydney, Australia,

---

[85] "A Dream Deferred," *The Economist* (September 9, 2017), 27–28.

[86] Editorial, "The TrumpRyanCare Debacle," *Times Digest* (March 25, 2017), 8.

[87] Mark Zimmerman, "Catholic Health CEO Calls Push to Dump Obamacare 'Heartbreaking,'" *Crux* (January 5, 2017).

[88] Julie Hirschfeld Davis and Alan Rappeport, "Tax Overhaul Would Aid Wealthiest," *Times Digest* (April 27, 2017), 1.

[89] Charles M. Blow, "100 Days of Horror," *The New York Times* (April 17, 2017), 17.

[90] Emily Durup, Alia Wong, and Hayley Glatter, "Learning in the Aftermath of a Divisive Election," *The Atlantic* (November 15, 2016).

who were as young as five, received "art therapy" after they were heard chanting "We hate Trump." The school confirmed that it had held special lessons to comfort students upset at the result of the presidential election. "They wrote cute stuff but there was a lot of wishing for no war and no fighting."[91] Also in Australia, the corporate giant PricewaterhouseCoopers offered counseling to staff who had become worried by Trump's election win. The chief executive, Luke Sayers, said: "Partners and staff have reached out to me already concerned by reports of women being denigrated on the streets in the US, or Muslims being told to go home."[92]

Prior to Trump's election *The Economist* described the contemporary corruption of truth in politics as

> "post-truth" politics—a reliance on assertions that "feel true" but have no basis in fact. . . . Once, the purpose of political lying was to create a false view of the world. The lies of men like Mr. Trump do not work like that. They are not intended to convince the elites, whom their target voters neither trust nor like, but to reinforce prejudices.[93]

If lies reward politicians or corporate leaders, then that is fine, according to this philosophy. Sabrina Tavernise notes, "News that is fake . . . has lurked online for years, but never before has it played such a prominent role in an American election and its aftermath."[94]

Theological Reflection: The Common Good

Today, everything comes under the laws of competition and the survival of the fittest, where the powerful feed upon the powerless. As a consequence, masses of people find themselves

---

[91] Sam Buckingham Jones, "Trump Puts Kids in Therapy," *Sydney Morning Herald* (November 16, 2016), 3.

[92] Cameron Stewart, "PwC's Australian Staff Worried by US Poll Offered Trump Therapy," *The Australian* (November 19, 2016), 1.

[93] "Art of the Lie," *The Economist* (September 10, 2016), 11.

[94] Sabrina Tavernise, "As Lies Spread, More Readers Shrug at Truth," *Times Digest* (December 7, 2017), 3.

excluded and marginalized; without work, without possibilities, without any means of escape. (*Evangelii Gaudium,* no. 53)

The real test for determining if governments and other agencies are working for the common good will be whether or not they give special consideration to citizens who are the most socially and economically vulnerable. As noted by Pope John XXIII, the common good "embraces the sum total of those conditions of social living, whereby people are enabled more fully and more readily to achieve their own perfection" (*Mater et Magistra,* no. 65). As this chapter shows, the rags-to-riches trope of the American founding myth and its Trumpian expressions fail this test in often dramatic ways. As a consequence of the attitudes and decisions of Trump and his supporters, millions of Americans are being excluded, marginalized, and forced into social, economic, and political loneliness.

Laudato Si': Summary

The ecclesial document that best critiques today's inveterate cultures of individualism, as described above, is Pope Francis's 2015 encyclical *Laudato Si' (On the Care of Our Common Home).* In the first paragraph of the document we are reminded that the earth is "our common home," and that it "is like a sister with whom we share our life and a beautiful mother who opens her arms to embrace us" (par.1); that it is a home for trees, flowers, animals, and human beings. It is not a commodity, an inanimate object to be assessed according to neoliberal profit values.[95] The words "common good" are used thirty times in the encyclical.

In the encyclical's opening Francis places the blame for our climate crisis right where it belongs. We humans have violated the earth, but sin has violated us: "The violence present in our hearts, wounded by sin, is also reflected in the symptoms of sickness in the soil, in the water, in the air and in all forms of life" (par.2). The encyclical's six chapters delineate the climate crisis and our roles as creation's stewards. For example, Chapter 1 describes what is happening to our common home: "We cannot adequately combat

---

[95] See Kevin W. Irwin, *A Commentary on* Laudato Si' (New York: Paulist Press, 2016), 95–96.

environmental degradation unless we attend the causes related to human and social degradation" (no. 48). Chapter 2 describes the Gospel of Creation: "We are not God. The earth was here before us and it has been given to us" (no. 67), reminding us that we are the earth's stewards. "The harmony between the Creator, humanity and creation as a whole was disrupted by our presuming to take the place of God and refusing to acknowledge our creaturely limitations. This in turn distorted our mandate to 'have dominion' over the earth (cf. Gen 1:28), and to 'till it and keep it' (Gen 2:15)" (no. 66). He does not apologize for his assessment of what is happening: "Doomsday predictions can no longer be met with irony or disdain" (no. 161). And he argues that the people on the margins of society, the powerless, are those who suffer the most, as when he observes, "The warming caused by huge consumption on the part of the rich countries has repercussions on the poorest areas of the world, especially Africa, where the rise in temperature, together with drought, has proved devastating for farming" (no. 51).[96]

Political Action Needed

The encyclical challenges us to action at two levels: political and individual (no. 202). Francis is critical of governments that ignore what is happening. At the same time he recognizes that there is a need for a robust role for governments in regulating their economies and protecting the environment according to ethical principles. "A healthy politics needs to be able to take up this challenge" (no. 197). Summarizing what he calls the "weak responses" of global leaders to the environmental crisis, Francis states: "The problem is that we lack the culture needed to confront the crisis. We lack leadership capable of striking out on new paths and meeting the needs of the present with concern for all and without prejudices towards coming generations" (no. 53).

---

[96] Robinson Meyer notes that according to recent studies global warming will intensify regional inequalities in the United States, particularly in the southern states. "The American South Will Bear the Worst of Climate Change's Costs," *The Atlantic* (June 29, 2017). Trump's anti-environmental policies will only further this development.

Individual Action Needed

Despite his call to action, Francis notes that "not everyone is called to engage directly in political life" (no. 232). What then can we do individually? "The ecological crisis is also a summons to profound interior conversion" (no. 217), he observes, and "an awareness of the gravity of today's cultural and ecological crisis must be translated into new habits" (no. 209). What do these two statements mean for us?

Jean Vanier—the founder of L'Arche, an international network of communities for people with developmental disabilities and their caretakers—provides a compelling answer to this question. Like Pope Francis, he is intensely sensitive to the seductive power of culture. Left unchallenged, the cultures of L'Arche communities can insidiously drift away from their authentic founding story and its primary gospel roots. Therefore, he sees the ever-present need for *refounding* L'Arche communities—the need to be constantly inspired by the primary roots of L'Arche.[97] Those roots include love, especially Christ's loving concern for people who are on the margins of society.

The same is true for us—we need to be reminded of our roots as well. Refounding means returning to, and re-owning, the founding story of our faith: love of God and love of our neighbor.[98] It is this love for one another that should impel us to respond to the ecological crisis in whatever way we can.

A sense of deep communion with the rest of nature cannot be real if our hearts lack tenderness, compassion and concern for our fellow human beings. . . . Concern for the environment thus needs to be joined to a sincere love for our fellow human beings and an unwavering commitment to resolving the problems of society. (no. 91)

---

[97] Jean Vanier, *The Founding Myth and the Evolution of Communities,* Prophetic Papers, 2 (1993), 8–9.

[98] See Gerald A. Arbuckle, *Catholic Identity or Identities? Refounding Ministries in Chaotic Times* (Collegeville, MN: Liturgical Press, 2013), 89–198.

The test of this love, therefore, will be our concern for people on the margins who suffer most from the ecological crisis. "The mindset which leaves no room for sincere concern for the environment is the same mindset which lacks concern for the inclusion of the most vulnerable members of society" (no. 196). From loving will automatically follow an effective desire to do something—big or small—to relieve our climate crisis. "Love, overflowing with small gestures of mutual care . . . makes itself felt in every action that seeks to build a better world. . . . Social love is the key to authentic development" (no. 231).

Summary

- Cultures that emphasize individualism to the detriment of the common good foster individual and group loneliness; such is the case with the mythology of the American Dream.
- In libertarian economic theory everything is assessed in terms of the profit motive; minority groups and individuals that are assumed to be unable to contribute economically are pushed aside.
- The ideology of Trumpism energetically encourages the culture of inveterate loneliness by increasing conflictual divisions within the American society. Discrimination is legitimized by the gravely divisive aspects deep within the founding mythology of the United States. The innocent people who are subjected to this behavior feel increasingly demeaned, socially, politically, and often economically, excluded, and thus more and more lonely.

Reflection Questions

- Do you think an excessive concern for individual rights makes it difficult for people to work together for the sake of the common good and, thus, lessen loneliness in society?
- Pope Francis in *Laudato Si'* links concern for the poor with the need to care for the environment. What does he mean?

- What does Francis mean by an "ecological spirituality," and in what ways can it motivate us to an ardent concern for the protection of our world?
- Ponder the final paragraph above ("The test of this love . . .") and ask: In my life, what can I change? What can I do?

4

Poverty as a Trigger of Loneliness

We are seeing the consequences [in the United States] of the lack of hope in rising suicide rates and addiction to opioids and other drugs, in crime and health care outcomes, and in differential educational attainment, among many other measurable outcomes.
  —CAROL GRAHAM, *HAPPINESS FOR ALL?*

One of the main limitations of conventional poverty research has been . . . diverting attention away from causal factors.
  —PETER SAUNDERS, *THE POVERTY WARS*

Since even the most common men have souls, no increase in their material wealth will compensate for arrangements which insult their self-respect and impair their freedom.
  —R. H. TAWNEY, *EQUALITY*

This chapter explains:

- Poverty is a trigger for social exclusion and loneliness.
- The various definitions of poverty.

- The need to assess poverty primarily for its dehumanizing qualities.
- The notion of poverty in the Old Testament.

Triggers for social exclusion of people from mainstream political, social, and economic life that lead to individual and/or cultural loneliness can take a wide variety of forms. Some examples of exclusionary triggers are poverty, racism, disability, gender, ethnicity, age, sexual orientation, and religious affiliation. Social exclusion is the social hardship and relegation of individuals or groups to the borders of society.[1] People are unjustly forbidden to participate in key activities of the society in which they live, thus evoking levels of alienation and loneliness. While they might be able to maintain support from and friendship with members of their own kind, they are alienated from the group with the dominant power. They are made to feel left out, lonely. A multitude of ritual actions tell them they do not belong. The following definition of social exclusion highlights these points:

> Social exclusion is a process that deprives individuals and families, groups and neighborhoods of the resources required for participation in the social, economic, and political activity of society as a whole. This process is primarily a consequence of poverty and low income, but other factors such as discrimination, low educational attainment and depleted living environments also underpin it. Through this process people are cut off for a significant period in their lives from institutions and services, social networks and developmental opportunities that the great majority of a society enjoys.[2]

Consider the biblical story of Bartimaeus. A blind beggar, he has been socially excluded by his poverty and disability. Bartimaeus is sitting by the roadside, a sure symbol of his social rejection (Mark

---

[1] The term *social exclusion* is commonly used in Europe and Australasia. In the United States authors tend to use such terms as *ghettoization* or *marginalization*. See Tania Burchardt, Julian Le Grand, and David Piachaud, "Introduction," in *Understanding Social Exclusion*, ed. John Hills, Julian Le Grand, and David Piachaud (Oxford: Oxford University Press, 2002), 1–12.

[2] John Pierson, *Tackling Social Exclusion* (London: Routledge, 2002), 7.

10:46–52). He is trapped in absolute poverty and so is forced to beg on the fringes of his former community. He has been expelled and now is shunned not only because of his poverty but also because of his blindness. He is judged to be ritually endangering the clean. For his family and former friends he no longer exists. His blindness was like HIV for us in the 1980s—a reason to exclude the sufferers from society. The only identity he possesses is that of a beggar, which is indeed a very precarious form of existence. As Jesus passes by, Bartimaeus cries out for healing. The crowd does its best to silence him, "but he only shouted the louder" (Mark 10:48). People who are poor, especially those who are ritually unclean, are expected to remain silent and accept their fate as (it was falsely believed) a punishment by God for their sins.

Racism and Sexism—Triggers of Exclusion

Maxine Clarke, an Australian writer and poet and a daughter of a Jamaican academic and a Guyanese mother, describes her experience of racism in Australia in the 1980s and 1990s.[3] She was prevented from receiving a well-deserved public-speaking prize, mercilessly teased, excluded by some of her peers, and told by a geographically challenged teacher that her mother's family must be from Ghana not Guyana, that she cannot be "from India" as she has those "striking African looks." Sexism is another trigger for exclusion. Kelly Dittmar claims that "masculine dominance in the Republican Party [in the United States] is not only in numbers but in culture."[4] In July 2017, two female senators who disapproved of their party's proposed healthcare legislation were subjected to demeaning sexist comments.

This chapter focuses on poverty as a ritual trigger for social exclusion and as a cause of consequent loneliness for people who are rendered powerless. How a problem is articulated and then elucidated

---

[3] See Maxine Beneda Clarke, *The Hate Race: A Memoir* (Sydney: Corsair, 2016).

[4] Cited in Elise Viebeck, "Female Senators Are Increasingly on Receiving End of Insults from Male Officials," *Washington Post* (July 27, 2018). Kelly Dittmar, Center for American Women and Politics, Rutgers University, is the author of *Navigating Gendered Terrain: Stereotypes and Strategy in Political Campaigns* (Philadelphia: Temple University Press, 2015).

strongly affects what is actually done about it. Inaccurate assessments of and defective attitudes toward poverty unvaryingly result in bad policies and practices that can intensify alienation and loneliness. Frequently, poverty is measured only in quantifiable terms such as low income, inadequate housing, sickness, and level of educational achievement. This gives an inadequate picture of the realities of poverty. Qualitative analysis is also essential; thus, there are four additional definitions of poverty in the following list. However, all five are interconnected and reinforce one another:

- poverty as quantifiable
- poverty as deprivation of opportunities
- poverty as stigmatizing and discriminating, with racist connotations
- poverty as cultural breakdown
- poverty as a culture of violence

Poverty as Quantifiable

On the basis of income there is a distinction between absolute and relative poverty. *Absolute poverty* is defined by a set income measure below which people experience complete destitution and so cannot meet even minimum needs for food and shelter. The United Nations Development Programme has set this measure as one US dollar a day for people living in third- and fourth-world countries. Below that income threshold people experience severe malnutrition and perilous levels of ill health.

In the United States in 2015 "19.4 million people reported family income below one-half of the poverty threshold."[5] In 2016, it was estimated that there were over half a million people in the United States classified as homeless, 8 percent of whom were veterans.[6] But these statistics are inadequate by themselves because they do not tell

---

[5] Bernadette D. Proctor, Jessica L. Semega, and Melissa A. Kollar, "Income and Poverty in the United States: 2015" (Washington, DC: US Department of Commerce, September 2016).

[6] This is a drop of 35 percent since 2009. Social Solutions, "2016's Shocking Homelessness Statistics," blog (June 21, 2016).

us, for example, about "how much income [people] actually have, [and] how reduced their children's chances are of developing skills for climbing into the middle class."[7]

Relative poverty, on the other hand, is more helpful in assessing material and income levels and their impact on people's lives. The term *relative poverty* refers to "the lack of resources needed to obtain the kinds of diet, participate in the activities and have the living conditions and amenities that are widely approved and generally obtained by most people in a particular society."[8] Those who experience this form of poverty, as Bartimaeus did, have resources so below others in society that they are effectively excluded from ordinary and essential living arrangements and activities.

Lack of equality of educational opportunity is a significant contributor to the rigidity of poverty. Educational needs in socioeconomically depressed areas require significant input of finance and specialized staff, but, in fact, they get less than what is needed in terms of buildings, facilities, equipment, and teachers (particularly those with training in special needs). People with no housing, or inadequate housing, find it extremely difficult, if not impossible, to obtain ordinary services such as a bank account or a credit card, or to develop a regular relationship with local schools and doctors. In Australia the lack of affordable housing is making low-income households spend 30 percent and some as much as 50 percent of their income on rent. Most jobs are in metropolitan areas, far away from low-cost housing. Thus, increased travel costs add to the financial burdens of living in poorer housing. Those living on low incomes have incidences of illness and poor health at much higher rates than people on high incomes. The causes are many; they include stress, poor and/or overcrowded housing, poor nutrition, and lack of money.

People can become so imprisoned by their low income that it is incredibly hard for many to break through its crushing circumstances. We speak of a cycle of poverty, simply because the factors referred to are interconnected and self-perpetuating.[9] This vicious cycle, in

---

[7] Jeff Madrick, "America: The Forgotten Poor," *The New York Review of Books* (June 22, 2017), 49.

[8] Pierson, *Tackling Social Exclusion*, 9.

[9] See Gerald A. Arbuckle, *Culture, Inculturation, and Theologians: A Postmodern Critique* (Collegeville, MN: Liturgical Press, 2010), 53.

which poverty breeds poverty, transmits its effects from one genera-
tion to another. There is no beginning to the cycle and no conclusion.
A financially poor family leads to a poor diet, inadequate housing,
limited access to health and educational facilities, unemployment and
underemployment because of a lack of qualifications, and reduced
energy levels. Bartimaeus was ensnared in this cycle. He would have
been suffering from a poor diet, the effects of unemployment, poor
health, and reduced energy levels.

Poverty as Deprivation of Opportunities

Since poverty prevents or obstructs people from participating as full
members of society, it can be defined as a "deprivation of opportunities" or a "capability deprivation." All have the right to work, to
participate in society, and to grow intellectually, emotionally, and
spiritually. All people have responsibility for one another's well being;
all people should have opportunities to meet their responsibilities and
to contribute to society.[10] But structures of society can render these
rights and responsibilities impossible for groups in society to achieve.
People who are trapped in the circle of poverty have a restricted range
of choices available to them. To be poor is "to be denied the chance to
enjoy the consumption of goods, or the ability to achieve and maintain
good health, or participate in social activities or other aspects of community life."[11] Such was the fate of Bartimaeus in the time of Christ.
Such is still the fate of millions of people in the world today.

Unless we look at poverty from this structural, cultural, entrapping
perspective, then we will tend to blame the victims for their poverty,
social exclusion, and loneliness. Statements like "the poor can get
themselves out of poverty, if they truly want to" are dangerously
simplistic and do nothing to clarify our understanding of the complexity of poverty and its ability to crush initiative and self-respect. For
example, in Australia poverty is commonly viewed by people from
an affluent culture as the victim's problem and not as a multifaceted

---

[10] See Mary Jo Bane, in *Lifting Up the Poor: A Dialogue on Religion,
Poverty and Welfare Reform*, ed. Mary Jo Bane and Lawrence M. Mead
(Washington, DC: Brookings Institution Press, 2003), 22–23.

[11] Peter Saunders, *The Ends and Means of Welfare* (Cambridge: Cambridge
University Press, 2002), 143.

cultural issue.[12] Likewise, in the United States, people who are poor, especially if they are single mothers, African Americans, or Hispanics, are frequently blamed for being poor by members of the dominant culture. In March 2017, United States congressman Roger Marshall cited scripture in defense of the unsuccessful Republican proposal to repeal Obamacare, despite the fact that it would deprive twenty-four million Americans of health insurance: "There is a group of people that just don't want healthcare and aren't going to take care of themselves."[13] The impact of cultural factors on the health of the marginalized is ignored.[14]

Poverty as Stigmatizing and Discriminating: Impact on Victims

The third definition of poverty describes it from the perspective of the people who experience it. Let me first clarify what I mean by *stigmatizing* (further explained in Chpater 5). A *stigma* is a culturally recognized quality that is used by people who hold power to differentiate and discredit others: "It is the phenomenon whereby an individual with an attribute which is deeply discredited by his/her society is rejected as a result of the attribute. Stigma is a process by which the reaction of others spoils normal identity."[15]

The particular stigma disqualifies those so marked from full social acceptance. The stigma may be physical (a bodily deformity), mental, age, behavioral, or social (in the sense of membership in a group, for example, an ethnic group or people of low income). The identification of the stigma is used to reduce the person from a complex whole to a single, tainted, and discounted trait, upon which all social interaction with the person by the dominant power group will be based.

---

[12] See Alastair Greig, Frank Lewins, and Kevin White, *Inequality in Australia* (Cambridge: Cambridge University Press, 2003), 94.

[13] Roger Marshall, quoted in Jeff Madrick, "America: The Forgotten Poor," *The New York Review of Books* (June 22, 2017), 50.

[14] See Joel F. Handler and Yeheskel Hasenfield, *Blame Welfare, Ignore Poverty and Inequality* (Cambridge: Cambridge University Press, 2007), 1–16.

[15] Erving Goffman, *Stigma: Notes on the Management of Spoiled Identity* (New York: Simon and Schuster, 2009), 8.

A stigma is a highly subjective issue, both for the stigmatized and the stigmatizers, as Gillian Paterson reminds us.[16] It is engraved on people's identity at the deepest level. Both groups have internalized the scripts that inscribe some as having less than full humanity, and others as having full humanity. Note that the process of stigmatizing people who are poor is done by those with the political and economic power to do so (see Chapter 5). The tragedy is made worse when those who are stigmatized begin to believe the negative stereotypes given them by stigmatizers.[17]

Those who are trapped in a cycle of poverty and are stigmatized by society can feel shamed, pushed to the margin, considered of no importance, as having nothing to contribute to society, worthless, of no credibility, and blamed for their own poverty—they can even be made to feel genetically inferior as human beings. It has been found that many people using a food bank in England "see themselves as failures, excluded from normal society, and often claim to be ashamed that they cannot provide for their families."[18] In an Oxford University study into poverty and shame, "The words 'awkward,' 'embarrassed,' 'guilty,' 'rotten,' 'degraded,' 'crap,' 'useless,' 'worthless,' 'a failure,' 'uncomfortable,' 'funny,' and 'dirty' were all used to convey how people felt about themselves or were made to feel in certain social interactions."[19]

Most of us would at some stage experience these feelings, but people who are stigmatized by society, such as people who are socioeconomically poor or are struggling with mental illness, are made to

---

[16] Gillian Paterson has developed a timely study on the relationship among stigma, stigmatizing, and discrimination relating to HIV/AIDS in Africa and the moral and theological implications for the churches on this tragic issue. See *AIDS Related Stigma: Thinking Outside the Box: The Theological Challenge* (Geneva: Ecumenical Advocacy Alliance, 2004).

[17] In 1976, in a study of attitudes of senior indigenous Maori college students in New Zealand, I found that 73 percent accepted the dominant culture's view of their inferiority. They agreed to the statement: "Maoris have above-average gifts for manual or semi-manual work." Teachers said that when these students found their studies hard, they would quickly lose confidence in themselves, saying: "What's the use! We Maoris don't have the skills anyway."

[18] Pat Caplan, "Big Society or Broken Society? Food Banks in the UK," *Anthropology Today* 32/1 (2016): 5–9.

[19] See Kayleigh Garthwaite, *Hunger Pains: Life Inside Foodbank Britain* (Bristol: Polity Press, 2016), 145.

experience these feelings *every day* of their lives. A sense of fatalism and hopelessness can grip them, as their sense of self-worth and self-respect disintegrate. We need to ponder and become keenly aware of what happens to human dignity once hope is a forgotten word and a person's spirit is enslaved. The psalmist describes the inner pain of people who have been stigmatized and socially marginalized because of their poverty: "You have deprived me of my friends, made me repulsive to them, imprisoned, with no escape" (Ps 88:8). You can sense the pain also in the cry to Jesus by Bartimaeus: "Let me see again" (Mark 10:51).

Sociologist Harriet Bradley aptly illustrates how society stigmatizes the poor while rewarding the wealthy for their own mistakes:

> While bailiffs come round to impound furniture and electrical appliances from the homes of the poor who fall behind with their bills, when the Royal Bank of Scotland faced financial crisis in 2008, the UK government used taxpayers' money to bail them out. But the public gained nothing from this, and the bankers continued to pay bonuses to themselves and their favored employees on top of big salaries (the bonuses received by women . . . are smaller).[20]

Look further at the Australian scene, at how quick governments and the public are to stigmatize people who are poor for their own misery, at how the problem of poverty is reduced to blaming people on welfare. This then legitimizes discrimination against them. In January 2002, reports Mark Peel, the Melbourne *Herald Sun* condemned four thousand welfare cheats but failed to point out that this represented a minuscule fraction of those seeking benefits.[21] One month later, the minister for Family and Community Services reinforced the popular, but incorrect, stereotype that a huge percentage of people on welfare cheat the system. She will personally ensure, she said, that

---

[20] Harriet Bradley, *Fractured Identities: Changing Patterns of Inequality* (Cambridge: Polity Press, 2016), 266.

[21] See Mark Peel, *The Lowest Rung: Voices of Australian Poverty* (Cambridge: Cambridge University Press, 2003), 172; Peter Saunders, *The Poverty Wars* (Sydney: University of New South Wales Press, 2005), 95; Rodney Whyte, *Australia's Artful Dodger: Centrelink* (Wollongong: Welfare Watchdog Publications, 2005), 103.

cheats are caught and punished. Other politicians have also played on the stereotype. As Peel comments: "Some politicians and public policy-makers [have] even created fictional stories to demonize welfare recipients; in the absence of sufficiently dramatic empirical evidence, fiction does just as well."[22] When people are demonized, they are quickly defined to be in some way or other innately inferior. This is equivalent to racism. The categorization legitimizes governments denying them their fundamental rights.[23]

People can give up trying to cope with the endless stigmatizing pressures of prejudice, poverty, unemployment. Human dignity cannot be subjected to endless indignities and remain intact. In the United States a recent study by Carol Graham convincingly argues:

> The empirical findings . . . confirm the increasingly consistent story of "two Americas" with the poor much less likely to be optimistic about their futures than the rich. . . . Lack of hope and faith in the future may seem intangible and far from the realm of policy, but is reflected in real-world outcomes. . . . The recent increase in mortality rates for middle-aged, uneducated whites is a stark marker of this ill-being and lack of hope.[24]

One Australian Aboriginal person declared with sadness: "Look at me—I'm coloured and I'm dirty, drunken, lazy and irresponsible, like they say—that's my privilege, because I'm Aboriginal—I can do as I like, because that's what they expect of me anyway." Little wonder if at times this sense of hopelessness can be a catalyst for violent outbursts of frustration.

Poverty as Cultural Breakdown

As we have seen, people who lose hope and faith in the future can fail to accept incentives and interventions even in instances where

---

[22] Peel, *The Lowest Rung*, 172.

[23] See Evelyn Kallen, *Social Inequality and Social Injustice* (New York: Palgrave, 2004), 32.

[24] Carol Graham, *Happiness for All? Unequal Hopes and Lives in Pursuit of the American Dream* (Princeton, NJ: Princeton University Press, 2017), 118, 147.

policy changes make them available. Indigenous cultures such as the First Nations in North America, the Maori people in New Zealand, and Aborigines in Australia still struggle to find their cultural roots after centuries of exploitive contact with Western colonizing powers.[25] People whose culture has been destroyed lose heart and energy, because a culture provides people with a sense of identity, belonging, and self-respect. They die emotionally and psychologically, and their physical health further disintegrates (see Chapter 2). "'Beside the waters of Babylon,' cried the Israelites in exile, 'we sat down and wept when we remembered Zion. . . . For there our captors asked us for songs, and our tormentors asked for mirth, saying, 'Sing us one of the songs of Zion.' How could we sing the Lord's song in a foreign land?" (Ps 137:1).

When British settlers first arrived in Australia in 1788, they concluded that the country was *terra nullius*—a land without a people—and therefore it was theirs for the taking. They took the land by forcibly removing the Aboriginal peoples, and we know what happened to Aboriginal peoples in consequence.[26] Because the identity of Aboriginal peoples is intimately related to the land, they lost their sense of belonging and meaning in life. Such was also the experience of Native Americans and other indigenous peoples around the world. We cannot grasp the reasons for their contemporary poverty if we ignore cultural history. Likewise, it is impossible to understand the poverty of African Americans and the loss of hope for many of them if we forget the years of slavery and ongoing prejudice and discrimination that still continue today.

Robyn Eversole notes that there is a world pattern linking indigenous peoples to poverty and racism:

> When dominant groups impose their culture (e.g. market capitalism and sedentary lifestyles) and destroy aspects of indigenous culture (e.g. access to land and language), poverty tends to increase. Indigenous poverty is related to racism. . . . Racist

---

[25] See Henry Reynolds, "New Frontiers: Australia," in *Indigenous Peoples' Rights in Australia, Canada, and New Zealand*, ed. Paul Havemann (Oxford: Oxford University Press, 1999), 129–40.

[26] See a summary of the controversial use of the term *genocide* in Bain Attwood, *Telling the Truth about Aboriginal History* (Sydney: Allen Unwin, 2005), 87–105.

assumptions may be used by members of the dominant society to justify the appropriation of indigenous people's resources. . . . Indigenous poverty is related to social marginalization.[27]

The impact of cultural disintegration is also a reality for people who feel left behind in the economic changes of their countries. For example, Baltimore, a former steel and manufacturing center, has lost seventy-five thousand factory jobs since 1990. Consequently, about a quarter of the population "are stuck in poverty, with few obvious exits."[28] It is estimated that about fifty thousand residents are addicted to opioids.[29] A twenty-five-year study of 790 children in the city found that from 1982 to 2007, only 4 percent of poor children succeeded in obtaining a college degree.[30]

Poverty as a Culture of Violence

Normalization of Violence

Violence, like fundamentalism, is rather slippery to define. Violence is not about damaging or destroying *things*. It is about abusing *people*. Violence crushes the spirit of people and makes them submissive to violators. It is not confined to killing or physical violence, but the creation of *cultural* conditions that materially or psychologically destroy or diminish people's dignity, rightful happiness, and capacity to fulfill basic material needs. Cultures of violence can also be called "cultures of bullying,"[31] because the conscious or unconscious intention of the powers that politically control the cultures is to intimidate people into submission or to make them feel that they can develop no

---

[27] Robyn Eversole, "Overview: Patterns of Indigenous Disadvantage Worldwide," in *Indigenous Peoples and Poverty: An International Perspective,* ed. Robyn Eversole, John-Andrew McNeish, and Alberto Cimadamore (New York: Zed Books, 2005), 34–35.

[28] "On Murderous Streets," *The Economist* (July 1, 2017), 29.

[29] Ibid., 30.

[30] Ibid.

[31] See Gerald A. Arbuckle, *Confronting the Demon: A Gospel Response to Adult Bullying* (Collegeville, MN: Liturgical Press, 2003), 65–94.

rational control over their lives. Such degrading intimidation results in distressing loneliness.

Neo-capitalism, which is so popular today (see Chapter 3), begets a culture of violence, and the poor and vulnerable in society are the first to suffer its impact.[32] Its ideological assumption is that profit is the sole measure of value. It is cultural violence. Walter Wink, a social and scriptural commentator, pinpoints this tragic reality of our times: "Violence is accorded the status of religion and it, not Christianity, is the real religion."[33] It is increasingly taken for granted in many quarters that violence is the only and final means to security, victory or revenge.

Little Lisa, the saxophone-playing daughter of Homer on *The Simpsons* television show, at one point becomes squeamish about watching television violence. Her delinquent brother, Bart, replies: "If you don't watch the violence, you'll never get sensitized to it."[34] What Lisa is complaining about is the "normalization of violence" or the "normalization of deviance."[35]

An Example of Normalized Violence: Baltimore

Baltimore is one of the least safe cities in the United States; the city saw 343 murders in 2017, in most of which both the victims and their murderers were African American. Violence has become normalized. Why is this so? "The answer lies in some combination of poverty, family instability, epidemics of drug use in the wretched inner-city districts into which many blacks [are] corralled by racist

---

[32] For a fuller development of the relationship between postmodernity and violence see Gerald A. Arbuckle, *Violence, Society, and the Church: A Cultural Approach* (Collegeville, MN: Liturgical Press, 2004), 153–214.

[33] Walter Wink, *Engaging the Powers: Discernment and Resistance in a World of Domination* (Minneapolis: Fortress Press, 1992), 13.

[34] Quoted in Chris Turner, *Planet Simpsons* (London: Ebury Press, 2004), vi.

[35] Sociologist Diane Vaughan used the phrase "normalization of deviance" to describe a cultural drift in which circumstances classified as "not okay" are gradually reclassified as "okay." She illustrated this with what led to the space-shuttle *Challenger* disaster. See Diane Vaughan, *The Challenger Launch Disaster* (Chicago: University of Chicago Press, 1996).

housing policies, and bad, or non-existent, policing."[36] The last of these, which goes well beyond occasional instances of police violence, harkens back to America's public racist history. The murders of black Americans did not particularly bother police because black lives were considered of less value than white lives. While this may have changed today, it is difficult to recruit and train inner-city police officers because of the existing culture of violence.[37]

Normalization of Gambling: Violence against the Poor

James Doughney asks:

> Is it right for our society to license, literally, a form of institutional banditry against those less well off?[38]

Consider the normalization of violence against poor people that occurs in significant parts of the world—for example, the United States, Australia, Britain—because of the neo-capitalist gambling policies of governments. A disproportionate share of problem gamblers are drawn from the lower socioeconomic sections. People are unwittingly being encouraged to believe that gambling is a personally and socially rewarding and relaxing experience. Governments have become so dependent on taxes from gambling to balance their budgets that it is difficult for them to be open to its social costs—especially to the costs for people who are already poor and disadvantaged. For example, in 2011, Australia's six state governments reaped "$A5 billion a year in taxes from gambling. They have been wishy-washy in calling for curbs."[39]

Under the influence of neo-capitalist ideology the primary purpose of casino operators and associated agencies is to maximize their

---

[36] "On Murderous Streets," 28–29.

[37] Ibid.

[38] James Doughney, "Socioeconomic Banditry: Poker Machines and Income Redistribution in Victoria," in *Competing Visions: Refereed Proceedings of the National Social Policy Conference 2001*, ed. Tony Eardley and Bruce Bradbury, SPRC Report 1/02, Social Policy Research Centre, University of New South Wales, Sydney, 153.

[39] "Gaming and Politics in Australia," *The Economist* (January 28, 2012), 26. This rose to $A6 billion in 2014–15.

profits and make every effort to exploit the weaknesses of potential patrons and motivate patrons to gamble large amounts.[40] Where this exploitation occurs, there is a culture of violence. As elsewhere, gambling in the United States, through parimutuel betting, the lottery, Indian reservation casinos, or luxury resorts, is now considered a normal form of relaxation. Yet, "lotteries are played disproportionately by the poorest and most disadvantaged groups, with the unemployed, the low paid, the undereducated, the elderly, the minority groups spending more than others." This means that "various projects and services funded by lotteries are paid for primarily by the poorest members of their communities."[41]

As in the United States, the casino and associated agencies in Australia target depressed or lower socioeconomic geographical areas, especially through electronic gaming machines (EGMs).[42] When gambling sites are placed disproportionately in these poorer suburbs, the consequence is that less-well-off people frequent them. "Local government areas [in Australia] with the lowest socio-economic indicators have the highest densities of gaming machines and losses per adult. . . . Household expenditure survey data confirms that gaming expenditure [on EGMs] accounts for a disproportionate share of the household income of the bottom 60% of households, and is least significant amongst the richest 20%."[43] Only 41 percent of EGM players surveyed claim to limit their gambling to what they can afford.[44] Over a quarter of respondents to a survey wrongly believed that "a poker machine is more likely to pay out soon if someone has been playing it for an hour and lost their money."[45]

---

[40] Germain Grisez, *The Way of the Lord Jesus: Difficult Moral Questions* (Quincy, IL: Franciscan Press, 1997), 3:838.

[41] Gerda Reith, "Pathology and Profit," in *Gambling: Who Wins? Who Loses?*, ed. Gerda Reith (New York: Prometheus Books, 2003), 12.

[42] Australians lose more than US$20 billion a year gambling, about two-thirds of that on EGMs. "Gaming and Politics in Australia," *The Economist*, op. cit., 26.

[43] David Hayward and Bev Kliger, *Breaking a Nasty Habit? Gaming Policy and Politics in the State of Victoria*, a report commissioned by the InterChurch Gambling Taskforce (2002), 9.

[44] Roy Morgan Research, *Seventh Survey of Community Gambling Patterns and Perceptions* (Melbourne: VCGA, 2000), 80.

[45] Hayward and Kliger, *Breaking a Nasty Habit*, 34.

Machines are programmed to ensure that over a given period of time the machine wins. Skill has no role in this form of gambling. The longer people play, the more chance they have of losing,[46] and the possibility of losing massive sums of money on EGMs is a reality.[47] "About 600,000 Australians (4% of adults) play [EGMs] at least once a week. On average they pour an astonishing \$A8,000 [per player] each year into the machines."[48] Statistics have shown that "problem or compulsive gamblers" provide a *significant* source of profits. It has been estimated because "the problem gamblers account for over 40% of losses, it can be safely concluded that of the \$A2.4b that was lost on poker machines [in 2001], between \$A1b and \$A1.4b is likely to be accounted for by this group of players. A disproportionate share of these people are drawn from lower income groups."[49] With such a massive number of machines in Australia (200,000), and given that the lower socioeconomic areas are targeted, it is extremely difficult for people who are poor or unemployed to escape the impact of the culture of violence fostered by institutional gambling companies.

The industry's owners in the United States and Australia aim to create an atmosphere in which gambling is socially acceptable and a pleasant experience by providing a variety of recreational and entertainment services, such as theaters and dancing facilities, at venues like casinos and hotels. Their transfer of some profits from these venues into the community—for example, through well-publicized donations to sporting clubs and charitable activities—can help to blind the public to the primary purpose and social consequences of this type of institutional gambling. One could be excused for thinking that the executives are providing recreational facilities. But behind this facade, the real industry is gambling. Everything is window dressing—executives and advertisers use the term *gaming* rather than *gambling* to help disguise what is really going on. The latter word has a harsh note of reality to it, but the former evokes playful behavior, something safe

---

[46] Ibid., 5–6.

[47] John Dalziel, communications director of the Salvation Army, noted in a personal communication to the author that it is now "possible to lose up to \$5,000 in an *hour* by playing multiple machines which you can do at the push of a button" (March 22, 2004).

[48] "Gaming and Politics in Australia," 26.

[49] Hayward and Kliger, *Breaking a Nasty Habit,* 37.

that children can participate in.[50] Who are the real winners? People who are economically and socially excluded and marginalized in society are not the winners. The social damage of gambling costs Australia between \$A1 billion and \$A5 billion a year. One in ten problem gamblers have contemplated suicide; the marriages of one in four have broken up due to gambling.

Responding to Poverty

Efforts to eradicate poverty as a trigger for social exclusion and loneliness are of two types, though the line between them is not always clear: emergency and developmental community programs. Emergency aid concentrates on working *for* people. Developmental projects emphasize collaborating *with* people. Emergency efforts are short term, aiming to respond to a specific and urgent crisis, and generally have little direct impact on the structural causes of poverty. Community development programs, however, are more long term and are directed at the causes of poverty and injustice, attempting to change personal and social perceptions and to promote self-reliance.

It is not our task here to suggest particular projects for implementation, because this can only be done by each system or facility in close partnership with the people it is called to serve. But it is within the scope of this chapter to remind readers of some basic guidelines that should be followed in choosing and implementing projects. Goodwill alone is no guarantee that involvement in community development will succeed. By way of background to these guidelines there are two fundamental requirements for the success of any community developmental program: first, the need to foster the ongoing participation of the people the project seeks to serve; second, the need for change agents to have the right attitudes to development.[51]

Guideline 1: Aid Is a Two-Way Process

The most important gift of a would-be change agent in community development is the willingness to listen. The word most used in the

---

[50] Ibid., 42–43.

[51] See Gerald A. Arbuckle, *Earthing the Gospel: An Inculturation Handbook for Pastoral Workers* (Maryknoll, NY: Orbis Books, 1990), 196–202.

scriptures after the name of God is the word *listen* and its many expressions such as *harken, attend,* and *open your ears.* Without the gift of listening in a change agent, it is impossible to develop the mutual trust that will ultimately be the foundation for development. Real listening is tough and grinding work, especially in a world where there is so much stress on being busy *doing* things. Serious and deliberate listening to people who are marginalized takes time and a willingness to avoid hasty analyses and answers. Above all it demands of change agents an awareness that those who experience injustice may have insights into its causes that they do not have. Development is a two-way process of learning. Change agents may have far more to learn than the people they seek to aid.

Indeed, people who struggle against poverty and marginalization have much to teach those of us who are privileged with human and material resources. In a particularly touching scene Jesus reminds his disciples of the teaching power of people society brands as weak. For example, he settles a dispute about who should be the greatest among them by placing a child in their midst. He then insists that they must become like a child, who socially is equal in status to a slave (Matt 18:1–5).[52] Yet, by their powerlessness, children can teach the powerful something fundamental about life—joy, simplicity, a yearning for love and respect.

Pope Francis writes that people who are poor "have much to teach us" about coping with their marginalization and loneliness:

> Not only do they share in the *sensus fidei,* but in their difficulties they know the suffering of Christ. We need to let ourselves be evangelized by them. . . . We are called to find Christ in them, to lend our voice to their causes, but also to be their friends, to listen to them, to speak for them and to embrace the mysterious wisdom which God wishes to share with us through them. (*Evangelii Gaudium,* no. 198)

Jean Vanier also invites us to work *with* people on the margins, but with a warning: We must be prepared to learn from these people, not just to give them the benefits of our expertise. Jean Vanier believes

---

[52] See Bruce J. Malina and Richard L. Rohrbaugh, *Social-Science Commentary on the Synoptic Gospels* (Minneapolis: Fortress Press, 1992), 117.

that people with mental disabilities, for example, have by "their very weakness and their call to friendship and communion the ability to touch the hearts of the powerful and strong, calling them to love and to a deeper recognition of their fundamental humanity. They possess thus a healing power, bringing people to unity, renewing the church and humanity."[53] Jesus Christ has truly chosen the foolish and the weak of this world to confound the wise and the strong (1 Cor 1:27).[54]

I recall two incidents in which I felt particularly powerless and dependent on people who themselves had become marginalized. The first occurred in a poor Fijian village in 1965 where I was about to begin research into credit unions that were owned and operated by local people. I asked a gathering of people what they had gained by their membership in these unions. I expected a reply detailing loans for material goods. Not so! Tears streaming down his face, one man replied, "For the first time in my life I could be trusted by people. The colonial government has been telling us for years that we cannot manage our own affairs and that we do not trust one another with money matters. I received a loan from my credit union on the basis of my character alone. Never before have I felt trusted by people! This is my experience." No book could have taught me in more eloquent language that sustained poverty destroys a people's spirit of self-worth and mutual trust and that the ultimate aim of development is growth in self-reliance and shared trust.

Later, in 1968, on a rugged island between New Zealand and Antarctica remote from any settlement, my vehicle had become impossibly bogged down in the mud of an unpaved road. I was rescued eventually by a family living close by in considerable poverty and isolation. I became totally dependent for several days on their generosity. My academic skills were useless—even at card games I was their inferior! They had the power, not me, yet they treated me as an honored guest, sharing what little they had with me until

---

[53] Jean Vanier, *The Founding Myth and the Evolution of Community,* Prophetic Paper 2 (1993), 7. See also reflections by Hans S. Reinders, "Being with the Disabled: Jean Vanier's Theological Realism," in *Disability in the Christian Tradition: A Reader*, ed. Brian Brock and John Swinton (Grand Rapids, MI: Eerdmans, 2012), 467–511.

[54] See Jean Vanier, *Letter to My Brothers and Sisters in L'Arche* (Trosly, 1996), 7.

I could be rescued and returned to New Zealand. My lectures on poverty changed in response to this and other similar incidents.

In summary, authentic listening requires a direct effort to share in a significant way in a people's experience of being mistreated, bypassed, left helpless. It involves a choice to express compassion more radically by sharing to some degree in the sufferings of people on society's margins. Without some experience of solidarity, it is easy for aid givers to view people on the margin as "them," the impersonal objects of our sympathy. There is a danger of acting in a paternal way toward these people, thus forcing them into a harmful culture of dependency. "It is easy to tell the poor to accept their poverty as God's will," writes Thomas Merton, "when you yourself have warm clothes and plenty of food and medical care and a roof over your head and no worry about the rent. But if you want them to believe you, try to share some of their poverty and see if you can accept it as God's will."[55]

Ultimately, the commitment to work with people who are poor is a spiritual one. It necessitates a struggle for total personal and institutional transformation, a letting go of the desire to dominate people and to use God's creation exclusively for one's own personal or institutional advantage. It means a constant willingness to analyze *together* what is happening and how best to move forward *together* according to gospel values. If we do, we can confidently hope that "the light [will shine] in the darkness, and the darkness [will] not overcome it" (John 1:5).

Guideline 2: Listen to Discover the People's Needs

This guideline is often overlooked because the temptation is to decide what is best for others. In brief, the process of assistance must begin at the point of the needs of the people, not the needs as perceived by the aid giver, no matter how objectively important they may be. When this basic guideline is neglected, any effort at community change is doomed to fail. In order to discover people's real needs in today's complex societies, the assistance of appropriate professional personnel may be necessary. This may be time

---

[55] Thomas Merton, *New Seeds of Contemplation* (London: Burns and Oates, 1961), 139.

consuming, but respect for the dignity of people and the correct stewardship of resources demand it.

Guideline 3: A Project Must Affect the Whole Group

A change agent who wishes to help a group of people to develop must seek to involve all sections. If not, factions will emerge and endanger whatever cooperation is emerging. Also, people are apt to lose interest or become discouraged or suspicious of others if they are unable to see that each step in a project is related to the overall goals. While the vision for a project can be grand, the steps toward its achievement need to be small and readily identifiable by those involved.

Guideline 4: Ongoing Local Leadership Structures Must Be Established so that the Project Is Owned by the People Themselves

The temptation is for aid givers to attempt to do everything themselves, thus forcing people into an unhealthy dependency situation.

Guideline 5: Change Requires Rituals of Group Mourning

Frequently groups that have been marginalized by successive governments and other agencies experience a significant unarticulated grief that is the accumulated sadness, fatalism, and anger resulting from their humiliation and rejection. When grief is kept hidden and unprocessed in a community, we can be sure that hopelessness is a consequence. There is no energy for constructive change. Grief remains like a powder keg waiting to be ignited into all kinds of individually harmful and community-destroying behavior. The first-century Roman poet Ovid aptly described the reality of unnamed grief: "suppressed grief suffocates."[56] Unfortunately, grieving in the Western world tends to be treated as "a weakness, a self-indulgence, a reprehensible bad habit instead of a psychological necessity."[57] Yet,

---

[56] Ovid, *Tristia,* book V. eleg. 1, line 63.

[57] Geoffrey Gorer, *Death, Grief, and Mourning in Contemporary Britain* (New York: Doubleday, 1965), 85.

rituals of mourning remain an essential precondition for successful community development projects. In both the Old and New Testaments we see many examples of people who, once they begin to name their grief in public, discover new hope and new visions of society.[58] This public proclamation of grief can be silenced from two different sides—from beneath by those too crushed to cry, and from outside by those who fail to recognize that people are in pain.[59] Some in dominant power positions may, however, recognize this pain, but they may fear for their position if it is acknowledged. The change agent must be skilled in perceiving this pain and be able collaboratively to develop constructive rituals, in order to allow grief to be named so that hope can emerge.

Theological Reflection:
Poverty in the Old Testament

The righteous know the rights of the poor;
    the wicked have no such understanding. (Prov
    29:7)

This reflection offers us the chance to learn from the poor in Old Testament times. What is God saying through them? How does God judge wealth? Why does God show in this Testament a special love of the poor in their loneliness? Society in the times of both the Old and New Testaments is polarized: wealth is concentrated in the

---

[58] For an understanding of the significant relationship between ritual and cultural change, see Gerald A. Arbuckle, *Change, Grief, and Renewal in the Church: A Spirituality for a New Era* (Westminster: Christian Classics, 1991); idem, *Refounding the Church: Dissent for Leadership* (Maryknoll, NY: Orbis Books, 1993), 180–200; idem, *Healthcare Ministry: Refounding the Mission in Tumultuous Times* (Collegeville, MN: Liturgical Press, 2000), 271–341; idem, *The Francis Factor and the People of God: New Life for the Church* (Maryknoll, NY: Orbis Books, 2015), 91–124. In rituals of mourning in traditional cultures and in the scriptures there is a twofold dynamic: the naming of loss or sadness, and then the identification of what is new and positive in the experience of the group, however faint it might be.

[59] See Walter Brueggemann, *Hope within History* (Atlanta: John Knox Press, 1987), 72–91.

hands of a minority, and the rest of the population live in degrading poverty.[60]

Poverty Defined

Poverty means two things: lack of the material goods necessary for life, and lack of power to defend oneself against the oppression of the wealthy. Thus, to equate poverty with "spiritual poverty" is biblically incorrect. People who are poor are made to feel socially and humanly inferior and unwanted in a society that defines status on the basis of wealth. They are forced to remain in the loneliness of their poverty because of the arrogance, avarice, and godlessness of the rich, who are corrupted through storing up treasures for themselves instead of becoming rich in the sight of God (Luke 12:21).

The scriptures are not against wealth, but they are opposed to its misuse. Capital must be at the service of the common good; in aiding people on the margins believers are expected to give not only from their surplus goods but also from their capital. People are just when they are in right relationship with God and with other people. The ultimate test of this right relationship is one's loving concern for people who are economically deprived in society and who suffer the consequent social and political powerlessness. In both Testaments there is a strong condemnation of well-to-do people who fail to use their wealth appropriately. People are entrapped in poverty and rendered politically powerless because of the greed of people who are wealthy.[61]

Involuntary Poverty Condemned

In the Old Testament involuntary poverty with its material and immaterial aspects is contrary to the fundamental truths of God's special relationship with the Israelite nation. All people are equal in dignity before God. All have the right to an equitable use of this world's resources, and all are called to work collaboratively to ensure that this right is respected. For example, we read in Isaiah:

---

[60] Portions of this section are adapted from Gerald A. Arbuckle, *A 'Preferential Option for the Poor': Application to Catholic Health and Aged Care Ministries in Australia* (Canberra: Catholic Health Australia, 2007), 24–26, 31–32..

[61] See Ben Witherington, *Jesus and Money* (London: SPCK, 2010), 7–16.

> Ah, you who join house to house,
>   who add field to field,
> until there is room for no one but you,
>   and you are left to live alone
>   in the midst of the land. (Isa 5:8)

The prophet is condemning the rich for swallowing up small indebted farms, "leaving the landless poor at the mercy of the employment practices of the landed rich. . . . Biblical law addresses the question of social welfare by giving as many people as possible the capacity to produce and hence to look after themselves."[62] Ultimately, God owns the land. From God's standpoint this means that even those people who have access to property are "aliens and tenants"[63]:

> The land shall not be sold in perpetuity, for the land is mine; with me you are but aliens and tenants. Throughout the land that you hold, you shall provide for the redemption of the land. (Lev 25:23–24)

The test of the community's faithfulness to God is its concrete daily respect for these truths. "You shall love the Lord your God," says God, describing how the Israelites are to relate to him, "therefore, and keep his ordinances, and his commandments always" (Deut 11:1). Thus "to love God" is to be inseparably linked with "serving him" in building a community of justice and compassion (Deut 11:13). In return, God promises that the Israelites "would eat to their hearts' content" (Deut 11:15). However, God warns about letting their hearts be "seduced into turning away" by the gods of wealth and power (Deut 11:16).[64] If temptations lead them politically and economically to exploit the poor, thus marginalizing vulnerable widows, orphans, and refugees, they are acting hypocritically. For this they are to be punished (Amos 8:4–6).[65] "Ah, you who make iniquitous decrees, who

---

[62] Jonathan Burnside, *God, Justice, and Society: Aspects of Law and Legality in the Bible* (Oxford: Oxford University Press, 2011), 207, 251.

[63] Ibid., 219.

[64] See Delbert R. Hillers, *Covenant: The History of a Biblical Idea* (Baltimore: Johns Hopkins University Press, 1969), 152.

[65] See Mary Elsbernd and Reimund Bieringer, *When Love Is Not Enough: A Theo-Ethic of Justice* (Collegeville, MN: Liturgical Press, 2002), 41–46.

write oppressive statutes, to turn aside the needy from justice, and to rob the poor" (Isa 10:1–2).

The prophet Amos scathingly decries the Israelites "who oppress the poor, [and] crush the needy" (Amos 4:1). In the time of Amos a small political group had robbed people of land that had been in their families for generations. Now they were being charged exorbitant rents as tenant farmers and pressured to grow crops that their masters needed to enrich themselves further through the international market. Speaking through Amos, God condemns the hypocrisy of the rich oppressors for their fine acts of worship while neglecting the rights of people who are poor: "I hate, I despise your festivals, and I take no delight in your solemn assemblies. . . . Take from me the noise of your songs; I will not listen to the melody of your harps. But let justice roll down like waters, and righteousness like an overflowing stream" (Amos 5:21, 23–24). By "justice" and "righteousness" Amos means that people must meticulously avoid oppressing the poor and crushing the needy. Instead they are to pursue systematically steadfast love in their regard.

Vulnerable Groups: Special Concern

Three vulnerable groups are often singled out for special concern: widows, orphans, and migrant aliens. In the patriarchal cultures of those times only free adult males have rights. Others have to depend on male patrons for protection. Hence, women and children who have been widowed or orphaned and lack an adult male to defend them have no legal rights. They become particularly vulnerable to all kinds of oppression (Job 22:9; 24:21; Ezek 22:7). In the Book of Exodus the Israelites are left in no doubt as to what they must do: "You shall not wrong or oppress a resident alien, for you were aliens in the land of Egypt. You shall not abuse any widow or orphan. If you abuse them, when they cry out to me, I will surely heed their cry; my heart will burn" (Exod 22:20–23). God reminds the Israelites that they were once vulnerable aliens in Egypt until they were rescued from their slavery (Exod 24:17–18).[66]

---

[66] Walter Brueggemann, the Old Testament scholar, notes: "It is important to accent that something like 'God's preferential option for the poor' is deeply rooted in Israel's speech about God. The claim is not a belated, incidental addendum to Israel's ethical reflection, but belongs integrally and inalienably to Israel's core affirmation of the character of Yahweh." *Theology of the Old Testament: Testimony, Dispute, Advocacy* (Minneapolis: Fortress Press, 2005), 144.

Hospitality to Strangers

Hospitality is one of the most important virtues for Jewish people—for example, it is more important than fasting (Isa 58:7). This is because hospitality is an application of the fundamental truth that all creation belongs to God and all have the right to share equitably in its fruits. The Israelites, since they had been strangers in Egypt, are to show hospitality in turn to strangers in their midst: "You shall not oppress a resident alien; you know the heart of an alien, for you were aliens in the land of Egypt" (Exod 23:9), and "The alien who resides with you shall be to you as a citizen among you; you shall love the alien as yourself, for you were aliens in the land of Egypt" (Lev 19:33–34). The prophets often speak of the duty of giving to the poor as an expression of hospitality, but their emphasis is primarily on its justice quality and not on what we would call today philanthropy—the giving from one's surplus. Philanthropy, however, is also encouraged (Prov 3:27–28; 28:27).

In brief, God is not against wealth or power as such but condemns their exploitation. However, the danger of being seduced by material goods is so great that their ownership is problematic. When people become selfishly attached to wealth and power, refusing to use them in the service of the community, then evil exists. They no longer have a right relationship with God (Ps 49:6). God has a preferential love for people who are economically poor, that is, for the powerless, because they have no one to trust but him: "This is the one to whom I will look, to the humble and contrite in spirit, who trembles at my word," and "The Lord . . . will have compassion on his suffering ones" (Isa 66:2, 49:13) because they have cried to the Lord and have been "heard by the Lord" (Ps 34:6). The poor are to be God's loved ones that the Messiah will draw together in a new relationship.[67] And God so identifies with people who are poor that caring for them is like helping God: "Whoever is kind to the poor lends to the Lord, and will be repaid in full" (Prov 19:17).

---

[67] See X. Leon-Dufour, *Dictionary of Biblical Theology* (London: Geoffrey Chapman, 1967), 386–87.

Summary

- Poverty excludes people from participating in the social, economic, and political activity of society as a whole, forcing them into a world of powerlessness and loneliness. Poverty thus degrades their dignity.
- In responding to poverty, Pope Benedict XVI's warning must be heeded: "We are dealing with human beings, and human beings need something more than technically proper care. They need humanity. They need heartfelt concern" (*Deus Caritas Est,* no. 31).
- At the heart of the Old Testament's teaching on wealth, property, and poverty is the fundamental principle that the world and everything within it belongs to God. Some ethical implications of this for the Israelites are: no interest is to be charged on loans to members of the community (Deut 23:19–20); permanent hospitality is to be given to escaping slaves (Deut 23:15–16); wages must not be held back from the poor (Deut 24:14–15); injustices must not be committed against a resident alien or an orphan (Deut 24:17–18); the community must provide food for the needy and the marginalized (Deut 24:19–22).[68]

Reflection Questions

- Have you ever felt excluded from a group? What did it feel like?
- In your experience how are people who are poor portrayed in the mass media? by politicians?
- Who in your society are poor because they have little or no power to change? What political changes should be made to help them?
- Should the justice system give them rights to this help?
- Is there something, however small, that you can do to relieve the loneliness of people who are poor?

---

[68] See Walter Brueggemann, *Journey to the Common Good* (Louisville, KY: Westminster John Knox, 2010), 39–40.

5

"You Are Not Us!": The Loneliness of Strangers

There are many markers of the high cost of being poor in the land of the American Dream. . . . And all of these combine to make it difficult for children born into families with these markers to exit poverty.

—CAROL GRAHAM,
HAPPINESS FOR ALL?

Authoritarianism is creeping back as new radical parties bring about a renewed emphasis upon ethno-politics, which establishes a sharp distinction between "members" and "strangers," those who belong and the rest.

—MONTSERRAT GUIBERNAU,
BELONGING

Various subcultures exist side by side, and often practice segregation and violence. . . . There are many "non-citizens," "half-citizens," and "urban remnants."

—*EVANGELII GAUDIUM*, NO. 74

This chapter explains:

- Why all cultures are tempted to ethnocentric reactions.
- How dominant societies develop exclusion triggers and loneliness.
- Multiculturalism as a ritual process of sharing power with minority groups.
- The meaning of a "preferential option for the poor" in the New Testament.

In a previous publication I described how fundamentalism in many shapes and forms is very much present in our Western societies.[1] There are abundant fundamentalist economic, political, nationalistic, and religious movements in the West. Right-wing, populist, anti-immigrant movements are on the rise in Europe, the United States, Australia, and elsewhere. One thing common to all fundamentalist movements is this—they set up rigid inclusion/exclusion boundaries. One is either *in* or *out*, excluded and cast into the liminality of loneliness. However, this ability to set up rigid boundaries that exclude is not a quality of fundamentalist movements alone. On the contrary, any dominant society holds the power to exclude people unjustly from belonging. This chapter describes the various ways in which this power is exercised against people who are unable to defend themselves. It begins with an anthropological analysis of the dynamic behind this exclusion process.

Theoretical Considerations

Ethnocentrism

Through symbols, myths, and rituals, all cultures have an inbuilt tendency to create boundaries with potentially powerful feelings dividing "us" from "them," unless they work actively to prevent this from occurring. This is the social disease of ethnocentrism, the definition of which (by G. Sumner in 1906) remains valid today: "the view of

---

[1] See Gerald A. Arbuckle, *Fundamentalism at Home and Abroad: Analysis and Pastoral Responses* (Collegeville, MN: Liturgical Press, 2017).

things in which one's group is the centre of everything, and all others are scaled and rated with reference to it."[2] The English poet Rudyard Kipling describes ethnocentrism in this way: "All nice people like Us are We, and everyone else is They."[3] The media can play a key role in developing the language of ethnocentric exclusion through their cutting back of complex realities to simplified binaries such as black/ white, young/old, and rich/poor, "which are then joined to estimations of moral worth such as degenerate/civilized . . . respectable/rough. This contributes to the creation of images of the 'other' as abnormal, distant, outside and not us."[4] Since the "other" is not like us, they can be treated with disdain. Sociologist Jock Young describes this as a method of cultural essentialism that "allows people to believe in their inherent superiority while being able to demonise the other, as essentially wicked, stupid or criminal."[5]

Anthropological Explanation

Anthropologist Mary Douglas's explanation throws further light on this potential problem. She focuses on a people's understanding of "purity" and "pollution."[6] Her language appears at first to be some-what dramatic, but her insights are of significant importance to read-ers. Her concept of pollution does not refer to the intrinsic hygienic properties of things but rather to their symbolic qualities as "matter out of place."[7] For Douglas, when explaining her understanding of pollution, the object of our deepest anxieties is everyday dirt. It evokes an attitude—"ugh!"—and demands a response—"clean up!" What is considered dirty in some way or other pollutes or defiles what is clean and must be put aside. An appreciation of what causes things to be called dirty or clean, Douglas argues, may uncover the deepest

---

[2] William G. Sumner, *Folkways* (Boston: Ginn, 1906), 13.

[3] Rudyard Kipling, *Debits and Credits* (London: Macmillan, 1926), 327–28.

[4] Daphne Habibis and Maggie Walter, *Social Inequality in Australia: Discourses, Realities and Futures* (South Melbourne: Oxford University Press, 2015), 125.

[5] Jock Young, *The Exclusive Society* (London: Sage, 1999), 109.

[6] See Mary Douglas, *Purity and Danger: An Analysis of the Concepts of Pollution and Taboo* (London: Routledge and Kegan Paul, 1966).

[7] Ibid., 36.

mysteries of the moral order itself, the reasons that some societies renew and reaffirm their fundamental collective feelings and beliefs, while others do not even bother.[8]

The question is—why are some things considered dirty and other things clean? Why are shoes judged dirty when placed on the table but clean when on the floor? It is the location that defines their dirtiness and its power to evoke a reaction. Ideas of dirt and feelings of being disgusted arise when things are outside their usual boundary system. Examples include how we consider our relation to hair, fingernails, and skin taken from the body, or pots and pans being placed in the bedroom away from the kitchen. As Douglas writes: "Dirt is the by-product of a systematic ordering and classification of matter, in so far as ordering involves rejecting inappropriate elements."[9] This means that what is thought to be dirty is relative. Douglas comments: "Shoes are not dirty in themselves, but it is dirty to place them on the dining-table. . . . It is dirty to leave cooking utensils in the bedroom. . . . In short, our pollution behaviour is the reaction which condemns any object or idea to confuse or contradict cherished classifications."[10]

It is not just a question of factual location that condemns something as dirty or clean. Shoes are not dirty just because they are on the table rather than on the floor, but because they *should* be on the floor and *not* on the table. There is a moral quality to reality that renders the issue of classification, and misclassification, also as a matter of right and wrong. When we say that shoes should be on the floor we are not only stating a fact about "the mechanical appropriateness of nature, but a moral evaluation of that order."[11] Dread of pollution is like fear of immorality or sin.

Scriptures: Pollution and Exclusion

The Israelite tradition required that people must show compassion, especially to people who are poor and marginalized (Isa 58), but

---

[8] See Robert Wuthnow, James D. Hunter, Albert Bergesen, and Edith Kurzweil, *Cultural Analysis* (London: Routledge and Kegan Paul, 1984), 85.

[9] Douglas, *Purity and Danger,* 48.

[10] Ibid.

[11] Wuthnow, Hunter, Bergesen, and Kurzweil, *Cultural Analysis,* 87.

Jewish fundamentalists discarded this obligation, developing instead a religion that focused on external conformity to rituals of accidental importance.[12] So, to touch a dying person, a leper, or a blind person causes ritual impurity in a would-be aid giver. In the parable of the Good Samaritan (Luke 10:25–37), the priest sees the dying man on the roadside but declines to help because he is not prepared to be defiled by touching the victim (v. 31). The victim has become socially a nonperson. The Levite, who belongs to an order of cultic officials "for the service of the Lord" (Exod 32:28), also declines to help, for the same reason (v. 32). Jesus several times touched ritually impure people to heal them, and consequently he himself became ritually dirty and risked being excluded from society. For example, when he healed a leper, "he could no longer go into a town openly, but stayed out in the country" (Mark 1:45). People feared they themselves would become ritually impure in his presence.[13]

Pollution and Ethnic Boundaries

Every human society and organization subscribes, mostly *unconsciously*, to rules of purity and pollution in some form or other. A culture (or subculture) is a purity system—that is, it tells people what is pure and clean, or evil and therefore dangerous or polluting. The fear of pollution defines and protects the boundaries of a group. Pollution, as opposed to purity, interferes with the acceptable equilibrium, destroys or confuses desirable boundaries, and evokes destructive forces or conditions. As Douglas writes: "In short, our pollution behaviour is the reaction which condemns any object or idea likely to confuse or contradict cherished classifications."[14] Contemporary refugees trying to land in the United

---

[12] See John J. Pilch, *Healing in the New Testament: Insights from Medical and Mediterranean Anthropology* (Minneapolis: Fortress Press, 2000), 111–17; and Gerald A. Arbuckle, *Violence, Society, and the Church: A Cultural Approach* (Collegeville, MN: Liturgical Press, 2004), 242–47.

[13] See Richard L. Rohrbaugh, "The Social Location of the Markan Audience," in *The Social World of the New Testament: Insights and Models,* ed. Jerome H. Neyrey and Eric C. Stewart (Peabody, MA: Hendrickson, 2008), 143–62; Louise J. Lawrence, *Sense and Stigma in the Gospels* (Oxford: Oxford University Press, 2013).

[14] Douglas, *Purity and Danger,* 36.

States, Australia, or Europe are daring to break orderly boundaries and thus are creating among citizens a fear of being "polluted." They are "them," and the self-righteous citizens are "we."[15]

For example, a 2004 survey in Australia found that 96 percent of respondents accepted the statement, "It is good for children of different ethnic and religious backgrounds to mix at school."[16] This is a public myth of Australians, but the operative myth is significantly different because there is an increasing ethnic segregation in Australian schools. In her research of secondary schools Dr. Christina Ho concluded that

> there is a growing unofficial creed among many Australian parents that a "good school" for their children is one where minorities are in the minority. And public schools are increasingly viewed as ghettoes, whether they are the disadvantaged schools of the poorer suburbs, or the high achieving selective schools that top all the league tables.[17]

It would seem, therefore, that a significant percentage of Anglo-Australian parents view ethnic minorities as endangering the "purity" of their culture and community. If this pattern continues, school communities will fail to reflect the full diversity of Australian society.

From Gossip to Scapegoating: Triggering Exclusion

Gossip is the forerunner of witch hunting or scapegoating.[18] Gossip is the liminal stage between private and public worlds, but

---

[15] See Richard Alba and Nancy Foner, *Strangers No More: Immigration and the Challenges of Integration in North America and Western Europe* (Princeton, NJ: Princeton University Press, 2015), 2–16.

[16] Deb Wilkinson, Richard Denniss, and Andrew Macintosh, *The Accountability of Private Schools to Public Values,* discussion paper no. 71, The Australian Institute (2004).

[17] Christina Ho, "'My School' and Others: Segregation and White Flight," *Australian Review of Public Affairs* (May 2011).

[18] See Pamela J. Stewart and Andrew Strathern, *Witchcraft, Sorcery, Rumors, and Gossip* (Cambridge: Cambridge University Press, 2014), 203; Tom Douglas, *Scapegoats: Transferring Blame* (London: Routledge, 1995).

scapegoating formally takes malicious feelings toward others from a world of shared secrets directly into the public arena. For example, the chief priests had been gossiping about Jesus and the dangers he presented to their status, but finally they came out into the open and formally named Jesus as the object of their scapegoating: "The chief priests answered [Pilate], 'We have no king but the emperor.' Then they handed [Jesus] over to them to be crucified" (John 19:15–16). Self-preservation motivated this scapegoating; as Caiaphas shrewdly said, "It is better to have one person die for the people" (John 18:14).

Anthropologically, witch hunting is the simplistic search for agent(s) to be branded as responsible for individual or community afflictions. It fulfills several functions: to explain for individuals and cultures what cannot be understood; to control the uncontrollable; and to account for the problem of evil personally and in society. Envy, jealousy, and fear are among the powerful emotions behind scapegoating. The objects of scapegoating are branded as "dirt," as less than human, so that a society can act against them without feeling guilt. This is the evil of racism in all its hideous forms.[19] The victims are powerless to fight back. There seems to be a basic need in all cultures for human beings to avoid responsibility and to transfer evil to others. The comic dramatist W. S. Gilbert has the Lord High Executioner in *The Mikado* sing:

> As some day it may happen that a victim must be
>   found,
> I've got a little list—I've got a little list,
> Of society offenders who might well be under-
>   ground,
> And who never would be missed—who never
>   would be missed.

Sometimes the term *stigmatization* is used as a substitute for the word *scapegoating,* but there is a significant difference in meaning.

---

[19] Racism is "an ideological discourse based upon the exclusion of particular collectivities because of their biological or cultural make-up." Montserrat Guibernau, *Belonging: Solidarity and Division in Modern Societies* (Cambridge: Polity, 2013), 84.

Anthropologically a *stigma* is a social quality that devalues an individual, community, or culture. There are socially defined stigmas of the body (for example, deformities, learning disabilities), of assumed character (for example, having a criminal record, being gay), and of social collectivities (for example, youth, people who are poor, religions, tribes, minorities, immigrants, refugees, races). The fact that people suffer stigmas does not mean that at this moment they are being scapegoated. It does mean, however, that they are the ones most likely to be scapegoated and excluded, when the need arises, by the dominant power group for problems for which they are not responsible.[20]

For example, in the 1990s, "Pauline Hanson started a new nationalistic Australian political party, One Nation, and for a period of time it had significant impact on voters. Among the reasons she gave for the notable decline in incomes of white Australians were globalization, Asian immigration, and welfare payments to Aboriginal peoples. Hanson skillfully [drew] on the unarticulated feelings of envy and jealousy that many of her followers experienced. One observer commented that 'Ms. Hanson speaks to the subjectivities of men—tapping into their pervasive sense of loss . . . mourning for lost jobs, past glories, lost power and . . . loss of national sovereignty (due to globalization).'"[21] She claimed that others (migrants and city people, for example) had moved into positions of power, but that rural men had been sidelined.

The inclination for people to blame others for their own afflictions is a convenient way to avoid owning up to their own role in their development and to the accompanying guilt. Scapegoating can evoke such fears for self-preservation that even friends are falsely and often secretly accused of misdeeds, if this will prevent punishment for the scapegoaters. We have but to reflect on the operations of secret police in the former East Germany to see to what extent fear and secrecy can destroy family bonds and friendships. Little wonder that witch

---

[20] See Erving Goffman, *Stigma: Notes on the Management of Spoiled Identity* (Englewood Cliffs, NJ: Prentice-Hall, 1964); Arbuckle, *Violence, Society, and the Church*, 138.

[21] Marilyn Lake, "Pauline Hanson: Virago in Parliament, Viagra in the Bush," in *Two Nations: The Causes and Effects of the Rise of the One Nation Party in Australia,* ed. Robert Manne (Melbourne: Bookman Press, 1998), 118.

hunting transforms open cultures into worlds of jealously guarded, fear-evoking secrets, in which truth, trust, and friendships are shattered, even in schools. One further tragic consequence of scapegoating is that the victims can even begin to believe the negative stereotypes said about them.

Chaos Triggers Blaming

Anthropologists have discovered that this tendency to assign blame to others is particularly rife in times of cultural disintegration or chaos. Terms like *witches, enemies of the people, political subversives, conspirators,* and *polluters of orthodoxy* have been used throughout history to refer to individuals or groups who are targeted as the causes of the cultural malaise. Mass scapegoating movements, moral panics or crazes emerge out of the turmoil; putting aside the rules of rationality, people vengefully and simplistically search out and name people they believe cause their chaos. For example, there was the anti-Communist craze within the United States in the early 1950s under Senator Joseph McCarthy. The cultural and political climate within the United States was ripe for such witch hunting, because, as Eastern Europe and parts of Asia had succumbed to oppressive Communist dictatorships, many Americans wondered about their own future as a free nation. McCarthyism caused suffering for thousands of innocent people, with the unquestioning cooperation of many politicians and the Federal Bureau of Investigation, the mass media, and millions of American citizens.[22]

Another example may be found in President Trump's use of American residual racist mythology of Mexican people and others. In order to account for an assumed decline in the American economy and global power, he rails repeatedly against the stupidity of the nation's political leaders who, he says, have allowed "Mexican immigrants whom [Trump] called 'rapists'"[23] to cross the border and damage the economy.

---

[22] Gerald A. Arbuckle, *Intentional Faith Communities in Catholic Education* (Strathfield: St. Pauls Publications, 2016), 56

[23] "Election 2016: How It Happened," *The Economist* (November 12, 2016), 31.

Today, as Europe experiences high unemployment, people yearn for an explanation; ultra-right and nationalistic movements flourish, indiscriminately accusing immigrants for the rise of unemployment. Generally, marginalized peoples are particularly targeted in witch-hunting movements. Those who fear that their political or socioeconomic power is being undermined direct their anger against these outcasts because, it is believed, the latter are seeking revenge for their socioeconomic and political powerlessness. In the social, economic, and religious turmoil of the fifteenth to seventeenth centuries in Europe, the most marginalized were Jews, women, and the poor; these people readily became the scapegoats for the fears of the frightened political, social, and religious elite in society. Little wonder that today immigrants and refugees in Western countries are being falsely blamed for undermining the economies of those countries. And women remain objects of contemporary scapegoating. In fact anti-feminist movements are bound to intensify as supporters of oppressive patriarchal power in cultures feel their status and power threatened and eroded through the campaign for women's rights. Of course, the dynamic also works the other way. That is, outcasts are tempted to simplify the reasons for their misery by blaming a powerful person or group.[24]

The leaders of scapegoating crazes are people who are thought to have particular ability to name, ritually control, and punish society's enemies. Traditional cultures have different terms for these people, including *diviners, witch-doctors,* and *shamans.* In Western cultures their equivalents can be populist religious or political leaders such as Adolf Hitler or, on occasion, such sophisticated ritual activities as congressional hearings in the United States or state trials under Communist countries. These individuals or political rituals may tap into the fears of people by skillfully and publicly identifying particular people as scapegoats to account for society's social and economic problems.[25]

Today we see a "normalization of nationalistic, xenophobic, racist and anti-Semitic rhetoric, which primarily works with 'fear': fear of change, of globalization, of loss of welfare, of climate change,

---

[24] See Arbuckle, *Intentional Faith Communities in Catholic Education,* 534–57;

[25] See Ruth Wodak, *The Politics of Fear: What Right-Wing Populist Discourses Mean* (London: Sage, 2015), 3–4, 153–54.

of changing gender roles; in principle, almost anything can be constructed as a threat to 'us,' an imagined homogenous people inside a well-protected territory."[26] Every time there is a move to reinforce the "us," fed by fear, the scapegoated suffer yet more loneliness and have less power to change the situation.

Dominant Societies' Attitudes toward Outsiders

We can observe two types of policies in stances taken by dominant societies toward minority groups: the first appears in situations in which the political power of the former is *not shared with* minority groups (sometimes referred to as outsiders or strangers), who consequently are forced into cultural loneliness; the second appears in situations in which power is positively shared with minority groups.

Policies in Dominant Societies in which Power Is Not Shared

Enforced Ethnicity

Ethnicity is the existence of culturally distinctive, self-conscious groups (ethnic groups) within a society, each claiming a unique identity based on a shared tradition or common experiences and on social symbolic markers such as culture, language, religion, income, and physical characteristics such as skin pigmentation. Historically, the tendency has been to assume that social markers were determined by the physical qualities of people. Thus, the word *race* was incorrectly and frequently applied to separate ethnic groups. In recent times the term *ethnic group* has become preferable among many who seek to counteract the implied or overt xenophobia of the word *race*.

The ethnic identity of an oppressed group is called an *involuntary* or *ascribed* ethnicity; there is little or no escape from this negative labeling and oppression. In such cases of involuntary or ascribed ethnicity, the us/them dichotomy that is always present in ethnic relations

---

[26] Wodak, *The Politics of Fear,* x; see also Arbuckle, *Fundamentalism at Home and Abroad,* 1–29.

is especially strong. The dominant group ("us"), often out of a sense of fear of losing its position of power, pejoratively stereotypes the oppressed group ("them") and institutionalizes that oppression so that in key areas of life such as employment, education, and social relationships, the oppressed are excluded from equality with the dominant group. To develop and legitimize this discrimination, the in-group frequently brands the out-group racially or culturally inferior. This has happened to blacks in South Africa, African Americans in the United States, Jews in Nazi Germany, and immigrants in parts of contemporary Europe. Members of the dominant host group commonly tend to isolate themselves geographically and socially to avoid unnecessary contact with the immigrant groups.[27]

Under oppression, aggrieved ethnic groups may demand equality of opportunity, even going so far as to seek radical forms of political self-determination—one example of this is evident in the breakup of Yugoslavia into the violently opposed nationalistic states of Bosnia, Serbia, and Croatia. In Canada, Quebec nationalists think that total political independence is the only option left to them; they believe that the present federal government system cannot adapt sufficiently in order to allow them equality of opportunity. Many contemporary Scottish nationalists have similar thoughts. Ultimately, at the heart of the revival of ethnicity is the fundamental need for all peoples, whether oppressed or not, to develop a sense of community identity and self-worth. The more people are oppressed the more they yearn to belong.

Historical Policies for Indigenous Peoples and Migrants

Historically, the dominant society can act toward ethnic groups in one or more of the following ways: by annihilation, segregation, or assimilation, or by encouraging cultural pluralism or multiculturalism.

In the early years of European colonization, for example, the indigenous peoples in Australia experienced efforts to annihilate them. There were also attempts to segregate indigenous Australians by taking their lands and forcing them away from developing urban settlements. By segregating them so that they were out of sight, governments could ignore their human rights. Violence against the First Peoples was especially intense, tragically symbolized by the simple

---

[27] Arbuckle, *Violence, Society, and the Church*, 184.

fact that they were excluded from the democratic process until the late 1960s. They had to suffer "probably the crudest and most cruel form of cultural imperialism."[28]

Assimilation policies are either formal or informal, but the purpose is the same; that is, ethnic minorities are expected to acquire the symbols, myths, and rituals of the dominant culture. Phrases such as *melting-pot policy* and *cultural pluralism* became fashionable at various times. Up until the early 1920s in the United States it was assumed that indigenous peoples and immigrants should just melt into the mainstream of life, without concessions or supports, in order to pool their characteristics and develop an altogether new amalgam or American culture, and thus schools ignored diversity entirely.

The reality was very different. People with power were not interested in the customs and values of socioeconomically poor migrants. The policy was devastating for the welfare of immigrants. Then governments in Australia, Britain, and Canada slowly introduced the policies of *cultural pluralism*: core values and customs of the dominant culture were to be acquired, but ethnic minorities could preserve values and customs provided these did not interfere with the core values of the dominant society. In Australia, for example, the policy meant that "immigrants would be expected to agree publicly that all things Australian are best, to be greatly interested in sport and not to work too hard, and in return they would not be badgered if they privately practiced their native culture."[29] At heart, this policy of toleration of "nonessential" customs was merely an attempt to make cultural assimilation efforts in countries like Australia and Britain a little less nasty or disruptive for migrants. The long-term

---

[28] Christine Fletcher, "Living Together But Not Neighbours: Cultural Imperialism in Australia," in *Indigenous Peoples' Rights in Australia, Canada, and New Zealand*, ed. Paul Havemann (Auckland: Oxford University Press, 1999), 347. From the late 1800s to 1957 many Aboriginal children in Australia were forcefully removed from their parents in order to "Europeanize" them. The trauma of their loneliness remains vividly alive today in their cultural history. Canada adopted a similar policy toward indigenous children. See Colin Samson and Carlos Gigoux, *Indigenous Peoples and Colonialism: Global Perspectives* (Cambridge: Polity, 2017), 104–11.

[29] Martin L. Kovacs and Arthur J. Cropley, *Immigrants and Society: Alienation and Assimilation* (Sydney: McGraw-Hill, 1975), 123.

aim remained the same: ethnic minorities must adopt all aspects of the dominant way of life.

In 1951, assimilation became the naive, official Australian policy of the state and Commonwealth governments for Aboriginal peoples. Coerced assimilation aimed to eliminate them as a "culturally different ethnic presence in White Australia. . . . Mission stations, churches, government welfare organizations, and prisons were the chief assimilationist vehicles."[30] It was claimed that this assimilationist policy would raise the standard of living of the Aboriginal peoples "by integrating them into White society—a move based on the assumption that assimilation would provide [them] with access to good housing, health care, and education."[31] However, the cultural differences between Aboriginal peoples and other Australians were so immense that the former "suffered devastating effects under the 'benign' onslaught."[32] It is not surprising that many were left without a sense of identity, cultural heritage, security, or a sense of self-respect or self-worth. No wonder they developed feelings of alienation and hopelessness and an abiding distrust toward governments.[33] "Assimilation was and is a massive abuse of human rights. . . . [Human rights] did not inherently accrue to Aboriginal people but were, instead, a reward if they would renounce their Aboriginality and embrace the dominant status quo. It was equality based, not on respect for racial difference, but on the denial of your race."[34] As Aboriginal activist Noel Pearson asserts, "Freedom for our people will not come as a result of progressive governments giving us our rights back or enacting 'social justice.' We will be free when we take back our right to take responsibility."[35]

---

[30] Ibid., 342.

[31] Ibid., 341.

[32] Ibid.

[33] See Charles D. Rowley, *Outcasts in White Australia* (Canberra: ANU Press, 1971), 234–36; Gerald A. Arbuckle, *Earthing the Gospel: An Inculturation Handbook for Pastoral Workers* (Maryknoll, NY: Orbis Books, 1990), 169–86.

[34] Mike Dodson, *Assimilation versus Self-Determination: No Contest*, NARU discussion paper no. 1 (Darwin, 1996), 6.

[35] Noel Pearson, *Up from the Mission: Selected Writings* (Collingwood: Black, 2011), 28.

Punishing Asylum Seekers/Refugees

Every year millions of people are compelled to flee their homes, and very often their countries, to find protection from tyranny and persecution because of their nationality, race, religion, political, or social convictions. Especially given the contemporary antagonism, even hatred, toward these people in general, there is often ignorance or confusion about the reasons why they are fleeing.

- An *asylum seeker* is a person who seeks protection because of a well-founded fear of being persecuted because of religion, nationality, race, political, or social convictions or membership in a particular social group.[36] Such persons may have actually suffered persecution, even torture, or other inhumane treatment. Not every asylum seeker may be eventually classed as a refugee, but every refugee is originally an asylum seeker.
- A *refugee* is one who has fled persecution, has achieved protection, and has been officially classed as a refugee. Such persons may be living in a refugee camp, hopefully waiting for the chance to return to their home country or to be settled in another country. For many people, such as those refugees trapped in Palestinian refugee camps, there is little hope of ever being resettled.
- Asylum seekers and refugees are radically different from *migrants,* because migrants have chosen to leave their country for reasons such as work or education and can theoretically return home whenever they wish.[37]

Today there 21.3 million refugees worldwide. One in every 113 people globally is now either seeking asylum, internally displaced,

---

[36] See Jo Coghlan, John Minns, and Andrew Wells, eds., *Seeking Refuge: Asylum Seekers and Politics in a Globalising World* (Sydney: Wollongong University Press, 2005).

[37] See Andrew and Renata Kaldor Centre for International Refugee Law (kaldorcentre website), "Debunking Myths," University of New South Wales–Sydney, September 30, 2015; William Maley, *What Is a Refugee?* (Melbourne: Scribe, 2016), 15–41.

or a refugee.[38] In 2015 over one million asylum seekers from Syria, Afghanistan, Iraq, and elsewhere fled to Europe, most to Germany and Sweden. Words cannot describe the enormous loneliness that these people experience—such as the loneliness that arises while trying to live in a country without adequate accommodation or language skills amid growing local antagonism. The appalling tragedy is that "despite the fancy international edifice of agencies, and the warm glow of media attention around them, *most* of the world's refugees receive virtually no material assistance at all from any of them."[39]

There has been an alarming move toward harsher treatment of refugees in many countries. The policies of most of the developed world toward refugees have either ignored the crisis or been miserly in seeking just solutions. There is a common assumption that refugees should have sought protection closer to their own countries before embarking on their journeys. Yet the real issue is that "all too often, we fail to treat [refugees] as human, something that says more about us than about them."[40]

The Trump administration planned in 2017 to curtail severely the number of refugees accepted by the United States, the lowest since 2007. In 2016 the United States accepted about ten thousand Syrians fleeing their country's civil war—far fewer than other Western countries. In 2017, President Trump proposed to suspend refugee admissions from Syria indefinitely, claiming Syrian refugees posed a security risk.[41]

Possibly the worst example is Australia. In order to deter refugees from fleeing to Australia, the government devised a process in which "dehumanization is a central element of the policy of deterrence, both in terms of how the public see refugees, and how refugees are treated."[42] The policies are punitive, the message being that refugees should not have attempted to enter Australia. They are transferred to

---

[38] See these and related statistics on the Refugee Council of Australia website, www.refugeecouncil.org.au/statistics.

[39] Alexander Betts and Paul Collier, *Refuge: Transforming a Broken Refugee System* (Milton Keynes: Allen Lane, 2017), 7.

[40] Maley, *What Is a Refugee?* 195.

[41] See Krishnadev Calamur, "Donald Trump's Other Wall," *The Atlantic* (September 20, 2017).

[42] Maley, *What Is a Refugee?*, 190.

detention centers in two developing countries—Papua New Guinea and Nauru. "Amid catastrophic human rights consequences, including prolonged child detention and high suicide rates, the scheme was abandoned, only to be reintroduced in 2012."[43] Amnesty International describes the situation:

> Mental illness and incidents of self-harm . . . are shockingly commonplace. . . . What drives so many people to this level of despair? One factor that plays a significant role in people's hopelessness is the fact that they are trapped ʼ . . . and face debilitating uncertainty about their future. . . . A 19-year-old Syrian refugee said: "I felt like I was a slave. Being detained is like feeling you did something wrong—like you are a criminal." Treatment for people suffering psychological trauma is inadequate. Beyond serious human rights abuses . . . refugees and asylum seekers have also been subjected to countless daily humiliations that have cumulatively served to dehumanize them and violate their dignity.[44]

Punishing people for being refugees and asylum seekers makes little sense—yet it is the modus operandi in a number of global situations.

Blaming People with Disabilities

When society perceives disabled people as useless, it is because in society's judgment they lack engagement in mainstream economic activities. They are seen as "abnormal" or "deviant," and therefore need to be marginalized from "normal" social interaction.[45] It is "politically convenient to have the problem located in the individuals

---

[43] Betts and Collier, *Refuge*, 51.

[44] Amnesty International, *Island of Despair: Australia's "Processing" of Refugees on Nauru* (London: Amnesty International, 2016), 4, 5, 6. In June 2017, the Australian Government, under pressure from the Federal Court, agreed to compensate nineteen hundred asylum seekers for their inhuman treatment in detention centers.

[45] See Colin Barnes and Geof Mercer, *Disability* (Cambridge: Polity, 2003), 1–41.

who are blamed for their failure to adjust to disability,"[46] thus becoming a financial and social burden for the rest of society.[47] As L'Arche founder Jean Vanier has skillfully indicated, people with learning disabilities are often stigmatized by society because they are judged incapable of offering valued services. But people with disabilities can teach us about the urgent, society-wide need for love, community, and celebration.[48] Society has the problem, not people with disabilities.

Ignoring Human Trafficking

Human trafficking uses violence, deception, or coercion to recruit, harbor, or transport people into a situation of exploitation, such as prostitution, forced labor, domestic servitude, forced marriage, forced organ removal, or forced criminality. About 2.5 million people around the world are ensnared in the web of human trafficking at any given time.

Stereotyping Aging

Ageism is the term that describes the negative stereotyping of and/ or discrimination against people by reason of their age.[49] The victims

---

[46] See Michael Oliver and Bob Sapey, *Social Work with Disabled People* (Basingstoke: Palgrave, 1999), 31; Carol Thomas, *Sociologies and Disability and Illness: Contested Ideas in Disability Studies and Medical Sociology* (New York: Palgrave Macmillan, 2007), 49–82. In a media release John Falzon of the St. Vincent de Paul Society berated the Australian Government for proposing to exclude from support people with disabilities caused by drugs or alcohol: "It is calculated to punish and exclude people who are living with a chronic disability and further force them into deeper poverty" (June 20, 2017).

[47] French anthropologist Michel Foucault blames the disciplines of medicine, psychiatry, biology, economics, and linguistics for inflexibly defining their "proper" subjects, dividing the world into ordinary, normal, controllable entities. For example, once people are defined as mad, they must be controlled accordingly. It is a question of knowledge and power. See Gerald A. Arbuckle, *Culture, Inculturation, and Theologians: A Postmodern Critique* (Collegeville, MN: Liturgical Press, 2010), 11–12.

[48] See Jean Vanier, *Jean Vanier: Essential Writings* (London: Darton, Longman, and Todd, 2008).

[49] This section is adapted from Gerald A. Arbuckle, *The Francis Factor and the People of God: New Life for the Church* (Maryknoll, NY: Orbis Books), 37–38.

may be young or old. Robert Butler, when considering the status of older people in the Western world, concludes that ageism "allows the young generations to see older people as different from themselves, thus they subtly cease to identify with their elders as human beings."[50] Older people may lose adult titles like Miss, Ms., or Mr. and be treated like children, being summoned by their Christian names "or given diminutive titles like 'dear' or 'love.'"[51] Little wonder that the self-esteem of aging people is undermined by this nasty stereotyping, thus increasing their feeling of loneliness. The fact is that most older people remain active, relishing their independence, often providing significant assistance within families, such as childcare, or continuing paid employment, if possible (many countries insist on compulsory retirement at sixty-five, and some employers discriminate against older people).[52] Unfortunately, since the emphasis in Western societies is on young people, sociologists have for the most part given insufficient time to studying aging and old age, however it is defined.

Gender Discrimination

People belonging to LGBT communities have long suffered marginalization, even persecution. The United States government has officially recognized that the military was wrong to condone prejudice against Americans based upon skin color or sexual orientation. However, in July 2017, Donald Trump suddenly banned transgender people from the armed forces without warning Congress, the public, or rank-and-file members of the military. He embraced the marginalizing prejudice of the past, overlooking the fact that these people are willing to defend their country with their lives.[53] Father James Martin, SJ, writes that

---

[50] Robert Butler, *Why Survive? Being Old in America* (New York: Harper & Row, 1975), 35.

[51] Mike Featherstone and Mike Hepworth, "Images of Ageing: Cultural Representations of Later Life," in *The Cambridge Handbook of Age and Ageing*, ed. Malcolm L. Johnson (Cambridge: Cambridge University Press, 2005), 358.

[52] See Christina Victor, *The Social Context of Ageing* (Abingdon: Routledge, 2005), 400.

[53] See Colbert I. King, "Trump's Retreat to a Rancid Past," *Washington Post* (July 28, 2017).

the marginalization of LGBT Catholics is present even in many local churches: "Over the years, I've discovered a great divide. I lament that there isn't more understanding and conversation between LGBT Catholics and the institutional church. . . . Many LGBT Catholics have told me that they have felt hurt by the institutional church—unwelcomed, excluded and insulted."[54]

Dominant Societies in which Power Is Shared through Multiculturalism

In 2016 Pope Francis said at a prayer vigil in Krakow, Poland, for World Youth Day: "Today, adults need you to teach us how to live in diversity, in dialogue, to experience multiculturalism not as a threat but an opportunity."[55]

Significant ethnic diversity is increasingly evident in most Western countries. From the late 1970s in countries such as Canada, Australia, and Britain the new policy of multiculturalism, like that of ethnicity, emerged at political, religious, and educational levels as a consequence of pressures from migrant and minority groups to have their cultural backgrounds respected. Assimilation was not working. Human rights were being ignored. But the words *multicultural* and *multiculturalism* invariably evoked, and still evoke, strong emotional reactions among members of dominant cultures.[56] In recent times the questioning of multiculturalism has been intimately tied to problems of Islamic and Muslim integration, leading to a backlash against multiculturalism.[57]

---

[54] James Martin, "Why I Wrote about the Catholic Church and the LGBT Community," *Washington Post* (May 31, 2017); and idem, *Building a Bridge: How the Catholic Church and the LGBT Community Can Enter into a Relationship of Respect, Compassion, and Sensitivity* (New York: HarperOne, 2017).

[55] Pope Francis, quoted in "Francis Makes Rousing Call for Millennials to Get Off Couch and Fix World," *National Catholic Reporter* (July 30, 2016).

[56] See Roger Hewitt, *White Backlash and the Politics of Multiculturalism* (Cambridge: Cambridge University Press, 2005), 1–17.

[57] See Christian Joppke, *Is Multiculturalism Dead?* (Cambridge: Polity Press, 2017), 36; Nasar Meer, *Citizenship, Identity, and the Politics of Multiculturalism: The Rise of Muslim Consciousness* (Basingstoke: Palgrave, 2010), 24–30.

For many conservatives in society multiculturalism has come to signify a very disruptive, unsettling, and dangerous force. For them, different cultures are something to be at best tolerated, but given the present backlash against multiculturalism this tolerance is being viewed as political and social weakness. Peace and order, some conservatives claim, have existed in the past and will continue to do so only when a dominant group has insisted on conformity to a monocultural ethos.[58] But this monocultural emphasis is having the opposite effect. Minority groups feel increasingly marginalized and lonely in the presence of the dominant culture. Hence, the policy of multiculturalism needs to be better understood. [59]

Defining Multiculturalism

Theologically, multiculturalism is the process of interaction between the gospel and cultures whereby cultures are so transformed and remade into "a new creation" (2 Cor 5:17) that they interact with one another in justice and charity in service of personal and community growth.

Political philosopher Bhikhu Parekh provides a helpful working definition that respects the pastoral theological approach:

Multiculturalism does not simply mean numerical plurality of different cultures, but rather a community which is creating, guaranteeing, encouraging spaces within which different communities are able to grow at their own pace. At the same time, it means creating public space in which these communities are able to interact, enrich the existing culture and create a new consensual culture in which they recognize reflections of their own identity.[60]

---

[58] See Henry A. Giroux, "Insurgent Multiculturalism and the Promise of Pedagogy," in *Multiculturalism: A Critical Reader*, ed. David T. Goldberg (Oxford: Basil Blackwell, 1994), 336.

[59] Multicultural policies have often overemphasized maintaining diversity and neglected the importance of encouraging positive interaction among cultures. The term *interculturality* seeks to restore the balance between diversity and interaction. See Ali Rattansi, *Multiculturalism* (Oxford: Oxford University Press, 2011), 148–64.

[60] Bhikhu Parekh, cited in Giroux, "Multiculturalism and the Promise of Pedagogy," 336.

Parekh's definition rejects two popular definitions, namely *demographic* and *holistic* multiculturalism. The former connotes that a particular society merely contains different cultural groups living side by side. If they are not positively interacting, such groupings intensify loneliness.[61] The second, *holistic* multiculturalism, means that a society values cultural diversity but gives higher priority to group-wide cohesion. Thus, while ethnic groups need to commit themselves to their receiving society, they also must make a reciprocal commitment to them.[62]

The definition provided by Parekh does support *political* multiculturalism, however. This is a social philosophy that acknowledges the legitimate concerns of ethnic groups within a society or an organization, and the need for these interests to be expressed in adequate politico-economic structures that permit minority peoples *by right* to be fully involved in decision making in matters that affect their lives. A balance is sought between the demands of overall group cohesion and inner cultural diversity. Without dialogue and power sharing the talk of multiculturalism, at the levels of government and other institutions, is simply a fad and true multicultural communities cannot exist.

Historically, political multiculturalism is a reaction against policies of cultural oppression, in which phrases or terms such as *cultural pluralism* and *integration* are often synonymous with covert or overt programs to destroy minority cultures by forcing them to be assimilated into the dominant culture. Critical decisions are made about minority peoples and their future without their participation. As a result, individual and group alienation and loneliness intensify.

Multiculturalism and Power

Power is the ability to influence negatively or positively. If there is to be authentic multiculturalism, three types of *positive* power must be exercised by dominant and ethnic groups: *nutritive* power, enabling power whereby people are given the chance to develop their own inner capacities; *integrative* power, the working together of individuals

---

[61] For an excellent critique of multiculturalism, see Anthony J. Gittins, *Living Mission Interculturally: Faith, Culture, and the Renewal of Praxis* (Collegeville, MN: Liturgical Press, 2015).

[62] See Bhikhu Paretkh, *A New Politics of Identity: Political Principles for an Independent World* (London: Palgrave Macmillan, 2008), 80–98.

and groups for the benefit of all; and *relational* power, the working together of all involved to learn from one another. Jesus Christ, the master educator, exercised all three powers in his role as the servant of God, the listening one, the one open to respond to the marginalized, the unwanted. Thus the genuine multiculturalist is one who is open to hearing, to dialogue with, to learn from, and to encourage people of different cultures.

In the United States the dominant policy remains assimilation— this seems to be what is truly meant by *Americanization.* The assumption is that all immigrants are to be thrown into the mainstream of American life without concessions or supports in order to pool their characteristics and to form a new American culture. The result has been that poor migrants were forced, for the sake of survival, to adopt as quickly as possible the existing dominant culture, the white Anglo-Saxon Protestant culture. The policy of assimilation has been devastating for many immigrants.

In Australia and Canada, however, multiculturalism, as defined above, has been over several decades part of a nation-building project for indigenous people and foreign immigrants.[63] So far the multicultural policies of these governments have weathered the contemporary backlash.[64] In Britain, multicultural educational policies have been introduced over time at local levels and have survived despite "a hardened context of counter-terrorism and worries about ethnic segregation."[65] Elsewhere in Europe, particularly in Holland and Germany, multicultural policies continue in the face of rising criticism.[66]

Fostering Multiculturalism: The Role of Educators

In an address to international nongovernmental organizations on July 9, 2015, Pope Francis said: "The world's peoples want to be artisans

---

[63] See Joppke, *Is Multiculturalism Dead?* 33–75.

[64] Mary Hawkins and Anne Matthews comment: "Australia's policy of managing ethnic diversity through multiculturalism has survived, and Australia rates either first or second (behind Canada) on the global scale of successful integration of migrants." *Identity and Belonging* (London: Palgrave, 2016), 23.

[65] Joppke, *Is Multiculturalism Dead?* 47.

[66] Ibid., 37.

of their own destiny. . . . They want their culture, their language, their social processes and their religious traditions to be respected."

Educators such as teachers and pastoral workers have a critical role in fostering multicultural communities. The real challenge in multicultural or cross-cultural education is to help people empathize with the feelings of others about ethnicity. Empathy should beget a genuine desire to struggle with and for people so that they have the chance to become agents of their own destinies. When this happens, the educational process is having some success. A knowledge of cultural lifestyles is helpful but of very limited value if empathy fails to develop.

An outsider can know far more about the history, cultural externals, or even language of an ethnic group than its members but still be thoroughly alien to those people because of a lack of empathy. Empathy is not something that one automatically learns; rather, it is the fruit of ongoing conversion in attending to, and learning from, one's own weakness and vulnerability. Only through the gift of empathy is one able to begin to touch the depths of a people's culture. Here are five anthropological guidelines to assist educators in fostering multiculturalism that increases people's feelings of belonging and helps to develop their sense of self-worth.

Guideline 1: Two pivotal anthropological principles must influence educators. First, only from a position of cultural strength can a people begin with dignity and self-confidence to share with other cultures and develop a common community. Second, only if ethnic groups have access to the power structures of society, for example, the political, economic, and educational institutions, will the achievement of full ethnic self-confidence be possible.

Guideline 2: People, provided they respect values such as justice and religious liberty, have a fundamental human right to foster their own cultural identities within a wider multicultural society; at the same time, they have the obligation to contribute to the development of this multicultural society to the best of their ability.

Guideline 3: For this process of cultural identity to advance freely, an atmosphere of trust needs to develop slowly between people from minority cultures and members of the dominant power culture. This mutual trust can emerge only through empathy and authentic dialogue.

Guideline 4: An awareness of one's personal values, prejudices, biases, and worldview, which have their origin in one's culture, will immensely assist one's understanding of and communication with other cultures.[67]

Guideline 5: Educators need to be alert to the following realities and cautions. If they are understood and accepted in practice, this will contribute to the development of communities that are truly based on equity and justice. Power will no longer remain in the hands of the dominant culture alone.

- Every effort must be made to develop educational and pastoral communities that truly represent the cultural diversity of a nation.
- People from minority cultures, on entering a dominant cultural domain, may immediately develop a sense of their own powerlessness, along with an awareness of their inability to communicate easily in this unfamiliar environment; this can lead to a "culture shock" that adds to their sense of alienation.
- Being aware of one's own personal biases, values, interests, and worldview, which all have cultural roots, as well as knowing one's culture, will significantly improve one's feeling for other cultures.
- It is easy for members of the dominant culture to impose their own identity on peoples of minority cultures in subtle and unconscious ways; extreme sensitivity is required on the part of members of the dominant culture to be aware of their own prejudices and how they can interfere in the educational process.
- Educators must be sensitive to how prejudice and discrimination operate, both within themselves and in their communities, and be prepared to counter such negativity.[68]
- Ethnic groups, like cultures, must not be thought of as discrete, frozen in time, resistant to external influences, homogeneous, and without internal conflict. Individuals belonging to ethnic groups will differ in their commitment to the distinguishing qualities of these groups.[69]

---

[67] See Don C. Locke and Deryl F. Bailey, *Increasing Multicultural Understanding* (Los Angeles: SAGE, 2014), 2–3.

[68] See Arbuckle, *Fundamentalism at Home and Abroad*, 162–84.

[69] See Arbuckle, *Culture, Inculturation, and Theologians*, 107.

- Educators need to be aware that individuals belonging to culturally different groups are simultaneously members of these groups *and* unique persons; they must strive to maintain a wholesome balance between their perception of individuals as cultural beings and as unique persons.[70]

Responsibilities toward Refugees and Migrants: Pope Francis

Francis writes that "our shared response may be articulated by four verbs: to welcome, to protect, to promote and to integrate."[71] By *welcoming* he means "above all, offering broader options to migrants and refugees to enter destination countries safely and legally. . . . The principle of the centrality of the human person . . . obliges us to always prioritize personal safety over national security."

By *protecting* he means "a series of steps intended to defend the rights and dignity of migrants and refugees." For Francis, "*promoting* essentially means a determined effort to ensure that all migrants and refugees—as well as the communities which welcome them—are empowered to achieve their potential as human beings, in all the dimensions which constitute the humanity intended by the Creator."

Finally, "*integrating* concerns the opportunities for intercultural enrichment." This significantly does not mean "an assimilation that leads migrants to suppress or to forget their cultural identity. Rather, contact with others leads to discovering their 'secret,' to being open to them in order to welcome their valid aspects and thus contribute to knowing each one better. This is a lengthy process."

Theological Reflection: Option for the Poor and Inclusivity in the New Testament

The theological reflection in the previous chapter concentrated on the notion of poverty, the purpose of wealth,[72] and God's concern for

---

[70] See Locke and Bailey, *Increasing Multicultural Understanding,* 305.

[71] This and the following quotations in this section are from Pope Francis, "Message for the 104th World Day of Migrants and Refugees 2018."

[72] See Ben Witherington, *Jesus and Money* (London: SPCK, 2010).

the powerless, as seen in the Old Testament; God demands action to relieve this powerlessness. The following reflection focuses on the teachings and actions of Jesus Christ, as recorded in the New Testament, particularly in the Gospel of St. Luke. Luke is especially strong in insisting on inclusivity.[73]

Preferential Option for the Poor

Luke speaks even more forcefully than does Matthew about riches, poverty, and the appropriate use of resources.[74] He is writing for Christian communities throughout the Greco-Roman empire that had a striking similarity with our contemporary world. It was a society in which a working person's wage never allowed the individuals to live far above the hunger line—one day for a person without employment would cause hunger.[75] There was great poverty for the majority of people, who were crippled by heavy taxes due to foreign invaders and rents to corrupt landholders. Temple taxes increased their misery. It was in this oppressive context that Jesus preached on the rights of the poor.[76]

In his teaching and lifestyle Jesus proclaims that the poor are to be the privileged "heirs of the kingdom" (James 2:5). He is to be the Messiah of the poor: "He has sent me to . . . let the oppressed go free" (Luke 4:18). After an ambiguous reaction on the part of his listeners (Luke 4:22), Jesus reiterates by way of examples taken from the lives of the prophets Elijah (1 Kings 17:17–24) and Elisha (2 Kings 5:1–19) that his mission is preferentially directed toward those who are underprivileged and marginalized. He maintains this theme in all his preaching, though he is severely criticized, even threatened with death, for doing so. Jesus Christ needs to be seen as one of "the poor" from the time of his birth to his death on the cross. In Hebrew times

---

[73] This section is adapted from Gerald A. Arbuckle, *A 'Preferential Option for the Poor': Application to Catholic Health and Aged Care Ministries in Australia* (Canberra: Catholic Health Australia, 2003), 27–34.

[74] See Christopher M. Hays, *Renouncing Everything: Money and Discipleship in Luke* (New York: Paulist Press, 2016).

[75] See Herman Hendrickx, *Social Justice in the Bible* (Quezon City: Claretian Publications, 1985), 85.

[76] See John D. Crossan, *God and Empire: Jesus against Rome, Then and Now* (San Francisco: HarperSanFrancisco, 2007).

God stands *beside* the oppressed, but in Christ there is to be total *identification* with the exploited. Jesus is himself the poor one, born in a stable (Luke 2:7), the vulnerable one who is to be killed for his concern for people who are poor (Luke 27:35).

In contrast to Matthew's version in the Beatitudes, in which people who are poor are generally referred to metaphorically ("Blessed are the poor in spirit," Matt 5:3), in Luke's text Jesus speaks of the materially or sociologically poor: "Blessed are you who are poor, for yours is the kingdom of God" (Luke 6:20) and "Woe to you who are rich" (Luke 6:24). The rich must use their resources to build a just community. These verses do not praise the lack of money or condemn people for having it; the Beatitudes address, as in the Old Testament, the gap between the two that makes people defenseless and lonely. The rich are challenged to renounce a significant amount of their wealth, and also to undertake unpalatable deeds, such as offering risky loans (Luke 6:35) and canceling debts (Luke 6:37).[77] Zacchaeus, the chief tax-collector of Jericho, following his conversion, is praised by Jesus for giving up half of his possessions to the poor, but Zacchaeus still remains a wealthy man (Luke 19:1–10).[78]

In Luke, Jesus is saying, more bluntly than in Matthew's text, that the chasm between the rich and poor cannot be justified, and that in the reign of God there will be an economic reversal.[79] Thus, those who are poor are called blessed, not because their poverty is something good in itself, but because when the kingdom of God takes shape, they will be the preferential beneficiaries of the changes that occur. Jesus says unambiguously that the ultimate indication of social good health is whether the community is committed to justice, especially justice to the powerless, the hungry, the oppressed, and the deprived in society. Jesus so identifies with the defenseless that when people refuse them justice they are refusing *him,* even if they are unconscious of this fact (Matt 25:40, 45).

---

[77] See David J. Bosch, *Transforming Mission: Paradigm Shifts in Theology of Mission* (Maryknoll, NY: Orbis Books, 1991), 103.

[78] See Rodger Charles, *The Social Teaching of Vatican II* (Oxford: Platter Publications, 1982), 302.

[79] See John L. McKenzie, *Dictionary of the Bible* (London: Geoffrey Chapman, 1965), 684.

In brief, Jesus describes a key sign of the reign of God—that those who are powerless will be in first place. Riches are evil whenever people become so preoccupied with them that they entirely control people's lives. There are five parables[80] in Luke's Gospel that are stories of social, economic, and political reversal, in which the marginalized are given preferential status:

- The Samaritan is good, not the status-proud priests and Levites (Luke 10:33–37);
- Lazarus is good, not the wealthy rich man (Luke 16:19–31);
- The tax-collector is good, not the Pharisee (Luke 18:10–14);
- The last-seated at the banquet are good, not the rich invited ones (Luke 14:15–24);
- The prodigal son is good, not his envious and self-righteous brother (Luke 15:11–32).

Inclusion: The Poor

As Mary Elsbernd and Reimund Bieringer observe, John's Gospel "presents an image of an inclusive community characterized by a variety of leadership roles, including representative figures from various ethnic groups, economic statuses, social locations, and genders."[81] Luke especially emphasizes the inclusive nature of the teachings of Jesus, often doing so in the context of a meal. His meals have a prophetic message; that is, contrary to the political and social hierarchies of Roman society and the polarities of daily Jewish life, molded by the rigid purity regulations that dictated that the sick, crippled, and maimed are pariahs, the meals of Jesus send a far-reaching message that all are welcome, and no one is to be excluded. "Go out at once into the streets and lanes of the town and bring in the poor, the crippled, and the lame. . . . Go out into the roads and lanes, and compel people to come in, so that my house may be filled" (Luke 14:21). Shortly before that, he insists: "When you give a banquet,

---

[80] Parables are fictitious stories told by Jesus Christ to explain his mission. They were given to stimulate discussions on fundamental values.

[81] Mary Elsbernd and Reimund Bieringer, *When Love Is Not Enough: A Theo-Ethic of Justice* (Collegeville, MN: Liturgical Press, 2002), 164.

invite the poor, the crippled, the lame, and the blind. And you will be blessed, because they cannot repay you" (Luke 14:13–14). What he taught, he practiced, breaking down purity and social barriers by eating with despised and stigmatized tax-collectors and sinners (Luke 5:29–30). As Marcus Borg writes: "The simple act of sharing a meal had exceptional religious and social significance in the social world of Jesus. It became a vehicle of cultural protest, challenging the ethos and politics of holiness."[82]

Inclusion: The Despised

At the time of Christ, Jews looked on Samaritans as stupid, lazy, and heretical—and Samaritans had similar views of their Jewish neighbors. Hence, when Jesus told the story of the Good Samaritan, his listeners would have had no doubt about its meaning (Luke 10:29–37). A Samaritan, considered by the Jewish people to be stupid, uncouth, and inferior, sees a dying Jew and immediately goes to his aid. Jesus's listeners would have been shocked to hear him say: "Go, and do likewise" (Luke 10:37). Two people, a hated Samaritan and a battered and bloodied Jew, excluded by Jewish society, are now to be unconditionally included.

Inclusion: Women

In the time of Christ women were second-class Jews, with status hardly above that of slaves. Though women are referred to in all four Gospels, it is Luke who gives them special prominence.[83] Women are models in prayer and discipleship during Christ's ministry. They had a public role in his traveling ministry (Luke 8:1–3), and women are paired with men in parables (Luke 15:4–10; 18:1–8; 21:1–4). It is Elizabeth and Mary, not Zechariah and Joseph, who are the first to hear of Christ's coming, who are extolled by angels, and who are the first to praise and prophesy about the Christ child. Often in his daily life Jesus expressed concern for the welfare of women

---

[82] Marcus Borg, *Jesus, A New Vision: Spirit, Culture, and the Life of Discipleship* (London: SPCK, 1993), 133.

[83] See Robert C. Tannehill, *The Narrative of Luke-Acts: A Literary Interpretation,* vol. 1, *The Gospel according to Luke* (Philadelphia: Fortress Press, 1986), 132–39.

in ways that were not condescending or prejudiced. He performed miracles for them, often breaking purity taboos, as in the case of the hemorrhaging woman (Luke 8:40–56). Women were noticeably among those at Christ's crucifixion (Luke 23:27,49); women prepared spices to anoint Jesus's body (Luke 23:55–56); women were the first to discover the tomb abandoned (Luke 24:1–3); angels told the women that Jesus had risen (Luke 24:4–8); and women were the first to carry the news of Jesus's resurrection to the other disciples (Luke 24:9–11).

The Magnificat: A Call to Inclusion

Mary's Magnificat—also called Mary's Song of Praise—in Luke 1:46–55 is the bridge between the Old and New Testaments. She states without ambiguity that Jesus has come especially for inclusion of the *anawim*, those who remain faithful to God in adversity. Her hymn is one of the most subversive statements in all of literature. For the faithful trapped in oppression and loneliness, it expresses a deep and dangerous hope of a better world.[84] The song proclaims three revolutions against forces of exclusion: a moral revolution ("He has shown strength with his arm; he has scattered the proud in the thoughts of their hearts," Luke 1:51); a political and social revolution ("He has brought down the powerful from their thrones, and lifted up the lowly," Luke 1:52); and an economic revolution ("He has filled the hungry with good things, and sent the rich away empty," Luke 1:53).[85]

Summary

- There is the potential within every individual and culture to assume that people not "like us" are inferior; such assumptions can lead to blaming or scapegoating these people.

---

[84] See Walter Brueggemann, *First and Second Samuel* (Atlanta: John Knox Press, 1990), 21.

[85] Gerald A. Arbuckle, *Healthcare Ministry: Refounding the Mission in Tumultuous Times* (Collegeville, MN: Liturgical Press, 2000), 169; see also Herman Hendrickx, *Bible on Justice* (Quezon City: JMC Press, 1978), 50; William F. Maestri, *Mary: Model of Justice* (New York: Alba House, 1987).

- Power is the ability to influence. It can be used by dominant societies in one of two ways: One is to refuse to share political, economic, or social power with others. This process of exclusion can take many different forms, such as annihilation, gender discrimination, and blaming. Or the power can be used positively for inclusion, that is, used in a sharing way so that people are able to realize their human dignity. One such way is through multiculturalism.
- Multiculturalism is a social philosophy that acknowledges the legitimate concerns of ethnic groups within a society or an organization, and the need for these interests to be expressed in adequate politico-economic structures that permit minority peoples, *by right,* to be fully involved in decision making in matters that affect their lives.

Reflection Questions

- What points in this chapter do you feel relate to your experience?
- Many millions of innocent people are being displaced, even abandoned, through wars, economic forces, and government decisions, thus becoming unskilled migrants, refugees, and asylum seekers. What can you do to make these injustices better known in your community?
- In Luke's Gospel a lawyer asks Jesus, "Who is my neighbor?" After answering this question by recounting the parable of the Good Samaritan, Jesus alters his emphasis on the neighbor as object (whom are we to love?) to neighbor as subject (*how* are we called to *be* neighbor?).[86] How would you answer these two questions?
- Pope John Paul II said that despite the problems in the world there is "no justification for despair or pessimism or inertia" (*Sollicitudo Rei Socialis*, no. 47). Why can a believer in Jesus Christ truly say this? Can you say it?

---

[86] See Thomas L. Schubeck, *Love That Does Justice* (Maryknoll, NY: Orbis Books, 2007), 49–50.

6

Tribalism, Polarization, and Loneliness: Healing in Society and Church

I have identified one impediment to good, safe care which infects the whole public hospital system. I liken it to the Great Schism of 1054. It is the breakdown of good working relations between clinicians and management which is very detrimental to patients.

—PETER GARLING,
*FINAL REPORT OF THE SPECIAL COMMISSION
OF INQUIRY ACUTE CARE SERVICES
IN NSW PUBLIC HOSPITALS: OVERVIEW*

The anti-Francis revolt . . . has acquired a newly vicious tone. A line has been crossed. I don't mean the line of good manners and respect. That was crossed some time ago, when four cardinals made public their letter challenging Francis's apostolic exhortation Amoris Laetitia, *and challenging him with a kind of public censure. Since then the tone of disrespect and contempt of some writers who back them has plumbed shocking new lows.*

—AUSTEN IVEREIGH,
"AS ANTI-*AMORIS* CRITICS CROSS
INTO DISSENT, THE CHURCH MUST MOVE ON"

This chapter explains:

- How tribalism encourages people and institutions to polarize relationships.
- How polarized relationships foster loneliness.
- The causes of polarization in the church.
- The antidote to polarization is faith-based dialogue.

This chapter examines tribalism and its inherent tendency to polarize relationships, along with the loneliness it causes in two institutions: hospitals and the church. Both institutions are in cultural chaos that is triggering loneliness for many people, and rival tribalism has become entrenched.[1]

At no previous period in the Western world has healthcare faced a more chaotic and threatening environment because of the demands being made upon it. Professionals locked in polarizing subcultures compete for limited resources, seeking tribal protection and advantage.[2] For Catholics, two worldwide cultural revolutions collided at the same time: Vatican II and the expressive revolution of the 1960s.[3] The long-overdue council altered the entire mythic structure of the church. A catastrophic cultural upheaval was inevitable.[4] Exposure

---

[1] This chapter is adapted and updated from *Refounding the Church: Dissent for Leadership* (Maryknoll, NY: Orbis, 1993).

[2] See Gerald A. Arbuckle, *Healthcare Ministry: Refounding the Mission in Tumultuous Times* (Collegeville, MN: Liturgical Press, 2000), xi–xii; idem, *Humanizing Healthcare Reforms* (Philadelphia: Jessica Kingsley, 2013), 11–20.

[3] For an understanding of the expressive revolution, see Gerald A. Arbuckle, *Violence, Society, and the Church: A Cultural Approach* (Collegeville MN: Liturgical Press, 2004), 157–79. "From the early 1960s to the early 1970s, the entire Western world experienced a dramatic, highly intense transformation of its cultural values and behavior patterns that started as a form of cultural revolution among a small group of committed radicals and climaxed by changing some of the most profound habits and assumptions of Western society" (157). No value or institution remained unchallenged.

[4] See John W. O'Malley, "Vatican II: Did Anything Happen?" *Vatican II: Did Anything Happen?* ed. John W. O'Malley (New York: Continuum, 2011), 52–91.

to the cultural disorder of the expressive revolution and its aftermath (the "culture wars") only intensified the chaos. Polarizing tribal tensions have emerged out of the cultural vacuum: clashes between those seeking to restore the church to its previous pre–Vatican II power structures and those committed to the council's values.

The term *tribe* implies a large element of cultural solidarity and belonging based on strongly shared symbols, myths, and rituals. Tribalism triggers loneliness at two levels—it forbids members from connecting with people not of their tribes; and it also ostracizes members who dare to break the boundaries to connect with outsiders. Bitter and divisive tensions among tribes leads to polarization. Each tribe cultivates negative emotionally charged stereotypes and prejudices about its tribal neighbors, making dialogue across the boundaries difficult, if not impossible. This cannot be resolved unless members of the opposing tribes learn the difficult art of dialoguing in order to collaborate for the common good. The difference between tribalism and fundamentalism is a narrow one; the former's boundaries are less rigid than those of the latter. However, tribalism can quickly morph into rigid fundamentalism.

Tribalism and Loneliness in Healthcare Institutions

To speak of tribal tensions in healthcare institutions may sound rather exaggerated.[5] Peter Garling, the author of the report of the commission that examined the crises within the acute care services of the public health system of New South Wales, Australia, concluded, "One impediment to good, safe care which infects the whole public hospital system . . . is the breakdown of good working relations between [medical] clinicians and management which is very detrimental to patients."[6] Distrust and deep antipathies divide the two groups. He

---

[5] In 2008 I was appointed to an independent panel by the Government of New South Wales, Australia, to oversee the reform of the public hospital system; in 2010 and 2011 I researched at Oxford University various tribal tensions within the National Health Service (NHS) of England. See Arbuckle, *Humanizing Healthcare Reforms.*

[6] Peter Garling, *Final Report of the Special Commission of Inquiry Acute Care Services in NSW Public Hospitals: Overview* (Sydney: Special Commission of Inquiry, 2008), 11.

likened the breakdown to the Great Schism, the lasting split between the Eastern and Western Christian Churches in 1054, when each side accused the other of having fallen victim to heresy and having started the division. An effective but frightening analogy. The author concluded that the tribal schism in the health system is "alienating the most skilled in the medical workforce from service in the public system."[7]

The operative myth for clinicians is their focus on the needs of individual patients to whom they are primarily accountable for their actions. To maintain this focus they expect to have sufficient resources allocated to them, but they persistently and strongly feel that managers are refusing to respond appropriately. Managers know that resources are limited, and for this reason their immediate operative myth is very different. Doctors are anxious about patient outcomes, whereas managers must be concerned "about patient experience (which includes outcomes, but only as part of a mix to be met out of finite resources)."[8]

The problem of the tribal split and tensions between medical clinicians and managers is not unique to Australia. It is a worldwide phenomenon, and both parties have been described as seriously unhappy with the tension.[9] There has even been talk of mass resignations by general practitioners from the National Health Service (NHS) in England, one major reason being their dissatisfaction with managers, who they feel are invading their professional territory. Serious discontent commonly exists also among managers, who complain that medical clinicians are financially naive and unwilling to acknowledge the immense complexity of contemporary healthcare institutions. The two subcultures are so mythologically diverse that the "potential for conflict arising from cultural differences is almost limitless."[10] Although

---

[7] Ibid.

[8] Nigel Edwards, Martin Marshall, Alastair McLellan, and Kamran Abbasi, "Doctors and Managers: A Problem without a Solution," *British Medical Journal* 326 (March 22, 2003): 609.

[9] See Richard Smith, "Why Are Doctors so Unhappy?" *British Medical Journal* 322 (May 5, 2001): 1073–74; and Nigel Edwards et al., "Unhappy Doctors: What Are the Causes and What Can Be Done?" *British Medical Journal* 324 (April 6, 2002): 835–38.

[10] James Drife and Ian Johnston, "Handling the Conflicting Cultures in the NHS," *British Medical Journal* 310 (April 22, 1995), 1054.

within the complex culture of a healthcare institution there are many other subcultures such as nurses, physiotherapists, radiographers, medical laboratory scientific officers, and hospital social workers, the dominant tribal subcultures in tension are clinicians and managers. This tension has an impact on every other healthcare subculture.

Even among physicians there are what might be called subtribes. They are often referred to as "medical silos,"[11] which are groups of specialists who keep to themselves, are overly sensitive to the importance of hierarchical status, and discourage the sharing of information with other medical professional silos.[12] This jealously guarded individualism is inimical to the development of teamwork among themselves,[13] across the silo barriers, between themselves and nurses, and between themselves and managers. Because of this individualism the degree of mutual support among medical clinicians is poor. The loneliness triggered by silo barriers intensifies, and the crossing of professional boundaries is looked upon with grave suspicion. Little wonder that many experience high levels of unaddressed stress and "seem to deny the effect of stress and fatigue on performance,"[14] further discouraging them from openly acknowledging and discussing their medical errors with their colleagues. For this reason the report into the acute care services of the public hospitals in New South Wales concluded that a "new model of teamwork [between medical professionals] will be required to replace the old individual and independent 'silos' of professional care."[15] Without teamwork, cultures of loneliness in healthcare systems will continue to grow to the disadvantage of all involved. But teamwork can only be achieved through dialogue.

---

[11] See Garling, *Final Report,* 4.

[12] See Henry Mintzberg, *Managing* (Harlow: Pearson, 2009), 169–70.

[13] See J. Bryan Sexton, Eric J. Thomas, and Robert L. Helmreich, "Error, Stress, and Teamwork in Medicine and Aviation: Cross Sectional Surveys," *British Medical Journal* 320 (March 18, 2000): 745–49; D. Bell, A. Paterson, and G. McAlister, "Prevention through Learning: Working Together to Drive High-Quality Care," *Journal of the Royal College of Physicians of Edinburgh* 47/2 (2017): 121.

[14] Sexton et al., "Error, Stress, and Teamwork in Medicine and Aviation," 745.

[15] See Garling, *Final Report,* 4.

Tribal Tensions in the Catholic Church—Schism Dangers

When Vatican II ended in 1965, Catholics were euphoric. It was the beginning of a new age of a prophetic church committed to dialogue with the world, collegiality, transparency in government, and social justice. The ghetto church of the Counter-Reformation was over. Now, over fifty years after the council, the euphoria is no more. "More and more American Catholics have been bemoaning the polarization in the church," writes Cathleen Kaveny, "but no one seems to have any idea how to address it."[16]

Why is this happening? There is a failure to understand that the church itself is a culture, and it does not escape the inevitable consequences of culture change. It is not some ethereal, nonhuman reality that is unaffected by the largely unconscious forces of culture.[17] Theologies do not exist in some heavenly vacuum. They are embedded in different cultural expressions. Pre–Vatican II theology was clothed in a culture that is radically different from Vatican II theology; the latter would demand its own cultural dress. Such cultural change does not, nor can it, occur overnight. Writers who assess the history of the impact of Vatican II on the life of the church rarely appreciate the fact that its documents would inexorably be the catalyst for continuing cultural chaos.[18] The documents demanded that the church interact with a changing world. If the world is in ongoing chaos, then we must expect the evangelizing church to be in chaos. The purpose of this section is to analyze these statements and why there is now so much unfriendliness and loneliness where there should be compassionate listening and dialogue.

Analysis in Brief

- Vatican II called for a *radical* cultural mythological change; such change was bound to be chaotic.

---

[16] Cathleen Kaveny, *A Culture of Engagement: Law, Religion, and Morality* (Washington, DC: Georgetown University Press, 2016), 167.

[17] See Gerald A. Arbuckle, *Culture, Inculturation, and Theologians: A Postmodern Critique* (Collegeville, MN: Liturgical Press, 2010), xix–xxiv.

[18] An interesting exception to this is the Jesuit philosopher B. R. Brinkman, "Due Vedute di Roma," *The Heythrop Journal: A Quarterly Review of Philosophy and Theology* 3/2 (1996): 176–92.

- The chaos has been intensified, first, by the failure of culturally appropriate leadership; second, by the impact of the expressive cultural revolution and the resulting, divisive "culture wars."
- The result has been a developing tribal division in the church: the surfacing of the residual mythology of the pre–Vatican II church on one side and Vatican II supporters on the other.
- Pope Francis stands in the middle, calling both sides to the mission of Christ to the world, but the polarizing continues in some parts of the church; the middle ground is in danger of shrinking.

Culture Models Set to Clash

Anthropologist Mary Douglas has produced a stimulating reflection on the interconnections among social structure, authority/power, ritualism, and cosmology that can aid our understanding of the tribal tensions within the church today. For example, Catholicism after Vatican II represents, from a cultural point of view, a distinct mythological swing from a highly articulated social system, existing within a powerfully condensed symbolic universe, to a more flexible and to some extent splintered social assembly within a far more diffuse symbolic universe. Douglas's typology is now further explained and then applied to the contemporary church.

Douglas builds her reflections on two independently varying social criteria that she terms *grid* and *group*. By *grid* she means the set of rules according to which people relate to one another. For example, there is a grid that regulates how crew members of an airplane should interact. In this case we speak of a *strong* grid, because the rules are unambiguous about how individual crew members must relate to the captain. They must obey or lose their jobs. The second variable is the *group*. This is a community's sense of identity in relationship with people beyond its boundaries; for example, the feeling of group identity of *this* particular plane's crew may be weak (though the *grid* remains strong), because individual members wish to fly with different personnel and may or may not do so on the next flight.

Douglas claims that cosmological ideals and the importance of ritual will differ predictably with the extent to which *group* and *grid* are stressed. The social body constrains the way the physical is seen; thus, if there are tight controls over how people are to dress and act bodily, then there will be a rigidly controlled social group, and vice versa. Obedience is demanded to the social order. If social control is weak, the body will be at ease, informal, untidy, and sloppy, as with loose-fitting clothes and unkempt hair. The relation of the individual to society differs with the restraints of *grid* and *group*; the more rigid the *grid* and *group* are, the more developed the idea of formal transgression and its dangerous results and the less preoccupation there is for the right of the inner self to be freely expressed.[19]

Model 1: Pre–Vatican II Church— Strong Group/Strong Grid Culture

Understanding the Culture Model

In a *strong group/strong grid* culture the boundaries of the group and how individuals are to relate to one another within the boundaries are sharply defined. People are expected to fit into a tradition-based, bureaucratic, hierarchical, and patriarchal system that is presumed to have, by right, a monopoly over knowledge; dependency and conformity are esteemed qualities. To maintain conformity there are detailed and rigid, morally sanctioned rules about how the human body (and thus the social body) is to be controlled. To break these rules is to risk ritual pollution that only the ritual guardians of the system can remove.

In terms of authority and power, the hierarchical leader's task is to maintain the status quo. For that, personal charismatic qualities are not needed; in fact, such qualities could risk drawing people away from tradition to a cult of the leader and set precedents for undermining the status quo in the group. Tradition, inasmuch as it sets boundaries and rules for living, can be said to have within itself a strong position of authority and power to coerce individuals into conformity. A potential for orthodoxy witch hunting exists, but it is infrequently used as long as the group/grid remains strong and the culture is stable; people are

---

[19] See Mary Douglas, *Natural Symbols: Explorations in Cosmology* (New York: Pantheon Books, 1970), 102. For a helpful review of the relationship among power, chaos, and ritual, see David Kertzer, *Ritual, Politics, and Power* (New Haven, CT: Yale University Press, 1988).

afraid to break customs lest the group socially punish them, such as by ostracizing or ridiculing them.

In the religious cosmology of the culture there is a hierarchy of transcendent gods/spirits that is intimately concerned with the well being of the culture and its stability. There are intermediary and more approachable spirits helping people to relate to the higher and more remote gods/spirits. The world is maintained in harmony by the gods/spirits, who keep the evil forces under control, but people can allow these same powers to enter their lives through sin. Sin is the conscious/unconscious breaking of detailed rules and laws established particularly to maintain the clarity of roles and boundaries within the culture; sexual sins are especially evil because if control over the body is broken, there is real danger that the social body will be fractured also. As far as the virtue of justice is concerned, it is *legal* justice that is stressed; that is, the rights of the group or tradition over its constituent members must be maintained at all costs or else the group will disintegrate. There are rituals under the firm direction of officials to remove the pollution resulting from sin and to ward off the evil forces endangering the predictability of daily life.

Examples of cultures approximating this model are the Israelites as described in the Book of Leviticus;[20] the Indian caste system; rural Ireland; and possibly the British class structure of the nineteenth century. In summary, it is a culture that allows no ambiguity. It is a culture of order and predictability.

Application to the Church

The Catholic Church prior to the council reflected many of the qualities of this culture model. For example, the church in the United States was considered by many, before 1965, to be "the best organized and most powerful of the nation's subcultures—a source of both alienation and enrichment for those born within it and an object of bafflement or uneasiness for others."[21] This statement is equivalent to saying

---

[20] See Mary Douglas, *Purity and Danger: An Analysis of the Concepts of Pollution and Taboo* (London: Routledge and Kegan Paul, 1966), 54–72.

[21] John Cogley, *Catholic America* (New York: Image, 1974), 135. For an overview of the pre–Vatican II Church in England, see Michael P. Hornsby-Smith, *Roman Catholic Beliefs in England: Customary Catholicism and*

that the group/grid typology within the American church was highly effective at that time. Membership qualifications were clearly stated; generally, one was born into the faith and, over time, one became enculturated into a very self-contained cultural milieu with its many distinguishing customs and institutions such as schools, clubs, hospitals, and universities. Certain particular customs, for example, the Friday abstinence from meat, marked Catholics off from Protestants across the boundaries.

In pre–Vatican II times the church's mission was also sharply focused and frequently articulated in sermons and popular literature: win pagan and Protestant souls for the Lord. Within the church, membership was hierarchically graded: pope, bishops, priests, religious, and laity. Members of the laity, who were passive receivers of the expert ritual/religious leadership of the clerical categories, were expected to go about saving their souls in the dangerous secular world through faithfulness to a set of intricate laws and customs. Sin was often synonymous with breaking these formally stated regulations, particularly some key ones related to the maintenance of the culture's boundaries. Thus sexual sins and the crossing of the barriers separating Catholics from non-Catholics were considered particularly heinous, with the Code of Canon Law having stopped "Catholics from participating in disputations or discussions with non-Catholics without permission of the Holy See" (Canon 1325, 3).

There also existed in the pre–Vatican II culture a complex regulative cosmology and a highly condensed and differentiated symbolic system of God and the saints, with their perceived qualities reflecting the culture's group/grid. God was presented as the remote Almighty and Unchanging One, Creator/Regulator; Christ as the King, Savior, and Judge of a people who "break the rules." Mary and the saints were depicted as approachable and understanding beings having particular cultic significance in various needs—for example, St. Anthony of Padua was the saint concerned for lost things—in contrast to the stern and remote God the Father and the sacrificing, judging Jesus Christ.

The hierarchical officials held positions of considerable authority and power. As the essential ritual intermediaries between the laity and Christ, they could threaten to withhold their services, even to the extent of excommunicating people from the body of the church, for

Transformation of Religious Authority (Cambridge: Cambridge University Press, 1991), 190–209.

such offenses as not sending one's children to a Catholic school. If the laity dared smudge the boundaries there were powerful symbols to indicate that they had moved to the edge of group life and were risking their salvation; thus, for a Catholic to marry a non-Catholic within the church, the ceremony had to be held in the sacristy, an uncomfortable and impersonal adjunct to the main church building. The group itself had similar coercive power over individuals; the Catholic community was so strongly bonded that one would fear to break the rules lest one become a subject of gossip, ridicule, or even ostracism.[22] In such an atmosphere it was only natural for justice to be considered primarily as legal justice, that is, stressing the rights of the group over the individual.

This model of church culture is open to obvious abuses. For example, the culture forced people into loneliness. People outside the church, including family members, were to be treated in many ways as strangers who risked the faith of insiders. Another problem is that external conformity to laws and rules can become more important than a personal relationship with Christ; morality is more concerned with sexual and private sins than with social issues of justice and human rights; scandals remain hidden to protect the good name of the church. The authority of the ritual/administrative leaders is also open to considerable exploitation; "creeping infallibility" becomes an approved way of administrative curial officers, bishops, and priests to avoid having to be accountable for their actions to laity and the church as a whole. And if one is the ritual expert in an unchanging church, then there is little need to cultivate dialogue with laity. One has all the answers before questions are even asked, so why listen to others for solutions to problems? There are no built-in public accountability systems for hierarchical officials. It is a culture insensitive to the demands of social justice. Inevitably this model, with its emphasis on the maintenance of tradition and the status quo, discourages pastoral innovation and dialogue with the world. A good symbol of this church culture is the barque (ship) of Peter, tossed around by hostile external forces, but safe, internally intact, and under the infallible captaining of the pope, the vicar of Christ on earth, assisted by the bishops, priests, and religious.

---

[22] See Hugh Brody, *Inishkillane: Change and Decline in the West of Ireland* (London: Faber and Faber, 1986), 178.

Model 2: The Vatican II Church—
Weak Grid/Weak Group Culture

Understanding the Culture Model

A culture of this type is strongly egalitarian in social relationships and in gender, with minimum pressure from structures within and at the boundaries of the group. Generally, communities of this type emerge only under the inspiration of some charismatic leader, who denounces the oppressive rigidity of the grid/group traditions or structures of a dominant culture from which escape is sought. Dress codes and rigid rules of conduct based on tradition are considered irrelevant; far more important are the interior conversion and effective commitment of members to the group's vision, mission, and values resulting in what sociologically are termed intentional communities. There is openness of the group to new insights and dialogue in order to achieve the mission. The culture type emphasizes collaboration for the common good.

Personal identity according to this model comes from an awareness of one's self-worth and potential for change, not from a culture's traditional internal and boundary structures. Religion is highly personalized; a personal relationship to gods/spirits and to other people who have the same values as oneself is what counts, and thus rituals are unimportant (unless they reinforce that sense of relationship or emerge out of the events of daily living, in which case they are very simple in structure). The world is inherently good, and if there are problems they are due to traditional grid/group structures that have stifled the good or prevented it from emerging in people's lives. Sin is not based on external measures alone, but rather on what one believes is wrong. If justice is stressed, it is in terms of the common pursuit of social justice so that all may benefit. This type of culture is open to considerable innovation, and dissent is also welcomed, because both are seen as essential requirements for growth.

Application to Church

Vatican II favored this culture model. Concrete examples of this model are the early Christian community in Jerusalem (see Acts 1:2ff.); religious congregations in the first stage of founding enthusiasm, such as the early followers of St. Francis of Assisi; and countercultural communities throughout history. If the fervor is to be maintained, members must face the challenge of building structures and group identity that do not crush the original enthusiasm. This is not an easy task, and it is rarely successful unless commitment to the ideals of the original founding group is vigorously maintained. The model is helpful in understanding the rise and inner dynamics of "churches from below" such as prayer groups, house churches, and small (or basic) Christian communities. Certainly, the spirit of Vatican II is to emphasize intentional faith communities in which there is collaboration for mission.

St. Paul further clarifies the qualities of an evangelizing, intentional community. He frequently speaks of the bonds of love that should bind people together in such a community. Like Christ, for Paul, love is something totally different from mere sentimentality or fine-sounding but hollow words. The main result of living the Gospel is the formation of entirely new relationships, similar to those among members of a family. When Paul says that he is carrying Christ's followers in his heart (Phil 1:7), he means that there exists between himself and them a unity similar to the one between himself and the risen Christ, and that this latter relationship is so deep that he can even write that Christ is living in him (Gal 2:20; Phil 1:2). For Paul, community consists of many subcultures and people with quite different gifts (1 Cor 12:12), but what binds them together is the commitment to the mission of Jesus Christ: "to testify to the good news of God's grace" (Acts 20:24). Paul was a realist. He knew from bitter experience that as the number of Christian communities developed there would be difficulties, even dissensions, in the communities he established.[23] Paul, who had trembled at the news of factions within the Christian community of Corinth, was devastated to discover yet more divisions (1 Cor 7:1–11, 8–10, 12–14).

When Paul said that converts to Christianity did not have to observe all Jewish laws, many Jewish people were annoyed. Thus, very early in its history the church started to experience conflict and polarization. Among the Christians in Antioch there was dysfunctional behavior. Paul saw that members simply had not clothed themselves with love, "which binds everything together in perfect harmony"

---

[23] See Ben Witherington, *Conflict and Community in Corinth* (Grand Rapids, MI: Eerdmans, 1995).

(Col 3:14). He spoke forcefully to those who forgot the mission of Christ and the call to "love your neighbor as yourself" (Gal 5:14): "If, however, you bite and devour one another, take care that you are not consumed by one another" (Gal 5:15). Paul became painfully aware that he had often not adequately formed his Christian communities. Hence, the fractious divisions.[24] For resolving community tensions and divisions, dialogue was needed: "The fruit of the Spirit is love, joy, peace, patience, kindness, generosity, faithfulness, gentleness, and self-control" (Gal 5:22–23).[25]

In summary, an intentional community is *a group of people who purposely and voluntarily coordinate and, if necessary, sacrifice their personal aspirations and actions for the common good. Intentional* means "deliberate" or "consciously chosen." Intentional communities acknowledge that members will be different from one another, but, in the words of Pope Francis, "We must walk united with our differences: there is no other way to become one. This is the way of Jesus."[26] An intentional community is not something that is achieved once and maintained as such without further effort. On the contrary, community is always in a state of becoming. It must be constantly willed by its members. Community only is alive when members are *willingly* and *actually* committing themselves to an agreed action.[27]

Reasons for Tribal Tensions: Rise of Restorationism

Why has the adoption of the Vatican II culture model been so problematic? Why is tribal polarization continuing to develop in parts of the church today, for example, in the United States, sometimes with the ferocity referred to by Austen Ivereigh in this chapter's epigraph?[28]

---

[24] See Jerome Murphy-O'Connor, *Paul: His Story* (Oxford: Oxford University Press, 2004), 111, 162–63.

[25] For an understanding of intentional communities and their pastoral application, see Gerald A. Arbuckle, *Intentional Faith Communities in Catholic Education* (Strathfield: St. Pauls Publications, 2016), 148–49.

[26] Pope Francis, interview with Antonio Spadaro, "A Big Heart Open to God," *America* 209/8 (September 30, 2013): 28.

[27] See Bernard Lonergan, cited in *Theology Digest* 14/2 (1966): 123.

[28] Austen Ivereigh, "As Anti-*Amoris* Critics Cross into Dissent, the Church Must Move On," *Crux* (December 11, 2016). Ivereigh is the author of *The*

Recall the warning of Rollo May: *"The loneliness of mythlessness is the deepest and least assuageable of all. Unrelated to the past, unconnected with the future, we hang as if in mid-air."*[29] The process of "myth splitting" in times of myth disintegration, familiar to anthropologists, helps to explain the complex process of tribalism and polarization within the contemporary church. This dynamic will now be more fully explained.

Built-in Ambiguities in Vatican II Documents

Vatican II radically affected the church's contemporary expression of its creation mythology in two ways, and the consequence had to be confusion or the malaise of chaos. First, it sought to reintroduce a much-needed balance within the mythology. For example, the principle of collegiality was highlighted in order to counter the centuries-long overemphasis on its polar opposite, namely, papal authority. The documents are filled with ambiguities and tensions resulting from the reintroduction of key myths within the creation mythology.[30] Gone are the many certainties of the pre-council apologetics constructed on the assumption that theological opposites did not exist. Table 6–1 on the next page shows some of the mythological ambiguities contained in the documents as expressed in pre–Vatican II and Vatican II understandings.

Nowhere in the documents does the council spell out precisely how these contradictions are to be balanced in real life. In reality, it simply could not do so. Rather, it rightly challenged all members of the church to struggle to develop in faith a living balance between the opposites through charity, ongoing mutual respect, and dialogue. For example, governing structures representing local and universal churches will work together *only* if they recognize that they must pursue a common mission: Christ's mission to the world. However, people who were used to being told expressly what to do by the

---

Great Reformer: Francis and the Making of a Radical Pope (London: Allen and Unwin, 2014).

[29] Rollo May, *The Cry for Myth* (New York: Delta, 1991), 99.

[30] One of the positive contributions of anthropologist Claude Lévi-Strauss to our understanding of mythology is his emphasis on polarities and the ability of myths to reconcile them. See Edmund Leach, *Lévi-Strauss* (London: Fontana, 1970), 54–82.

Pre–Vatican II Mythology	Vatican II Mythology
The church is universal,	*but* it is to be incarnated within local churches to reflect their diversities of culture.
The Catholic Church was established by Christ for the salvation of the world,	*but* Christians of other churches also belong to the church of Christ and can be saved through their traditions.
The church is an institution under the leadership of the bishops, who are committed to maintain order and unity,	*but* it is also the people of God, who as pilgrims are not concerned about rank.
The pope has full, supreme, and universal power over the church,	*but* the bishops collegially govern their dioceses with authority that is proper to them.
The aim of liturgy is to help us adore God our Creator,	*but* it must reflect the needs and customs of different peoples and cultures.
Heaven is our final destiny,	*but* for our salvation we must struggle for faith and justice in this world.
Priesthood is a sacrament and ministry established by Christ,	*but* all who are baptized share in Christ's priestly power.

Table 6–1. Mythological ambiguities expressed in pre–Vatican II and Vatican II documents.

church became confused. They opted, with growing emotional intensity, for one pole or the other in the myths. Theological, pastoral, and liturgical controversies rapidly emerged. Especially in the early years after the council protagonists used interest from the media to add fuel to the already existing tensions between opposing groups, which rapidly ceased to trust each another.

"Myth Splitting": An Explanation

Every myth contains opposites, for example, the rights of the individual and of the common good in the founding story of democracy. Anthropologist Claude Lévi-Strauss concluded that one key role of mythologies is to reconcile these opposites—that is, if they are allowed to interact, then tension between them will be creative. In practice, because of the uncertainties or ambiguities inherent in this tension, the common tendency (especially when the myths break down and lead to chaos) is for people to move toward one pole rather than the other; one is seen to be "good," the other "bad." One pole then tends to dominate to the detriment of the other.[31] This is the process of *myth splitting*.

Myth splitting is "a cultural and psychodynamic process whereby individuals and groups, in an effort to cope with the doubts, anxieties, and conflicting feelings [in the cultural chaos], isolate different elements of experience, often to protect the perceived good from the bad."[32] This division then forms a social defense,[33] that is, a system of relationships that people feel protects them from cultural disintegration or loss of meaning.[34] The contemporary rise of extreme

---

[31] See Gerald A. Arbuckle, *Catholic Identity or Identities? Refounding Ministries in Chaotic Times* (Collegeville, MN: Liturgical Press, 2013), 41–49.

[32] See Gareth Morgan, *Images of Organization* (Beverley Hills, CA: Sage, 1986), 206.

[33] The term *social defense* was first used by Isabel M. Lyth in 1961. See "The Functioning of Social Systems as a Defense against Anxiety," in *Containing Anxiety in Institutions: Selected Essays*, ed. Isabel M. Lyth (London: Free Association Press, 1988), 63–64.

[34] See Larry Hirschhorn and Donald R. Young, "Dealing with Anxiety of Working Defenses as Coping Strategy," in *Organizations on the Couch: Clinical Perspectives on Organizational Behavior and Change*, ed. Manfred F. Kets de Vries et al. (San Francisco: Jossey-Bass, 1991), 223.

nationalism in Western democracies, with its anti-immigrant dynamic, is an example of myth splitting. In the midst of rapid social changes, people feel threatened. They want to feel good again, so the more immigrants are seen as "bad," the more locals feel "good."[35]

We see a similar situation in the church today. As noted above, polar opposites exist in the documents of pre–Vatican II and Vatican II. The mythological opposites in both sets of statements are true, but without clear guidelines (which no one could give), chaos resulted. Today, there are people holding tenaciously to one view or the other and considering their opponents heretics.[36]

As chaos threatened, Rome reacted in an increasingly restorationist style to avoid ambiguities. For example, episcopal conferences and synods of bishops lost the power to act that had been given them by the council; the Roman Curia became more and more directive, and bishops continued to be appointed without proper consultation with local churches; control over liturgy given to bishops by the council eventually moved firmly back into the hands of Rome. In other words, in the above list of complementary mythic oppositions, the pendulum swung firmly in favor of the pre–Vatican II side.[37]

The second quality of the documents that intensified the chaos was the council's decision, in contrast to major previous councils, not to give a sharp focus at any stage to its deliberations. "Nothing," writes historian John O'Malley, "is more characteristic of Vatican II than the breadth of its concerns, never neatly packaged into a central issue."[38] Fundamentally, the council said to take the good news out to the world, but listen to its needs and be prepared to learn and be changed by it. It could not tell us how to respond to this imperative pastorally, just as it could not spell out how to reconcile the polar opposites in the myths listed above.

---

[35] See Melanie Klein and Joan Riviere, *Love, Hate, and Reparation* (New York: Norton, 1964), 13.

[36] See Arbuckle, *Healthcare Ministry*, 141–42.

[37] See Gerard Mannion, *Ecclesiology and Postmodernity: Questions for the Church* (Collegeville, MN: Liturgical Press, 2007), 43–74. Mannion uses the term *neo-exclusivism* as a synonym for *restorationism*.

[38] John W. O'Malley, "Developments, Reforms, and Two Great Reformations: Toward a Historical Assessment of Vatican II," *Theological Studies* 44/3 (1983): 395.

Inadequate Leadership

In times of chaos, well-formed residual myths commonly rise to the surface and become operative myths to fill the cultural vacuum. Following the council, due to inadequate leadership,[39] the pre-council residual mythology rose again to the surface. From a theological perspective I applaud the mythological changes of Vatican II, but as an anthropologist who is aware of the need to be sensitive to the complexities and uncertainties of cultural change, I remain deeply saddened. The resulting turmoil should have been expected and better catechesis prepared to explain the inevitable chaotic, yet potentially creative, consequences of the council's decisions.

The council failed to remind Catholics that the implementation of the council's thrusts would be a messy, painful, and grief-evoking process. For centuries Catholics had been treated like dependent children, instructed by their clerical leaders exactly how to win salvation by obeying detailed rules. Suddenly, the council announced that they had to stand on their own two feet and make decisions for themselves in light of the needs of the world, as well as the gospel and tradition. The world was no longer to be seen as evil in itself, and Catholics must now dialogue with people of good will, even with those who profess no faith at all. No longer could they identify themselves, or be identified by others, with rigid unchanging symbols of a ghetto culture. The council fathers did not foresee that cultures, especially the deeply embedded, longstanding, highly centralized and authoritarian culture of the pre-council church, do not change simply because a document says they should. The bishops and the curia were called to lead a massive cultural change, and they were totally unprepared for the task.

In fairness to the council fathers, they were but men of their times. We moderns, especially in the West, are rarely attuned to the devastating nature of radical mythological changes. We are accustomed to seeing entire landscapes being destroyed and redeveloped over a short time. In our naive appreciation of the power of technology, we assume that the same destruction and redevelopment can take place within cultures. We assume that symbolic landscapes of peoples can

---

[39] See Gerald A. Arbuckle, *The Francis Factor and the People of God: New Life for the Church* (Maryknoll, NY: Orbis Books, 2015), 165–72; Arbuckle, *Refounding the Church,* 39–43.

be destroyed—that the familiar sights, sounds, and routines in which peoples are nurtured can be obliterated overnight without particularly negative results for them.

The hard reality is that symbols, myths, and rituals are not replaced as quickly or easily as buildings and landscapes, or mass produced as readily as automobiles or toothbrushes. As we have seen, the uprooting of the inner framework of cultures, even when there is conscious and intellectual assent to what is happening, destroys a stable sense of belonging as well as people's individuality. People are bound to experience moments of intense loss. Remember this key fact: *myths relate to the heart*. We can change our ideas and make all kinds of rational plans with ease, but dramatic change in the mythic structure is in the last analysis the way people impose a felt order or meaning on the world and hold back anxiety-creating chaos. The council fathers could have saved themselves a good deal of trouble if they had taken to heart the advice of that shrewd political observer of change, Niccolo Machiavelli (1469–1527), in *The Prince*: "It must be considered that there is nothing more difficult to carry out, nor more doubtful of success, nor more dangerous to handle, than to initiate a new order of things."

Since the council had not established an appropriate process to implement its mythological changes, Pope Paul VI decided in 1967 that the curia would be responsible for the implementation of the council's major decrees.[40] That was unfortunate because the curia itself remained resistant to reform within itself and in the wider church; his decision has thus haunted the church ever since. Fifty years after the council, Pope Francis criticized the curia's culture and its faults, which were characteristic of modern bureaucracies,[41] such as deep-seated resistance to change, lack of accountability, departmental silos that refused to collaborate, membership based on like-minded thinking, and "creeping infallibility" in administrative decisions.

---

[40] Arbuckle, *The Francis Factor and the People of God*, 165; see also John W. O'Malley, *What Happened at Vatican II* (Cambridge, MA: The Belknap Press, 2008), 283; Hans Küng, *Can We Save the Church?* (London: William Collins, 2013), 201–5.

[41] See Gerald A. Arbuckle, *Violence, Society, and the Church: A Cultural Approach* (Collegeville, MN: Liturgical Press, 2004), 108–11.

The Expressive Revolution and "Culture Wars"

[The] social revolution of the 1960s brought two aftershocks. The first was the conservatism of the 1980s . . . which set up the culture war conflicts. The second . . . was the movement, particularly among young people, away from established religion.[42]

At the same time that Vatican II was becoming the catalyst for a cultural revolution within the church, the Western world was itself experiencing a most profound cultural shift from modernity to postmodernity; the visible sign of this dramatic cultural change was the expressive revolution of the 1960s. The expressive cultural revolution[43] of the mid-1960s was a massive, well-publicized attack on all that had been held sacred by modernity since the sixteenth century. No value, custom, or institution remained unchallenged and unaffected. Naive faith in science and technology disintegrated.[44] The expressive revolution was essentially an attack on boundaries of all kinds, gender differences, limits, certainties, taboos, roles, systems, styles, predictabilities, and traditions. There was widespread erosion of the legitimacy of traditional institutions: churches,[45] business, government, education, and the family.

---

[42] John I. Jenkins, CSC, cited in *Polarization in the US Catholic Church*, ed. Mary E. Konieczny, Charles C. Camosy, and Tricia C. Bruce (Collegeville, MN: Liturgical Press, 2016), 10; see also D. Putnam and David E. Campbell, *American Grace: How Religion Divides and Unites* (New York: Simon and Schuster, 2010).

[43] See Arbuckle, *Violence, Society, and the Church*, 157–72.

[44] See Hugh McLeod, *The Religious Crisis of the 1960s* (Oxford: Oxford University Press, 2007), 258.

[45] McLeod notes: "The nature, extent, and causes of this crisis [for the churches in most Western countries] are hotly debated, and historians are far from having arrived at any consensus. One of the most influential interpretations of the crisis is that advanced by Callum Brown and Patrick Pasture, which places gender, and specifically changes in women's consciousness and identity at its heart" (ibid., 186). See also Callum Brown, *The Death of Christian Britain: Understanding Secularisation 1800–2000* (London: Routledge, 2001); and Patrick Pasture, "Christendom and the Legacy of the Sixties: Between the Secular City and the Age of Aquarius," *Revue d'histoire ecclésiastique* 99 (2004): 82–117.

In brief, traditions were devalued, censorship dismantled, churches deserted, the family mocked. Countries, especially the United States, became polarized around issues such as abortion, homosexuality, recreational drugs, and gun politics. This polarization, which became known as the culture wars, was highly politicized: the Democratic Party followers were branded as the progressives, and the Republican Party devotees the traditionalists. The already existing polarization in the church deepened as Catholics became exposed to the expressive revolution, its assault on traditional values, and the divisive qualities of the culture wars. Restorationists reinforced their rigid position and were encouraged to do so by Rome. Pope John Paul II, followed by Benedict XVI, insisted on maintaining a culture of Catholic identity, "practices and beliefs that set Catholicism apart from contemporary American culture, not points of consonance."[46] There was to be no ambiguity.[47] Yet tribal divisions continued to expand. Sociologist Mary Ellen Konieczny, in her study of two American parishes, "one traditionally conservative, the other self-consciously progressive," observed "that views and practices related to sex, marriage, and child-rearing were crucial to the religious self-understanding of both groups and to their alienation from those on the other side."[48] Another cultural shift was needed to heal the divisions.

---

[46] Cathleen Kaveny, *A Culture of Engagement* (Washington, DC: Georgetown University Press, 2016), 3.

[47] See Arbuckle, *The Francis Factor and the People of God*, 165–82. Peter McDonough wrote in 2013: "Many progressives [in the United States], their ranks aging, their expectations dashed at the retrenchment following Vatican II, feel defeated. . . . Now that the traditional mores built into pre-sixties neighborhoods have eroded, an unspoken entente regarding the no-nos of the magisterium is the norm. The episcopal stonewalling that greets organized dissent is reciprocated by a perception, pronounced among younger cohorts, of the irrelevance of institutional Catholicism. . . . Attendance at weekly Mass is down to around 20–25 percent of American Catholics." *The Catholic Labyrinth: Power, Apathy, and a Passion for Reform in the American Church* (New York: Oxford University Press, 2013), 272.

[48] Mary Ellen Konieczny, *The Spirit's Tether: Family, Work and Religion among American Catholics* (Oxford: Oxford University Press, 2013).

Pope Francis: Rejection of Restorationism

The residual founding mythology of the church itself, not the pre-conciliar mythology, has slowly begun to resurface with more confidence under the leadership of Pope Francis, a wisdom figure.[49] Through his many actions and words he is leading the church in a massive ritual of letting go of attachments to a monarchical papacy and its theological foundations. Despite the cultural resistance from the curia and others, he struggles to build governance structures to ensure that Vatican II mythology is finally and firmly embedded in the church's culture. From the moment of his election he adopted a new style of leadership based on the founding mythology of the church. By his words and behavior he has said a definite no to deadening fundamentalist restorationism with its insistence on coercive rules, and an unambiguous yes to being involved in the hopes and frustrations of people and their cultures:

> If the Christian is a restorationist, a legalist, if they want everything clear and safe, they will find nothing. . . . Those who today always look for disciplinarian solutions, those who long for an exaggerated doctrinal "security," those who stubbornly try to recover a past that no longer exists—they have a static and inward-directed view of things. . . . God is in every person's life. Even if the life of a person has been a disaster. . . . You must try to seek God in every human life. Although the life of a person is a land full of thorns and weeds, there is always a space in which the good seed can grow. You have to trust God.[50]

A church that is fearful of the world becomes a church of protective rules, a fortress church of the pre-conciliar type (that is, the strong

---

[49] See Massimo Faggioli, *Catholicism and Citizenship: Political Cultures of the Church in the Twenty-First Century* (Collegeville, MN: Liturgical Press, 2017), 42–45. See also Arbuckle, *The Francis Factor and the People of God,* 182–92; and Gerald A. Arbuckle, *Fundamentalism at Home and Abroad: Analysis and Pastoral Responses* (Collegeville, MN: Liturgical Press, 2017), 118–20.

[50] Spadaro, "A Big Heart Open to God: An Interview with Pope Francis."

grid/strong group model). Francis will have none of this. As a cardinal, he had said that the church had become "too wrapped up in itself . . . too navel-gazing . . . 'self-referential,'" and that this had "made it sick . . . suffering a 'kind of theological narcissism.'"[51] As pope, he wrote: "I prefer a Church which is bruised, hurting and dirty because it has been out in the streets, rather than a Church that is unhealthy from being confined and from clinging to its own security" (*Evangelii Gaudium,* no. 49). Neither the church nor the evangelizer is to be the focus of our concern, but rather the "center is Jesus Christ, who calls us and sends us forth."[52] The church's primary task is to evangelize, not to protect itself from the sufferings of others—especially people who are poor and vulnerable:

> Mere "administration" can no longer be enough. . . . I dream of a "missionary option," that is, a missionary impulse capable of transforming everything, so that the Church's customs, ways of doing things, times and schedules, language and structures can be suitably channeled for the evangelization of today's world rather than for her self-preservation. (*Evangelii Gaudium,* nos. 25, 27)

Later, in his final speech at the conclusion of the 2014 Bishops' Synod on the Family, Pope Francis said: "It is the Church that is not afraid to eat and drink with prostitutes and publicans [tax-collectors]. The Church that has the doors wide open to receive the needy, the penitent, and not only the just or those who believe they are perfect!" His primary model of the church, therefore, is not hierarchical but the people of God (weak grid/weak group model): "The image of the church I like is that of the holy, faithful people of God. . . . There is no full identity without belonging to a people."[53] And Francis expresses this identity personally by openly proclaiming, "I am a sinner." Little

---

[51] Cardinal Jorge Bergoglio, 2013 Conclave. During the Easter rituals in 2013 Francis warned the clergy against becoming mere "managers" or "antique collectors" obsessed with liturgical niceties, urging them to leave their sacristies to change the secular world. See William Pfaff, "Challenge to the Church," *The New York Review of Books* (May 9, 2013), 11.

[52] Thomas Reese, "Pope Francis' Ecclesiology Rooted in the Emmaus Story," *National Catholic Reporter* (August 6, 2013).

[53] Spadaro, "A Big Heart Open to God."

wonder that Francis is such a powerful communicator—people feel he understands them.

The Synod on the Family and Dialogue

Francis returns to the importance of balancing polar opposites, an integral quality of the Vatican II documents.[54] For example, in his 2013 apostolic exhortation *Evangelii Gaudium (The Joy of the Gospel),* he uncompromisingly repeats the church's stand against abortion: "This is not something subject to alleged reforms or 'modernization.' It is not 'progressive' to try to resolve problems by eliminating a human life" (no. 214). But immediately he enters a different discourse: the world of human praxis, from which he has repeatedly stressed that doctrinal and moral certainties must never be divorced:

> On the other hand, it is also true that we have done little to adequately accompany women in very difficult situations, where abortion appears as a quick solution to their profound anguish, especially when the life developing within them is the result of rape or a situation of extreme poverty. Who can remain unmoved before such painful situations? (no. 214)[55]

"On the other hand," he writes. And in that lies a profound truth. For Francis is trying to balance two polar opposites in moral discourse: one that rightly takes an absolute view on the principle of human life, and another that rightly shows a compassionate appreciation for vulnerable people in the context of their lived human realities and the many pressures that influence moral decisions. What that means is that there can be no "monolithic body of doctrine guarded by all and leaving no room for nuance" (no. 40). Four times in the same document he uses the phrase "on the other hand."

The widespread preparation for the Synod on the Family that was held in 2014 evoked fears and hopes among Catholics. The desire to

---

[54] See Gillian Paterson, "'On the Other Hand . . . ': The Catholic Church and Some Discourses on Population," *The Heythrop Journal* 55/6 (2014): 1109.

[55] Pope John Paul II presents the same approach to abortion in *Evangelium Vitae*, nos. 183–84.

moderate the language used to speak about gay and lesbian Catholics, along with suggestions to permit some divorced and remarried Catholics to return to the sacraments, were received with elation by some but dismay by others. At the conclusion of the synod, Francis, on October 18, 2014, named several tensions and temptations that the synod participants experienced, for example:

- A temptation to hostile inflexibility, that is, wanting to close oneself within the written word (the letter) and not allowing oneself to be surprised by God . . . ; within the law, within the certitude of what we know and not what we still need to learn. . . . From the time of Christ, it is the temptation of the zealous, of the scrupulous . . . of the so-called—today—"traditionalists" and also of the intellectuals.
- The temptation to a destructive tendency to goodness, that in the name of a deceptive mercy binds the wounds without first curing them and treating them; that treats the symptoms and not the causes and the roots. It is the temptation of the "do-gooders," of the fearful, and also of the so-called "progressives and liberals."

For Francis, these temptations to become tribally trapped in mythological splitting can only be avoided through prayer-based discernment and dialogue. Authentic dialogue is able to break through the rigid borders that imprison fundamentalist theological thinking of the "right" or the "left"; this allows people to engage with the world beyond.

More polarizing tribal tensions erupted when Pope Francis published the post-synod apostolic exhortation, *Amoris Laetitia*. For restorationists, it contained many troubling instances of polar opposites in moral discourses, such as the following:[56]

- "'Principal tendencies' . . . are leading 'individuals . . . to receive less and less support from social structures than in the past,'" *but* "on the other hand, 'equal consideration needs to be given to the growing danger represented by an extreme individualism.'" (nos. 32, 33, internal quotations from *Relatio Finalis,* no. 5)

---

[56] See Arbuckle, *Fundamentalism at Home and Abroad*, 122.

- "It needs to be emphasized that 'biological sex and the socio-cultural role of sex (gender) can be distinguished but not separated,'" *but* "on the other hand, 'the technological revolution in the field of human procreation has introduced the ability to manipulate the reproductive act, making it independent of the sexual relationship between a man and a woman.'" (no. 56, internal quotations from *Relatio Finalis,* nos. 58, 33)
- "Those who know that their spouse is always suspicious . . . will tend to keep secrets . . . and pretend to be someone other than who they are," *but* "on the other hand, a family marked by loving trust, come what may, helps its members to be themselves and spontaneously to reject deceit, falsehood, and lies." (no. 115)

He does not, and cannot, say *how* the polar opposites are to be reconciled in particular situations. This shows how desperately we need appropriate catechesis and dialogue to avoid fundamentalism based on the exclusive emphasis on either one pole or the other in the tension. As Pope Francis writes: "We have been called to form consciences, not to replace them" (no. 37). Francis wholeheartedly believes in the importance of dialogue—something that is particularly abhorrent to fundamentalists. The word is mentioned over fifty times in *Evangelii Gaudium* and twenty times in *Amoris Laetitia.* For example:

Dialogue is much more than the communication of a truth. It arises from the enjoyment of speaking and it enriches those who express their love for one another through the medium of words. . . . Evangelisation . . . involves the path of dialogue . . . dialogue with states, dialogue with society—including dialogue with cultures and the sciences—and dialogue with other believers. (*Evangelii Gaudium*, nos. 142, 238)

Dialogue is essential for experiencing, expressing and fostering love in marriage and family life. Yet it can only be the fruit of a long and demanding apprenticeship. Men and women, young people and adults, communicate differently. . . . We need to develop certain attitudes that express love and encourage authentic dialogue. (*Amoris Laetitia,* no. 136).

Pope Francis's position is clear: He has moved away from the restorationist position of his predecessors. He stands in the middle, calling contesting tribes to focus on the mission of Jesus Christ to the world. Restorationists in particular are deeply annoyed by his stand; hence the rumors of possible schism. I doubt that we have yet reached the state of threatened chaos in the church that led the poet William Butler Yeats, following the horrific tragedies of World War I, to write: "Things fall apart; the centre cannot hold."[57] I am confident that Francis's image of a refounding church will remain; the middle will hold, though the remote risk of schisms may continue. Cohesiveness, focused on the mission of Jesus Christ, will emerge through faith-based dialogue, but it will continue to be a painful and uncertain journey.[58]

Responding to Tribalism: Dialogue

As Pope Francis has observed, "The Church is called to be at the service of a difficult dialogue" (*Evangelii Gaudium,* no. 74). Philosopher Martin Buber (1878–1965) distinguishes between two ways of relating to other people: "I-It" and "I-Thou." I-It relationships are characterized by the tendency to treat a person as "an impersonal object governed by causal, social, or economic forces."[59] An I-Thou relationship happens when there is mutuality, openness, presence, and directness.[60] The "I" relates to the "Thou" not as something to be studied, measured, or manipulated, but as an irreplaceable presence that responds to the "I" in its individuality. When this relationship

---

[57] William Butler Yeats, "The Second Coming," II.3.

[58] A January 2017 survey from the Pew Research Center "found that 87 percent of Catholics express a favorable view of Francis." As Thomas Reese comments on this finding, "It should be noted that these Catholics also liked John Paul and Benedict, [but] unlike the conservative dissidents, they did not abandon the papacy when Francis was elected." Thomas Reese, "Papal Loyalists Become Dissidents," *National Catholic Reporter* (November 8, 2017).

[59] Robert Audi, ed., "Martin Buber," *The Cambridge Dictionary of Philosophy* (New York: Cambridge University Press, 2009), 104.

[60] See Martin Buber, *Between Man and Man* (New York: Routledge, 2002), xii.

exists, participants in dialogue recognize the need for social bonding based on mutuality and interdependence in response to a common vision and mission. Dialogue aims to foster I-Thou relationships that are based on the need to work together to realize this need, and not on the narcissistic wishes of individuals. However, dialogue is a difficult journey, filled with dangers, so participants need to be aware of the following guidelines:

Guideline 1: Dialogue cannot begin unless people realize that individuals are not ethereal beings; they are encased in cultures that, at least unconsciously, influence the way they feel, think, and act. Theologians of different tribal schools meet not as "pure intellects" but as different cultures. That is, dialogue requires cross-cultural communication skills. Failure to recognize this will inevitably prevent dialogue. In fact, tensions are likely to increase.

Guideline 2: Dialogue is "that address and response between persons in which there is a flow of meaning between them in spite of all the obstacles that normally would block the relationship."[61] It is an interaction between people in which they aim to give themselves as they are and seek also to know the other as the other is. Therefore, it is authentic if three conditions are met: people feel they understand the position of others; they also feel that others understand their point of view; and, third, there is a readiness on the part of all to accept what is decided because it was reached openly and fairly. Scripture scholar Walter Brueggemann defines dialogue as follows:

> An honest facing of pluralism can be pastorally and usefully engaged only by an open-ended adjudication that takes the form of trustful, respectful conversation. Such a conversation is joined with no participant seeking to convert the other and no participant knowing the outcome ahead of time but only entering with full respect for the good faith of others and the willingness to entertain the troublesome thought that new "truth" received together may well be out in front of any of us.[62]

---

[61] Revel L. Howe, *The Miracle of Dialogue* (New York: Seabury Press, 1963), 37.

[62] Walter Brueggemann, *The Word Militant: Preaching a Decentering Word* (Minneapolis: Fortress Press, 2010), 22.

Guideline 3: Dialogue is not debate which assumes one already has the right answer; dialogue, however, is about seeking to discover common ground and it presupposes that "many people have pieces of the answer and that together they can craft a solution."[63]

Guideline 4: There are three qualities that distinguish dialogue from discussion:

- First, no matter what status people have they must participate as equals. If this equality does not exist, the all-important quality of trust cannot develop based on the mutual respect of participants.[64]
- Second, a profound capacity to listen with empathy is needed, flowing from respect and a sincerity "to think someone else's thoughts and feel someone else's feelings."[65] Listening demands that we not only hear what is said, "but also embrace, accept, and gradually let go of our own inner clamoring."[66]
- Third, dialogue requires that all participants are willing and able to bring to the surface their own assumptions for critical evaluation. The most noticeable difference, counsels Daniel Yankelovich, "between discussion and dialogue is this process of bringing assumptions into the open while simultaneously suspending judgment."[67]

Guideline 5: Because the aim in dialogue is to achieve an I–Thou relationship among participants, the process should take place in small groups, to be led by skilled cross-cultural facilitators. Dialogue is impossible in large groups.

Guideline 6: In religious dialogue it is advisable to begin every reflection with faith sharing—for example, sharing based on a parable from the Gospels. It is also advisable for members of opposing religious cultural groups to plan a small common gospel-inspired

---

[63] Daniel Yankelovich, *The Magic of Dialogue: Transforming Conflict into Cooperation* (New York: Simon and Schuster, 2001), 39.

[64] Ibid., 40–43.

[65] Ibid., 43.

[66] William Isaacs, *Dialogue: And the Art of Thinking Together* (New York: Currency, 1999), 83.

[67] Yankelovich, *The Magic of Dialogue*, 45.

action, such as working together once a week in a soup kitchen for homeless people.

Theological Reflection:
Dialogue at Jacob's Well (John 4:1–42)

Pope Francis tells us:

> We must . . . enter into a dialogue like that of our Lord and the Samaritan woman at the well where she sought to quench her thirst. . . . The Samaritan woman became a missionary immediately after speaking with Jesus and many Samaritans come to believe in him "because of the woman's testimony." (*Evangelii Gaudium*, nos. 72, 120)

The description of Jesus speaking to the Samaritan woman at a well is a particularly rich example of a cross-cultural religious dialogue.[68] All three qualities for an effective dialogue are present: equality, empathy, and the willingness to acknowledge difficult religious and cultural assumptions. The story reveals two clashing mythologies supporting two opposed cultures (John 4:1–42). The scene shows how the building of trust allows dialogue to become the catalyst for the transformation not just of the woman but also for Jesus, as they represent two antagonistic religious cultures. Simple and ordinary circumstances of daily life such as eating, walking, and even a request for a drink of water often become social dramas of special importance for Jesus in his ministry of evangelization. They become transformed into moments of revelation and grace. This is what happens in the event at the well.[69]

Dialogue Begins

The dialogue begins with a simple and respectful appeal to a stranger for water. Jesus is journeying through a part of Samaria with his disciples. Weary from his ministry, he pauses to rest beside a famous

---

[68] See Arbuckle, *Fundamentalism at Home and Abroad*, 173–75.
[69] See Arbuckle, *Culture, Inculturation, and Theologians,* 159.

Samaritan pilgrimage site, Jacob's Well (John 4:4–6). While the disciples are away buying food, a Samaritan woman of doubtful morality appears, and she and Jesus, now alone, meet, with Jesus taking the initiative in asking for a drink of water. This surprises the woman for two reasons: It is a dishonorable thing for Jews to greet women in public, and "Jews do not share things in common with Samaritans" (John 4:9). Jews look on Samaritans as stupid, heretical, and possessed by the devil (John 8:48). As Father John McKenzie, SJ, points out, there is "no deeper break of human relations in the contemporary world than the feud of Jews and Samaritans, and the breadth and depth of Jesus' doctrine of love could demand no greater act of a Jew than to accept a Samaritan"[70] as a brother or sister. Yet Jesus does this. By speaking respectfully to the woman, Jesus discards Jewish cultural, ritual, and religious prejudices. He speaks as an equal, and the woman, now not afraid to bring to the surface deep religious and cultural differences, responds: "How is that you, a Jew, ask a drink of me, a woman of Samaria?" (John 4:9). Samaritan women had the additional stigma of being regarded as menstruants from birth, that is, inherently unclean.[71] Not surprisingly, therefore, it would later be a deadly insult to Jesus to call him a Samaritan (John 8:48). The Samaritans had similarly degrading views of their Jewish neighbors. A Samaritan village would refuse him and his disciples hospitality on their way from Galilee to Jerusalem (Luke 9:52).

So, in this chance meeting between Jesus and a woman of such stigmatized cultural and personal origins, the questions are—how is Jesus to handle the situation? Will they end the process of dialogue that has just begun? Will Jesus continue to act respectfully even though this is contrary to the norms of Jewish culture?[72] Jesus fosters an atmosphere of empathy and trust between the woman and himself, which is a fundamental requirement of dialogue, by letting her know

---

[70] John L. McKenzie, *Dictionary of the Bible* (London: Geoffrey Chapman, 1965), 766.

[71] See Teresa Okure, "John," in *The International Bible Commentary,* ed. William R. Farmer (Collegeville, MN: Liturgical Press, 1998), 1468.

[72] See J. Martin C. Scott, "John," in *Eerdmans Commentary on the Bible,* ed. James D. Dunn and John W. Rogerson (Grand Rapids, MI: Eerdmans, 2003), 1171.

he is aware of her private life (vv. 16–19).[73] With confidence thus established, there are two key issues that Jesus wishes to explain to the woman—that knowledge of God is a gift likened to "living water" (v. 11), and the discovery of the true identity of Jesus himself (v. 14). Pleased with her trust in him, Jesus leads her to grasp these two realities through a conversational dialogue that is deeply respectful of her and of her ancestral and religious traditions. At the same time, he plainly points out that worship will not be confined to a definite place either in Jerusalem or on the sacred Samaritan mountain, but within Christ himself (vv. 20–26). It will be centered not on a special place or a particular group, but on a person.

The Disciples Fail the Test

At this point the woman is so transformed and energized by her conversion to Jesus, now recognized as the Christ, the Anointed One, that she leaves behind her water jug, a symbol of human thirst and affections that can never be satisfied without Jesus Christ, and hastens to share her faith with her kinsfolk (vv. 2–30, 39–42). There is a quite humorous touch to this incident because Jesus incongruously uses, as his messenger to these Samaritan people, a woman whose marital history is well known to them. However, there is a second drama that has yet to begin and it focuses on the disciples. When they return with food they react as Jewish men are culturally expected to behave. They are startled, even annoyed and ashamed, that Jesus is speaking to a woman and a Samaritan one at that (v. 27). This should not be! They urge him to eat, but he replies in a puzzling way by saying that his "food is to do the will of him who sent me and to complete his work" (v. 34). By contrast with the enthusiastic Samaritan woman who has gained so much through her dialogue with Jesus, the disciples ironically give the impression of being uninterested in the dramatic nature of his words and do not seem to want to learn from the incident. Still trapped in their Jewish prejudices, they are incapable of cross-cultural dialogue. They are not prepared to dialogue with Samaritans.

---

[73] Bishop Francisco Claver, SJ, has a short and helpful analysis of this incident from an inculturation perspective in *The Making of a Local Church* (Maryknoll, NY: Orbis Books, 2008), 116.

Abiding Lessons

The events at the well reveal two important themes of the evangelist John: his particular theological emphasis, and the missionary methods, including dialogue, that Jesus adopts. The latter involve beginning with the realities of everyday life and showing respect for people and their mythologies or traditions. Even when Jesus disagrees with those traditions, as in the case of the Samaritan belief in the place for true worship (John 4:20–24), he does so in a culturally respectful manner. At the same time evangelization calls us to struggle against the entrenched obstacles of theology, culture, race, sex, and class that exclude and degrade people.[74]

Summary

- For Catholics, two worldwide cultural revolutions coincided and collided at the same time: Vatican II, and the expressive revolution of the 1960s. The disruption of the entire mythic structure of the church and exposure to the cultural disorder of the expressive revolution and its aftermath only intensified the chaos. Polarizing tribal tensions have emerged out of the cultural vacuum creating increasing distrust and loneliness among members.
- Two major opposing tribal groups now exist: those seeking to restore the church to its previous pre–Vatican II power structures and those committed to the council's values.
- Pope Francis has said a definite no to deadening fundamentalist restorationism with its insistence on coercive rules and an unambiguous yes to being involved in the hopes and frustrations of people and their cultures.
- Intertribal, faith-based dialogue is essential.[75] Dialogue is an interaction between people in which they aim to give themselves as they are and seek also to know the other as the other is. It is authentic if three conditions are met: people feel they understand the position of others; they feel that others understand

---

[74] See Okure, "John," 1469.

[75] Pope Francis used the word *dialogue* twenty-five times in *Laudato Si'* and fifty-four times in *Evangelii Gaudium*.

their point of view; and there is a readiness on the part of all to accept what is decided because it was reached openly and fairly.

Reflection Questions

• Dialogue cannot occur unless we are prepared to listen to people. Also, two qualities of listening and hearing must be emphasized: hospitality and healing. The supreme exemplar of these qualities of hospitality and healing is Christ. From your experience, what do you feel about the following statements?

> True *hospitality* offers people the space to feel free to unburden themselves. "Hospitality," writes Henri Nouwen, "is not a subtle invitation to adopt the lifestyle of the host, but the gift of a chance for the guest to find his own."[76]

> Listening is also *healing* that is intimately connected to hospitality: "Healing means, first of all, the creation of an empty but friendly space where those who suffer can tell their story to someone who can listen with real attention."[77] True listening assumes a deep respect and concern for people. It means an unwillingness to offer solutions until the issues worrying people are fully listened to and heard.

• Can you think of a situation in your life when someone has confided something of his or her pain to you, and on reflection, you felt, in some strange way, nourished and uplifted by the experience?

---

[76] Henri J. M. Nouwen, *Reaching Out: The Three Movements of the Spiritual Life* (London: Collins, 1976), 69.

[77] Ibid., 88.

7

Authors in the Church: Triggers of Loneliness

I call on theologians to carry out this service [of evangelization] as part of the Church's saving mission. In doing so, however, they must always remember that the Church and theology exist to evangelize, and not be content with a desk-bound theology.
—*EVANGELII GAUDIUM*, NO. 133

I want to know Christ and the power of his resurrection and the sharing of his sufferings. . . . Not that I have already obtained this or have already reached the goal; but I press on to make it my own, because Christ Jesus has made me his own.
—PHILIPPIANS 3:10, 12

This chapter explains:

- Responsible dissent has often been a distressing experience.

- Social science research before Vatican II was commonly considered to be irrelevant.
- Social science research in the service of the gospel is now more acceptable.
- Jeremiah and St. Paul provide authors with consoling guides.

Though it is often an exceedingly enjoyable experience, an author's life in the service of the people of God can also be painfully lonely. Social scientists, for example, can spend weeks, months, even years, researching alone, not knowing whether or not their material will be taken seriously by those for whom it has been written. It can also happen that authors may never meet or connect with their readers. In addition, they may have to face severe criticism for what has been written, thus possibly adding to an author's sense of exclusion and loneliness. Interest groups can feel threatened whenever researchers highlight the gaps between rhetoric and reality. This chapter is devoted to the loneliness inherent in an author's vocation, particularly that of a social scientist, by which I refer primarily to sociology and cultural anthropology, whose task is to critique the church's culture from the perspective of their various disciplines.

Father Joseph Fichter (1908–94), renowned pioneer sociologist in United States, reflecting in 1973 on how some of his research projects had been received, noted that "the news media often appeared to be vicious, derogatory, and contemptuous"[1] when commenting on his publications. He continues: "I have had relatively little feedback from [my sociological studies], except sometimes to hear that they did 'more harm than good' by arousing suspicion, fear, and antagonism. In some cases . . . sending out the research report was like throwing it off a cliff on a dark night. It just seemed to disappear."[2] I have experienced similar, but less dramatic, reactions to the findings of some of my own sociological surveys.

What are some of the particular triggers of such an author's loneliness in serving the church? A faith-inspired author will call the people of God to identify and bridge the gaps between the gospel and the

---

[1] Joseph Fichter, *One-Man Research: Reminiscences of a Catholic Sociologist* (New York: John Wiley, 1973), 5.
[2] Ibid., 16.

world around them, including the church. It may mean the writer is to become a responsible dissenter[3] within the church. *Dissent* is a confusing and at times a highly emotive word, but here it simply means "the proposing of alternatives." As moral theologian Richard McCormick, SJ, notes, theoretically it should not be a threat "but an invigorating contribution to continued life and growth. To silence dissent is to exclude a possible source of correction and improvement."[4] In reality, however, responsible dissent in the church is commonly seen as a menace to people wedded to the status quo. The author then suffers the rejection and loneliness of many a prophet.

This chapter ends with a reflection on the loneliness that scriptural writers—Jeremiah and St. Paul—experienced, and how they maintained hope in the midst of the darkest moments in their lives.

Dissenting Authors: Experiences

There have been many writers over the centuries who have rightly critiqued the views and behavior of ecclesiastical representatives. Very frequently they have been ignored, silenced, or even excommunicated. Such actions by officials have been triggers for often incredibly long and painful periods of loneliness. Blessed John Henry Newman (1801–90) from the early days of his conversion to Catholicism began to feel the sorrows of loneliness as he viewed aspects of the church that failed to measure up to authentic gospel values. In 1843, two years after his conversion to Catholicism, he wrote: "You must bear in mind that, if I speak strongly in various places . . . against the existing state of things [in the church], it is not wantonly, but to show I feel the difficulties which certain minds are distressed with."[5] The

---

[3] For a fuller explanation of the meaning of "responsible dissent," see Gerald A. Arbuckle, *Refounding the Church: Dissent for Leadership* (Maryknoll, NY: Orbis Books, 1993), 1–10. The manner in which responsible dissent is done will be in accord with the gospel and with due respect for the divinely established structures of the church.

[4] Richard A. McCormick, SJ, "The Search for Truth in the Catholic Context," *America* (November 8, 1986), 276.

[5] John Henry Newman, letter to John Keble (September 6, 1843), cited in J. I. Gonzalez Faus, *Where the Spirit Breathes: Prophetic Dissent in the Church* (Maryknoll, NY: Orbis Books, 1989), 103.

feeling of loneliness is muted in this text, but in later years his sense of loneliness, even despondency, in regard to his new coreligionists is no longer muffled. In 1860 he wrote:

> I am nobody. I have no friend at Rome. I have labored in England, to be misrepresented, backbitten, and scorned. I have labored in Ireland, with the door ever shut in my face. . . . What I did well was not understood. I do not think I am saying this in any bitterness. . . . O my God, I seem to have wasted these years that I have been a Catholic.[6]

Three years later his loneliness is further intensified, triggered not directly by ecclesiastical officials but by fellow converts, an added source of great pain:

> O how forlorn & dreary has been my course since I have been a Catholic! . . . Persons who would naturally come to me, inquirers who would naturally consult me, are stopped by some light or unkind word said against me. . . . I shrink from a society which is so unjust towards me. I must say, that the converts have behaved to *me* much worse than old Catholics, when they might have had a little gratitude, to say the least.[7]

One can only imagine the loneliness experienced by later theologians such as George Tyrrell (1861–1909); Pierre Teilhard de Chardin, SJ (1881–1955); John Courtney Murray, SJ (1904–67); and Yves Congar, OP (1904–95). Under St. Pius X, Rome initiated a period of ecclesiastical McCarthyism against "modernists" who "were hunted down with a zeal that was as pathological as the paranoia that fed it."[8] Tyrrell daringly challenged the Roman, Jesuit, and English hierarchical authorities but was expelled from his Jesuit congregation and ultimately excommunicated. He was confronting the hegemonic abuse of power within the church.

---

[6] Newman, January 8, 1860, cited by Roland Hill, *Lord Acton* (New Haven, CT: Yale University Press, 2000), 118.

[7] Newman, January 21, 1863, cited in Hill, *Lord Acton*.

[8] Gabriel Daly, "Foreword," in George Tyrrell, *Medievalism* (Tunbridge Wells: Burns and Oates, 1994), 10.

In 1908, Tyrrell wrote the theological masterpiece *Medievalism* in defense of his position. One can still feel his personal loneliness in the text as he struggles to dialogue with people whom he once called his friends and colleagues. Today it is widely accepted that he anticipated many of the theological and structural reforms of Vatican II.[9] The brilliant paleontologist Pierre Teilhard de Chardin, SJ, sought to develop a synthesis of theology and science, yet for decades he was silenced by his Jesuit superiors at the behest of Rome. While secular experts applauded his work, Teilhard died before his major works were allowed to be published by ecclesiastical authorities. Particularly following Vatican II, Teilhard's writings have been applauded by theologians and popes, including Joseph Ratzinger, the future pope Benedict XVI.[10] Likewise, the major theological contributions of Murray and Congar to the post-council church have been widely acknowledged.

Every group, including the church, has the right to define its boundaries or what it considers to be its authentic symbols of identity and orthodoxy. But in setting boundaries two principles must be kept always in the forefront: that what is stated to be orthodox is in fact authentically orthodox and that the process of discerning what is or is not orthodox follows the religious and secular norms of truth, transparency, and objectivity. Anthropologists, however, point out that in times of cultural disintegration, when cultural boundaries are seriously threatened or break down, show trials[11] and scapegoating crazes[12] commonly occur. By passing the blame for their afflictions to others, people are able to distract themselves from the real causes of chaos and the efforts they must make to remove them.

Vatican II articulated a mythology of church that must guide the formulation of narratives of Catholic identities. However, there are two levels in the contemporary church at which the above two principles of setting boundaries have not always in practice been observed by people: at the grassroots level and at the hierarchical levels,

---

[9] See Anthony Maher, *The Forgotten Jesuit of Catholic Modernism* (Minneapolis: Fortress Press, 2017).

[10] See Joseph Cardinal Ratzinger, *The Spirit of the Liturgy* (San Francisco: Ignatian Press, 2000).

[11] See Arbuckle, *Refounding the Church,* 72.

[12] See Gerald A. Arbuckle, *Fundamentalism at Home and Abroad: Analysis and Pastoral Responses* (Collegeville, MN: Liturgical Press, 2017), 11–12.

especially in Rome.[13] The mythology they adopt, as the foundation of their narratives, is that of the pre-counciliar church. Both levels represent fearful groups in the church that seek to return to a bygone Catholic culture and witch hunt those who do not agree with them. The more that witch hunters at the grassroots level know that Rome favors restorationism, the more avidly they go about their work of scapegoating assumed unorthodox members of the church. They undertake their task in a variety of ways, such as direct communication to their bishops or to Rome itself.

At the church's hierarchical level, witch hunting is far more serious because it is deliberately planned and sanctioned from the top. Theologians have been particular targets of this witch hunting.[14] What James Provost, then professor of canon law at the Catholic University of America, wrote in 1989 is still very much true today: "The rejection of any type of 'dissent' from non-infallible positions has been severe, despite the exception made for many years in the case of Archbishop Lefebvre. There has been an on-going harassment of theologians . . . which often appears as an attempt to appease influential minorities." While acknowledging that issues of orthodoxy are a legitimate concern of papal authority, Provost commented that the way this authority is being used on occasions "has the appearance of a defensive effort

---

[13] The author has himself received two reprimands from Rome, one direct and the other indirect. In the late 1990s a dicastery contacted my superior general: "We are tired of receiving complaints about Father Arbuckle's writings on refounding. Please act!" The names of the complainers were not given. My superior general replied: "He writes as an anthropologist. Please indicate where he is offending!" They did not reply. My book *Refounding the Church: Dissent for Leadership* was translated into Spanish and published in 2000, *Refundar la Iglesia: Disidencia y liderazgo* (Santander: Sal Terrae). Major superiors conferences throughout South America then used the book as the foundation for a year's reflections on the church and religious life. Again Rome objected: "The Church has been founded. It does not need refounding!"

[14] See Daniel S. Thompson, *The Language of Dissent: Edward Schillebeeckx on the Crisis of Authority in the Catholic Church* (Notre Dame, IN: University of Notre Dame Press, 2003), 1–9; Bradford E. Hinze, "A Decade of Disciplining Theologians," in *When the Magisterium Intervenes: The Magisterium and Theologians in Today's Church*, ed. Richard R. Gaillardetz (Collegeville, MN: Liturgical Press, 2012), 3–39.

to exercise centralized control—defensive against the 'evil' world in contrast to the Second Vatican Council's views . . . defensive of a very limited school of theology."[15]

The victims of the theologians' "witchcraft" are thought by Rome to be the church itself and the integrity of papal authority. As in all orthodoxy crazes, respect for truth and human rights can suffer, as the following description of the judicial process established by the Congregation for the Doctrine of the Faith (CDF) indicates. The CDF remains substantially unchanged since it was inaugurated in 1971.[16] It is prosecutor, judge, and jury; persons being investigated are not told of the inquiry until stage thirteen (of eighteen stages) and may never know the identity of their accusers; defendants are unable to choose their defender or even know the latter's identity, nor is there access to material relating to the allegations against the accused; no publicity is permitted concerning the proceedings; and there is no right of appeal.[17] Serious injustices can occur. There is constant recourse to secrecy by the CDF in the judicial process. Secrecy is a powerful instrument of control in narratives of witch hunting, and it is particularly characteristic of cultures that are strongly hierarchical. It is used by elites in order to hold their position of power through the possession of special knowledge, and by non-elites in order to defend themselves against the intruding power of the elite. Egalitarian cultures, however,

---

[15] James Provost, "The Papacy: Power, Authority, Leadership," in *The Papacy and the Church in the United States*, ed. Bernard Cooke (New York: Paulist Press, 1989), 205.

[16] In 1997 the Holy See promulgated new procedural rules called "Regulations for the Examination of Doctrines," which modified previous norms governing the investigation of theologians. However, they do not substantially change the previous rules. The theologian Elizabeth Johnson had not heard that the Committee on Doctrine of the United States Bishops Conference had investigated and severely criticized her book *Quest for the Living God* until the day before the publication of their document. She had never been invited to enter into a conversation with the committee. See Richard R. Gaillardetz, "The Elizabeth Johnson Dossier," in Gaillardetz, *When the Magisterium Intervenes*, 178.

[17] B. Quelquejeu, quoted in Richard A. McCormick and Richard P. McBrien, "L'Affaire Curran II," *America* 163/6 (1990): 128; see also Jacques Dupuis, "Theologian on the Ropes," *The Tablet* (August 12, 2017), 8–9.

stress values of openness and publicity.[18] It is not surprising, therefore, that the more Rome tries to restore the pre–Vatican II hierarchically vertical structures, the more it opts for greater secrecy. Pope Francis is trying hard to change this bureaucratic behavior of the Roman Curia.[19]

There are times when secrecy is essential, such as to protect the rightful welfare of a person or group, but it must not be habitually used as a cloak for anything an organization does or wants to keep from the public gaze. And the habit of secrecy often leads to a very unpleasant quality—the justification of infringing laws and human rights "for the sake of the common good." Secrets give power of control over others, even more so when those who cultivate them are accountable to no public group; secrecy was used to intimidate victims of the Inquisition and this can still occur.

Serving the Church: Social Sciences

Theologians have not been the only targets of hierarchical disapproval. Prior to Vatican II "the hierarchs [in the church] looked on sociologists with suspicion and on their works with either scorn or fear." It was assumed that there "was nothing that social scientists could do for the church that could not be done better by bishops and their chancery officials, by canon lawyers, and even by moral theologians."[20] In 1948, Father Joseph Fichter, SJ, conducted a year-long sociological study of a southern American urban parish, and then his research was published in a report called "The Dynamics of

---

[18] See Don N. Levine, *The Flight from Ambiguity: Essays in Social and Cultural Theory* (Chicago: University of Chicago Press, 1985), 33; Gerald A. Arbuckle, *Confronting the Demon: A Gospel Response to Adult Bullying* (Collegeville, MN: Liturgical Press, 2003), 65–94.

[19] See Arbuckle, *Refounding the Church,* 74–75; see also Gerald A. Arbuckle, *The Francis Factor and the People of God: New Life for the Church* (Maryknoll, NY: Orbis Books, 2015), 183–92.

[20] Fichter, *One-Man Research*, 7. It did not help that most leading sociologists and anthropologists at this time considered the Christian faith, like all religious belief, to be erroneous and untenable. See Timothy Larsen, *The Slain God: Anthropologists and the Christian Faith* (Oxford: Oxford University Press, 2014), 10.

a City Parish." It described the manner in which the parochial clergy performed their sacramental, liturgical, and instructional functions. Fichter described the reactions to the report: "The book caused an uproar in conservative Catholic circles. The remaining three volumes of the series were suppressed. It appears that the American Catholic Church was not quite ready for a realistic account of the role of the parish priest."[21]

Later, in the documents of Vatican II the social sciences were acknowledged as essential aids in evangelization. It was felt that Christians must know the dramatically changing world they are to evangelize, and that common sense alone cannot grasp the complexity of culture or of change. So the social sciences must be used as instruments to assist evangelizers, both to understand the world and to discover how best to preach the gospel message.[22] Notably, papal support for the social sciences has continued since the council. Under Pope Paul VI ecclesial documents increasingly use insights from the social sciences. For example, he frequently uses the term *culture* in its cultural anthropological sense (see Chapter 2). This is particularly evident in his inspirational apostolic letter on evangelization *(Evangelii Nuntiandi)*. Written in 1975, when cultural anthropology is beginning its revolutionary reinterpretation of culture, the document reflects something of this radical rethinking. First, it no longer speaks of culture in the abstract sense but several times refers to "culture or cultures" (no. 20). Second, it refers to the need to use a people's "language, their signs and symbols" (no. 63). There is also the hint that cultures must not be considered as homogeneous or static because evangelization will be ineffective "if it does not answer the questions [the people] ask, and if it does not have an impact on their concrete life" (no. 63).

Similarly, from the beginning of St. John Paul II's pontificate he forthrightly focused on the fundamental importance of understanding

---

[21] Joseph Fichter, "Preface," in *Priests in Council: Initiatives Toward a Democratic Church*, ed. Francis F. Brown (Kansas City: Andrews and McMeel, 1979), xix.

[22] "In pastoral care, sufficient use must be made not only of theological principles, but also of the findings of the secular sciences, especially of psychology and sociology, so that the faithful may be brought to a more adequate and mature life of faith" (*Gaudium et Spes*, no. 62).

and interacting with cultures as the prerequisite for effective evangelization, though his use of the term *culture* often lacks the anthropological clarity of his predecessor.[23] Pope Francis has very openly supported the need for the social sciences as a service to evangelization
(*Evangelii Gaudium,* no. 133). For example, he uses the term *culture*
at least sixty times in *Evangelii Gaudium* in its cultural anthropological meaning.

The dramatic change in official theological thinking about the
evangelical potential of the social sciences, initiated by Vatican II,
at first brought joy to many professional social scientists. At the
beginning of Vatican II theologian Edward Schillebeeckx wrote en-
thusiastically that

> one might say that the integration of sociology into Catholic
> thought is today a fact, even though in some Catholic circles,
> not all reserve and suspicion have been overcome due to a
> misunderstanding of the real nature of sociological thinking.
> . . . The eager eyes of the church now look to this new science,
> because she is fully aware that every partial truth contributes to
> the total truth and therefore become important for the religious
> view and way of life.[24]

He was far too optimistic. Father Patrick J. O'Malley, the first
president of the newly formed National Federation of Priests' Councils, USA, complained in 1969 that "even in the most progressive
dioceses [social science] research has been limited and rarely followed
when accomplished." He commented that in some large dioceses "new
parishes were being planned on the basis of the telephone company's
projection of how many telephones will be needed" in newer areas.
He continued:

> This would be fine. But if parishes are to be the living pres-
> ence of Christ in the community such haphazard "planning" is
> nothing less than criminal. . . . The Church seems to follow the

---

[23] See Gerald A. Arbuckle, *Culture, Inculturation, and Theologians: A
Postmodern Critique* (Collegeville, MN: Liturgical Press, 2010), 142–46.

[24] Edward Schillebeeckx, cited in *Social Compass* 10/3 (1963): 257, 259.

ancient adage of "applying grease when the wheel squeaks" instead of attempting to identify needs in advance, to experiment with solutions and to implement workable programs.[25]

Fichter later commented: "The great awakening to the need for sociological research occurred among the American bishops" only when in 1971 they "finally accepted the obvious fact that seminaries were emptying and priests were departing."[26]

The social sciences are still accorded a very low priority by the church—in parish, diocesan, and congregational planning—and among theologians and liturgists. Theologians and liturgists continue to express with remarkable self-confidence views about how cultures are to be evangelized. Rarely do they seek, for example, the advice of anthropologists, whose specialized field of study is culture. Yet culture is most certainly a perplexing phenomenon—ubiquitous in presence, complex in detail, overwhelming and incomprehensible in its totality and intricacy. Any effort to grasp it through simplistic analysis is therefore doomed to failure. Throughout the world there are very few adequately trained cultural anthropologists or sociologists whose full-time task is to provide pastoral research material for local churches or religious congregations. This illustrates the overall continuing lack of interest in, and sometimes even hostility toward, what their disciplines offer to evangelizers today.

Case Study: Becoming a Nonperson

A lengthy study had been jointly commissioned by several dioceses into the pastoral needs of a number of minority groups. *Inter alia* it was discovered that these minorities were underrepresented in Catholic high schools and that the level of prejudice was significantly high among Catholic teachers. The report, in addition to being presented to relevant bishops and positively received, was tabled [that is, presented] by the researcher at a provincial chapter of a religious congregation, as the latter

---

[25] Patrick O'Malley, quoted in Francis F. Brown, "Introduction," in Brown, *Priests in Council,* xxi.

[26] Fichter, *One-Man Research,* 7. The bishops provided financial support for a study of seminarians.

maintained several of the schools surveyed. After the report was formally presented, a chapter member rose and severely attacked the report's findings without offering any proof for his allegations. "This is a most unscientific report . . . " and so on. Silence descended on the room and no one—not even the chapter's president who had asked for the report to be tabled [presented]—rose either to defend the report or to question the validity of the condemnatory comments. The chapter then passed to other business as though the report had never been tabled [presented].[27]

The researcher had become a nonperson. Commenting later on the incident, the researcher said: "It was a shattering experience. I left the room without even a word of thanks, ignored by chapter members."

This case study has several interesting features. The report showed clearly that the country in which the dioceses were located was about to experience a violent breakdown in race relations. This, and the evidence of prejudice among the teachers within the congregational schools, evoked so much anxiety that the chapter instinctively wanted to deny the facts. The person who attacked the report—that is, the "group-minder" or the informally appointed censor of troublesome incoming information—articulated the deep anxieties within the chapter's culture and conveniently found a scapegoat in the author and his report. Having disposed of the anxiety-evoking report, the chapter was able to get down to much less threatening issues that it could easily control. The chapter president did nothing to call the group-minder to order. They colluded with the denial in the chapter culture. Within five years the racial violence predicted by the report occurred, but it took a further eight years before another chapter admitted that the congregation must acknowledge the country's racial tensions. By then, this congregation had missed the chance to make a major contribution pastorally and educationally to racial harmony.[28]

[27] Arbuckle, *Refounding the Church,* 188–89.
[28] Ibid., 188.

Marginalizing Social Scientists: Some Reasons

Denial of Crises

The task of social scientists is to portray reality as it is, not as people would like it to be. Some aspects of reality—such as the ongoing, dramatic decline in vocations to the priesthood and religious life and the drop in the conversion rate—are very disturbing to church administrators and others. The very human reaction is to deny or avoid anxiety-provoking situations. The status quo, however dysfunctional it might be, is more comforting than the disorder that the presentation of reality evokes. Hence, some initial denial can normally be expected. The real problem occurs when this denial becomes chronic. Chronic denial leads to the "delusion that nothing has changed, causing a rejection of all information that might conflict with this assessment."[29] I have had incidents when religious and ecclesiastical clients have fallen into chronic denial when presented with uncomfortable statistical evidence. Never a pleasant experience for a researcher to observe!

Of course, denial can affect not just superiors but also whole groups of people—for example, religious congregations and dioceses. The tacit agreement of members in any group not to notice or openly acknowledge some troubling truth has been termed *group think.* It can plague organizations both large and small. For example, thoroughly prepared surveys can clearly indicate that a particular religious province is dying, yet its superiors and members refuse to accept the truth. They continue their work as though nothing is wrong. We call this denial *functional blindness*: the religious look at the statistics of rapid decline but see only growth.

At times people may attempt to cope with chaos by withdrawal into an unreal spiritual world. Or they may dream nostalgically of a return to a bygone age of power and glory. Both forms of denial are evident in the church today. We are surely experiencing a dark period of uncertainty about how to evangelize a postmodern world that is less and less interested in what the church has to teach. We evangelizers

---

[29] Manfred F. R. Kets de Vries and Danny Miller, *The Neurotic Organization* (San Francisco: Jossey-Bass, 1984), 142.

feel disoriented, directionless. Some of us turn to a spirituality that comfortably shuts out the world. Others opt for a new form of fundamentalism: the attempt to restore without change the symbols and rituals of a pre–Vatican II church (see Chapter 6). Both types of evangelizers see social scientists as dangerous compromisers with the world. "All we need," they proclaim, "is more faith, more prayer, and the Lord will see us through."

False Expectations

Normally, the task of the social scientist is to describe reality; it is then the task of administrators to make decisions for action on the basis of the information. When only information is provided, not action-oriented guidelines, administrators may condemn the analysis as a waste of time. Fichter wisely comments: "One of the persistent problems I encountered . . . was to clarify the difference between the person who does the research and the person who implements the findings. . . . [Research sponsors] wanted answers from the researcher without paying attention to the research data out of which they themselves would have to fashion the answers."[30]

Research Fatigue

In the years immediately following Vatican II, when there was a brief burst of interest in sociological surveys, people became weary, even cynical, at the prospect of filling out yet another questionnaire—especially when administrators did not know what to do with the collated material.

Self-Marginalization

Social scientists themselves can neutralize the effectiveness of their research by their own lack of professionalism. For example, the social scientist can use so much jargon that communication is impossible or is made unnecessarily difficult. Clients, when swamped with reports of this nature, abandon efforts to understand the material.

---

[30] Fichter, *One-Man Research*, 17.

Personal Experiences

Over several decades I have been involved in researching and writing pastoral survey reports for bishops, major superiors of congregations, and heads of particular ministries in the church. I have found that clients who fear "uncomfortable" information provided by social researchers may seek to keep the offending researchers at a safe distance or to neutralize the information in various ways. The following are several negative examples of reactions to survey reports. Each statement became a potential trigger for excluding or rejecting my expertise or that of other researchers.

- *Straight rejection:* "Your report has been received, but it has been decided that the time is not right to act on its conclusions." No reasons given.
- *The bottom-drawer method:* "We are most grateful for your fine report, and we expect to act on it in due course." Nothing is done.
- *The pass-the-buck method:* "Thank you. We are submitting your report to a subcommittee for its comments." Nothing is done.
- *"Minoritis":* "There are some minor inaccuracies in your report that really have us worried. Kindly explain." The hope is to discredit the entire report on the basis of minor inaccuracies. The major conclusions are not questioned, but they are quietly ignored.

A Cardinal Accepts His Authority

After finishing a major study of cultural prejudice among white Catholics in New Zealand at the request of the episcopal conference, I was asked by reporters of two television stations to answer questions for prime-time national news. I hesitated, fearing that on such a delicate topic I would unwittingly harm the church by the information I would give. I expressed my fears to Cardinal Reginald Delargey, then head of the bishops' conference, but he replied: "Gerald, this is our report, not yours. We commissioned it and we accept the responsibility for its findings. Go out and share what you think should be said, we support you!"[31]

The person who researches for ecclesiastical or congregational groups usually works alone in order to keep costs down. I recall one of the first sociological surveys I conducted in a large religious congregational province. I spent one morning just browsing through two hundred questionnaire responses. There, on one table, rested the hopes and frustrations of the individual religious of an entire province. Suddenly I felt overwhelmed and emotionally drained by the loneliness of the task, the enormity of the problems confronting the province, and the weight of the responsibility that now rested on my shoulders to present an accurate report.

Theological Reflection: Jeremiah

Lamentation's Gift

As authors contemplating the chaos both outside and inside the church, we can be tempted to despair and to lose zeal for our ministry. We would do well to ponder and embrace the power of hope-based lamentation so splendidly expressed in the life of Jeremiah. God will call us to a new way of writing and preaching the good news, if in admitting loss we are prepared to cry *to* and *with* him:

> O hope of Israel, its savior in time of trouble,
> why should you be like a stranger in the land,
> like a traveler turning aside for the night? . . .
> we are called by your name; do not forsake us!
>   (Jer 14:8, 9)

One can still feel the agony of Jeremiah as he pleads with God from the depths of his inner emptiness, when he becomes increasingly aware of his own sense of inadequacy and the enormity of the personal suffering his work will involve:

---

[31] Arbuckle, *Refounding the Church*, 116.

Cursed be the day on which I was born! . . .
Why ever did I come forth from the womb to see
    toil and sorrow,
and see my days in shame! . . .
But the Lord is with me like a dread warrior . . .
for to you I have committed my cause. (Jer 20:14,
    18, 11, 12)

This frightening cry of feeling utterly abandoned, similar to the cry from the cross centuries later, is not a curse on God or the refusal by Jeremiah of his vocation of mentoring, but a prayerful confirmation of his trust in God; he sees the depths of his own misery and need. In a spirit of total openness he offers himself to God, who alone can make up for his own weaknesses: "for to you I have committed my cause" (Jer 20:12).

Courageous

Jeremiah, as prophet and author, stands out in the Old Testament as a lonely, tragic person, but he has the skill of personally remaining strong and at the same time confronting the Israelites with their unruly ways. They must return to their covenant obligations or face the death of their culture and nation. For example, in one of the prophet's own personal laments or "confessions" (Jer 15:10–21), he gives vent to his anguish, describing the abuse he suffers because of his role as a prophet, condemning his enemies, and calling for his own vindication. He declares: "Woe is me, my mother, that you ever bore me, a man of strife and contention to the whole land! I have not lent, nor have I borrowed, yet all of them curse me" (Jer 15:10). He is depressed. He aggressively reprimands God for having deceived and deserted him in times of personal abuse at the hands of the mobs, for he has been flung into prison, beaten, shackled, and even lowered down a well: "Why is my pain unceasing, my wound incurable, refusing to the healed? Truly, you are to me like a deceitful brook, like waters that fail" (Jer 15:18).

When he then expresses sorrow for his failure as a prophet of God and also for his lack of gratitude, God immediately accepts his repentance—in fact, even before it is requested. Then Jeremiah's loneliness is sustained by his renewed hope in God, once more feeling the energizing or revitalizing embrace of God in his prophetic task: "Therefore, thus says the Lord: If you turn back, I will take you back, and you shall stand before me" (Jer 15:19). Jeremiah responds: "But the Lord is with me like a dread warrior; therefore my persecutors will stumble, and they will not prevail" (Jer 20:11). Jeremiah was "a naturally timid man, in no way suited by experience or by inclination to cope with the stony-hearted, unprincipled, timeserving advocates of the higher perversity with whom his prophetic office must inevitably involve him."[32] The tender-minded young man becomes strong and courageous; the sensitive, hesitant prophet becomes an "iron pillar, and a bronze wall against the whole land" (Jer 1:18). This is the newness, the transformation from despair to hope-filled loneliness.[33]

Divine Pathos

Abraham Heschel movingly speaks of the "divine pathos," the capacity of God himself to suffer because he has entered through the covenant into a personal relationship with the Israelites. As they suffer, so he suffers.[34] Through the love-inspired covenant God risks being hurt if his Israelite partners do not live up to their side of the agreement. And this is precisely what happens. God is forced to allow their destruction because the people are so sinfully stubborn. Yet, because of God's intimate union with them, God is also attacking himself: "Thus says the Lord: I am going to break down what I have built, and pluck up what I have planted, that is, the whole land" (Jer 45:4). God is thrown into a state of mourning for the loss of covenant friends and even of himself:[35]

---

[32] Bruce Vawter, *The Conscience of Israel Pre-Exilic Prophets and Prophecy* (London: Sheed and Ward, 1991), 241.

[33] See John Bright, "A Prophet's Lament and Its Answer: Jeremiah 15:10–21," in *A Prophet to the Nations: Essays in Jeremiah Studies*, ed. Leo G. Perdue and Brian W. Kovacs (Winona Lake, IN: Eisenbrauns, 1984), 325–47; Gerhard Von Rad, *The Message of the Prophets* (London: SCM Press, 1969), 24.

[34] Abraham Heschel, *The Prophets: An Introduction* (New York: Harper & Row, 1969), 24.

[35] Ibid., 111.

> Thus says the Lord of hosts: Consider, and call the
> mourning women to come: . . .
> let them quickly raise the dirge over us, so that our
> eyes may run down with tears. (Jer 9:17–18)

Yes, just when all seems to be totally lost, God in grief becomes the savior of himself and of the same people condemned to devastation. God's original words to Jeremiah are to be fulfilled: "See, today I appoint you over nations and over kingdoms, to pluck up and pull down, to destroy and to overthrow, to build and to plant" (Jer 1:10). Though God's heart is torn apart with the sorrow of mourning, God reiterates a willingness to build the nation anew, and the mocking of the Israelites by other nations cannot be tolerated for their weaknesses and destruction: "For I will restore health to you, and your wounds I will heal, says the Lord, because they called you an outcast: 'It is Zion; no one cares for her!'" (Jer 30:17). God is depicted as one who is so moved by the intensity of his anguish over the loss of his chosen people, that he can no longer hold back his re-creative power.

Relevance of Jeremiah

In this modern age, the task of confronting people and governments with their exclusion of millions of people into loneliness, as described in this book, is a most unpopular apostolate, just as it was in the days of Jeremiah. So we readily identify with Jeremiah as he cringes in fear at the very thought of such a burdensome challenge. Like him, we want to run away, to be spared the sniggers of those who think the prophetic role of challenging our contemporary nationalistic hegemonic forces is worthless, too bothersome, a relic of a bygone age. In the depths of our hearts we yearn for that Jeremiah-like openness with God, his repentance, his ongoing struggle to die to his own false attachments in order to proclaim joyfully: "For he has delivered the life of the needy from the hands of evildoers" (Jer 20:13).

Reflect on the way in which God and Jeremiah mourn together in the privacy of their solitude over the destruction of Israel. Jeremiah's duty is to call his people to a profound conversion of heart and action. The Babylonians are God's judgment on a highly unfaithful people. Because there is not the faintest move on the people's part of repentance, God, speaking through Jeremiah, insists their culture is doomed. This saddens Jeremiah to the depths of his heart: "For the hurt of my poor people I am hurt, I mourn, and dismay has taken hold of me. . . . Take up weeping and wailing for the mountains, and a lamentation for the pastures of the wilderness" (Jer 8:21; 9:10). Yet the people continue to deny they are committing evil. For the Israelites, vice is seen as virtue:

> From the least to the greatest of them
> everyone is greedy for unjust gain, and from
>   prophet to priest,
> everyone deals falsely.
> They have treated the wound of my people care-
>   lessly,
> saying "Peace, peace," when there is no peace. (Jer
>   6:13–14)

Jeremiah sees the coming doom as a consequence of the people's loss of friendship with God. This causes him painful anticipated grief, which he expresses in the graphic lament style that is so characteristic of Jeremiah: "My anguish, my anguish! I writhe in pain!. . . . My heart is beating wildly; I cannot keep silent. . . . I looked to the earth, and lo, it was waste and void" (Jer 4:19, 23). The reducing of Israel to chaos is inevitable because their "guilt is great. . . . There is no one to uphold your cause, no medicine for your wound" (Jer 30:15,13). We may, like Jeremiah, writhe in sorrow as we contemplate today's pandemic loneliness of millions of people and the injustices that cause it. But, as authors who are relying on the power of God, we in our loneliness will not be seduced into silence.

Theological Reflection:
St. Paul

At my first defense no one came to my support, but all deserted me. . . . But the Lord stood by me and gave me strength, so that through me the message might be fully proclaimed. (2 Tim 4:16–17)

Another patron for every writer committed to serve the people of God is St. Paul. Paul experiences loneliness, but in the above scriptural quotation we see him connecting with Christ in hope. For it is hope that sustains him in his loneliness: "If God is for us, who is against us?" (Rom 8:31). In another letter full of brilliant rhetoric and personal revelation, he demonstrates, both in what he says and how he says it, that the cross and resurrection of Jesus the Messiah really are the center and driving force of the life of the renewed humanity (2 Cor 6:4–10). The death and resurrection of Jesus the Messiah are not for Paul merely events in the past. They are the foundation of his, and the church's, daily existence.

Paul Criticized

The Corinthians question his legitimacy to preach Christ, an attack that deeply hurts Paul. In 2 Corinthians Paul faces severe criticism of his ministry and must reply to his accusers. Already in his first letter to this faith community there is a veiled indication that he is being censured: "But with me it is a very small thing that I should be judged by you or by any human court. I do not even judge myself. . . . It is the Lord who judges me" (1 Cor 4:3). On a visit to Corinth he is openly insulted by a Corinthian Christian and his attempts to resolve feelings against him fail. He is humiliated and disgraced by those who have attacked him (2 Cor 2:5–8; 7:12). He is thrown into loneliness.[36]

His grief-stricken letter devastatingly lists the assaults of his adversaries on his suitability for ministry, "on his honesty, steadfastness, sincerity, rhetorical sufficiency, and weak 'womanish' bodily presence."[37] He is attacked for dithering and acting capriciously (2 Cor 1:7; 10:1), being boorish and using offensive language (10:10; 11:6), and being manipulative (12:16). Genuine holiness is to be understood in light of dying and rising with Christ. In his letter in 2 Corinthians one can feel the loneliness and sorrow as he struggles

---

[36] See Ben Witherington, *Conflict and Community in Corinth: A Socio-Rhetorical Commentary on 1 and 2 Corinthians* (Grand Rapids, MI: Eerdmans, 1995), 360–410.

[37] Calvin J. Roetzel, *The Letters of Paul: Conversations in Context* (Louisville, KY: Westminster John Knox Press, 1974), 117.

with a community that has not understood this: "They don't want a suffering jailbird of a leader; they want someone with power and prestige, someone they can look up to."[38]

Paul Responds

Paul replies to these vicious insults with compelling language in defense of his right to preach about Jesus Christ. His most powerful self-defense, however, occurs after he has been mocked for his bodily weakness (2 Cor 10:10). Paul takes the word *weakness* used by his critics and uses it to defend himself. It is Christ who converts, not the bombastic eloquence of Paul (1 Cor 3:5, 18). When reflecting on the experience of his own hesitant journey of initiation away from a formalistic Judaism, he emphasizes the creative potential of acknowledging his inner chaos: "So, I will boast all the more gladly of my weaknesses, so that the power of Christ may dwell in me. . . . For whenever I am weak, then I am strong" (2 Cor 12:9–10). Christ is the new energizing force in his life. At another point he describes the rich potential of inner lostness as the springboard for accepting the creative newness of Christ's life, provided there is trust in the overwhelming power of God: "We are afflicted in every way, but not crushed; perplexed, but not driven to despair . . . always carrying in the body the death of Jesus, so that the life of Jesus may also be made visible in our bodies. . . . So death is at work in us, but life in you" (2 Cor 4:8, 10, 12).

As Pauline scholar Jerome Murphy-O'Connor observes, the sentiment just referenced

> is the summit of 2 Corinthians 1–9, and the most profound insight ever articulated as to the meaning of suffering and the nature of authentic ministry. . . . Paul's acceptance of his sufferings created a transparency, in which the authentic humanity of Jesus became visible. By grace in his comportment, Paul was to his generation what Jesus had been to his.[39]

---

[38] Tom Wright, *What St. Paul Really Said* (Oxford: Lion Hudson, 1997), 145.

[39] Jerome Murphy-O'Connor, *Paul: His Story* (Oxford: Oxford University Press, 2004), 184.

Paul's resilience in the face of loneliness-inducing adversity is an inspiring example for today's Christians to follow.

Relevance

Paul frequently refers to himself and other believers "as fools for the sake of Christ" (1 Cor 4:10). The message of Christ by worldly standards is incongruous: "For the message about the cross is foolishness to those who are perishing, but to us who are saved it is the power of God" (1 Cor 1:18). In a satirical way Paul says: "For Jews demand signs and the Greeks desire wisdom, but we proclaim Christ crucified, a stumbling block to Jews and foolishness to Gentiles" (1 Cor 1:22–23). From the perspective of worldly values Christ's message is nonsense. Christ bypasses those with power and embraces the weak; powerlessness is the model of true power and foolishness becomes the wisdom of God: "But God chose what is foolish in the world to shame the wise; God chose what is weak in the world to shame the strong; God chose what is low and despised in the world, and things that are not, to reduce to nothing things that are, so that no one might boast in the presence of God" (1 Cor 1:27–29). Paul asks the Corinthians to reflect on the paradox of his own life. They know well his weaknesses, yet the power of God shines through (2 Cor 12:10).[40]

We, following the example of Paul, enter into the regenerating mythology of Christ by acknowledging our unconditional dependence on him. There is then such oneness with him that we can say with Paul: "I have been crucified with Christ; and it is no longer I who live, but it is Christ who lives in me" (Gal 2:19–20). From our nothingness we become one in Christ, in his power, in his love. It takes the courage of faith, born of love, to confront in solitude our own inner darkness.

Summary

- There have been many writers through the centuries who have rightly critiqued the views and behavior of ecclesiastical representatives. Frequently they have been ignored, silenced, or even excommunicated. Respect for truth and human rights suffers.

---

[40] See Gerald A. Arbuckle, *Laughing with God: Humor, Culture, and Transformation* (Collegeville, MN: Liturgical Press, 2008), 88–90.

- In the documents of Vatican II, the social sciences are acknowledged as essential aids in evangelization. Because the research of social scientists often challenges the status quo in the church, they are in danger of being marginalized. However, when making their expertise available to the people of God, social scientists need to do so with respect, patience, and tolerance, gifts that are exemplified in the lives of prophets of old and in Jesus Christ.

Reflection Questions

- As writers and preachers, what are the implications for your ministry of the following statement by Pope Francis?

  More than by fear of going astray, my hope is that we are moved by the fear of remaining shut up within the structures which give us a false sense of security, within rules which make us harsh judges . . . while at our door people are starving. (*Evangelii Gaudium,* no. 49)

- Finally, Luke's Gospel states that "Jesus increased in wisdom and in years, and in divine and human favor" (Luke 2:52). How are these words true of the church and of each one of us?

Conclusion

Pastoral Responses

Exclusion ultimately has to do with what it means to be a part of society in which we live; those excluded are no longer society's underside or its fringes or its disenfranchised—they are no longer even a part of it. The excluded are not the "exploited" but the outcast, the "leftovers." . . . Almost without being aware of it, we end up being incapable of feeling compassion at the outcry of the poor, weeping for other people's pain . . . as though all this were someone else's responsibility and not our own.
—*EVANGELII GAUDIUM,* NOS. 53, 54.

There are two qualities that mark loneliness: (1) people feel excluded and rejected; and (2) at the same time they yearn to be intimately accepted or included by others. They crave belonging. Yearning or thirsting for a relationship is frequently and poignantly expressed by the psalmist: "O God . . . I seek you; my soul thirsts for you . . . as in a dry and weary land where there is no water" (Ps 63:1). Yet, it is not only individuals who experience this loneliness. Cultures do as well. Entire cultures can feel politically, economically, or socially excluded and oppressed.

What causes exclusion? It is true that individuals may cause their own loneliness, but more commonly cultural forces are the catalysts for social and political exclusion, as this book describes. We see this, for example, in racism, ethnic discrimination, the resurgence of non-democratic forms of nationalism across the West, marginalization because of economic and/or political inequalities, socially defined disabilities, refugee/asylum status, individualism and greed, demagogic and abusive leaders, fundamentalist movements, and tribalism. These increasingly polarizing forces establish a sharp distinction between "members" and "strangers," those who belong and the rest.

How are we to respond to the many triggers of exclusion discussed in previous chapters? How are we to cope with our own loneliness and the devastating loneliness of those around us, locally and globally? The following responses may help readers to find pastoral solutions to these questions.

Loneliness and Solitude

Response 1: Foster hope.

Gospel people are people of hope (see Chapter 1). To be held captive by the chaos within oneself and all around us only leads to increased cynicism and frustration. It is the gift of hope that will keep the soul focused and striving to be open to the loving presence of God. Pope Francis writes:

> One of the more serious temptations which stifles boldness and zeal is a defeatism which turns us into querulous and disillusioned pessimists, "sourpusses." . . . While painfully aware of our own frailties, we have to march on without giving in, keeping in mind what the Lord said to Saint Paul: "My grace is sufficient for you, for my power is made perfect in weakness" (2 Cor 12:9). (*Evangelii Gaudium,* no. 85)

Response 2: Relish moments of solitude.

Both loneliness and solitude are about yearning to make connections, but there is an important difference. Solitude is a yearning to connect with one's inner self in order to know oneself; it prevents one from becoming emotionally and spiritually overwhelmed by the pressures and desires of others. To relish solitude one does not have to become a hermit or spend long periods alone. When I was a young boy I recall what my father said to me: "It is my job to make all the beds of the family daily. Then, despite the noise in other parts of the house, I can be alone and I can ponder in these moments the challenges I and the family face. What is God asking of us?" Solitude offers us space to listen to ourselves and to God as the scriptures so frequently remind us: "When you are disturbed . . . ponder it, and be silent" (Ps 4:4). In solitude we can "test and examine our ways and return to the Lord" (Lam 3:40).[1]

Jesus Christ sets the example. Before he decides who to call to be his immediate disciples, he seeks solitude and prayer: "Now . . . he went out to the mountain to pray; and he spent the night in prayer to God. And when day came, he called his disciples and chose twelve of them" (Luke 6:12–13). Then there is the time when he confronts his future in the Garden of Gethsemane. What is the Father asking of him? He feels marginalized by his companions, who are content to remain asleep, ignoring his inner pain. "Father, if you are willing, remove this cup from me; yet, not my will but yours be done" (Luke 22:42). In his solitude he moves from resistance and hesitation to embrace lovingly the will of the Father and finds new reservoirs of courage. To his disciples he says with restored confidence: "Why are you sleeping? Get up and pray that you may not come into the time of trial" (Luke 22:46).

Response 3: In solitude we can discover the heart of our Christian faith: love.

St. John of the Cross writes:

> How gently and lovingly
> You wake in my heart,
> Where in secret You dwell alone;
> And in your sweet breathing,
> ˒ Filled with good and glory,
> How tenderly You swell my heart with love![2]

---

[1] See Anne Long, *Listening* (London: Darton, Longman, Todd, 1990), 3.

[2] St. John of the Cross, *The Living Flame of Love* (Stanza 4), in Kieran Kavanaugh and Otilio Rodriguez, *The Collected Works of St. John of the Cross* (Washington, DC: ICS Publications, 1979), 643.

Solitude offers within ourselves space for God's presence gently and lovingly to reveal itself. The soul discovers not just that God loves us intimately, but that God offers this love to all people if they are open to receiving it. This dynamic is evident in so many encounters that Jesus has with people. Consider the healing of Bartimaeus, the blind beggar (Mark 10:46). The episode uncovers the multidimensional nature of poverty (see Chapter 4). It also describes how Bartimaeus opens his heart to receive God's love, while the spectators to the event hesitate to do so.

Let us revisit the scene: Bartimaeus is "sitting at the side of the road" (Mark 10:46). In this one statement we have described for us two types of poverty: material and social deprivation. As a beggar Bartimaeus is caught in the poverty trap. Further, he is stigmatized and excluded by society as he ritually endangers the clean. For his family and former friends he no longer exists. He is assumed to have sinned and God is punishing him for this. The words "sitting at the side of the road" symbolically describe this social exclusion and stigmatization. The only identity he possesses is that of a beggar, which is a very precarious one indeed.

Jesus is passing by and Bartimaeus cries out for healing. The members of the crowd at first do their best to silence him: "Many sternly ordered him to be quiet, but he cried out even more loudly" (Mark 10:48). People who are poor, especially those who are ritually unclean, must remain silent, accepting their fate. Jesus calls Bartimaeus to his side and gently asks him what he desires: "My teacher, let me see again!" (Mark 10:51). Opening his heart to God's love, Bartimaeus immediately responds to this gift. He "sprang up and came to Jesus" (Mark 10:50). In contrast, the crowd at first remains blinded by its prejudice against people like Bartimaeus. Unlike Bartimaeus, the members of the crowd have to be prodded to open their hearts to receive God's loving presence: "Jesus stood still and said, 'Call him here.' And they called the blind man, saying to him, 'Take heart; get up, he is calling you'" (Mark 10:49).

Response 4: In solitude the soul opens itself to receive the gift of contemplation, which is an ever-deepening connection with God.

The relationship between contemplation and meditation has often been confused. In *meditation* the mind reflects on some Christian truth or scriptural passage or personal experience, using words and ideas in more or less logical progression, with the aim of reaching a fuller understanding and personal acceptance of the truth considered. Or the mind concentrates on some experience in the light of Christian faith in order to reach some decision, an awareness of God's will or reaffirmation of faith.

In *contemplation*, however, the mind functions in the opposite way. Words and thoughts in logical progression, reflections with the aim of coming to new insights or decision, are exactly what the mind does not want. Indeed, it finds them to be a barrier. What is desired is the chance simply to express to God one's loving, hoping, trusting, or thanking, in as few words as possible. One becomes aware of the presence of God apprehended not by thought but by love. In Psalm 131 the author describes in colorful imagery what happens to the soul in contemplation: "I have calmed and quieted my soul like a weaned child with its mother; my soul is like the weaned child that is with me" (v. 2). The image of a satisfied and peaceful child "snuggled into the shoulder of a mother" describes the soul no longer lonely but intimately connected to God's abiding love.[3]

Most simply, contemplation is being loved by God from within oneself and loving him with all one's being in return. God's dwelling within the soul incites in it a limitless thirsting for God and freely invites the soul to interpersonal communion. God calls the soul to come, to remain in rest free from the burden and labor of all action, lovingly attentive to God's presence. When this invitation is embraced in faith, the soul responds by allowing God to be increasingly active within it.[4] In summary, in the words of St. John of the Cross, "Contemplation is none other than a secret, peaceful and loving inflow of God, which, if not hampered, fires the soul in the spirit of love."[5]

---

[3] See Walter Brueggemann and William H. Bellinger, *Psalms* (Cambridge: Cambridge University Press, 2014), 553.

[4] See clarifications by Francis K. Nemeck and Marie T. Coombs, *Contemplation* (Collegeville, MN: Liturgical Press, 1982), 36–43; also idem, *The Spiritual Journey: Critical Thresholds and Stages of Adult Spiritual Genesis* (Collegeville, MN: Liturgical Press, 1991), 89–95.

[5] St. John of the Cross, *The Dark Night,* Chap. 10, v. 6, in Kavanaugh and Otilio, *The Collected Works of St. John of the Cross*, 318. For the reflections of St. Teresa of Avila on the difference between meditation and contemplation, see Peter Tyler, *Teresa of Avila: Doctor of the Soul* (London: Bloomsbury, 2013), 189–95.

Empathy for the Lonely

Response 5: Christian love evokes empathy without exception toward people who are lonely.

When we open our hearts to receive God's love, we are moved to extend that love to our neighbor without exception: "You shall love the Lord your God with all your heart, and with all your soul, and with all your mind. This is the greatest and first commandment. And the second is like it: You shall love your neighbor as yourself" (Matt 22:37–39). This twofold love evokes empathy, which demands more of us than sympathy. A sympathetic person acknowledges another person's emotional difficulties and provides comfort and assurance. Empathy, on the other hand, is the ability not only to understand but actually to share the feelings of another. Empathetic persons put themselves "in the shoes of others" because they have faced the same problems. Thus, they are able to identify with people who are lonely because they themselves have experienced in their own lives the sadness, even trauma, of loneliness. We are called to do likewise.

We see this dynamic portrayed again in the story of the healing of Bartimaeus by Jesus. Bartimaeus has been forced into social isolation and loneliness, his dignity as a human person denied him. Jesus sees Bartimaeus and immediately empathizes with him. There is no condescension. As we are confronted with the local and global disease of loneliness, what can we learn from this incident? In brief, there are four interconnected important lessons for us about empathy in this incident.

- Jesus by his attitude and action reassures Bartimaeus that he is a person of dignity. He empowers Bartimaeus to no longer accept the cultural stigma that pressures those who are poor to remain silent.
- Jesus asks Bartimaeus what he would like: "What do you want me to do for you?" (Mark 10:51). Thinking about justice begins by listening to those who know about injustice.[6] Jesus, having been rejected by society, already threatened with death, knows from personal experience the fears and loneliness of

---

[6] See Mark Peel, *The Lowest Rung: Voices of Australian Poverty* (Cambridge: Cambridge University Press, 2003), 11.

Bartimaeus. Jesus is thus able to reach out to Bartimaeus and compassionately touch his inner pains of exclusion and loneliness. Bartimaeus feels that Jesus understands and is empowered to act with courage in the face of the crowd's rejection.

- Jesus reacts in two prophetic ways to Bartimaeus's plight: he acts *for* and *with* the victim in order to break the several layers of poverty. By his actions Jesus is forcefully saying to the members of the crowd that their prejudices are contrary to his teaching about the dignity of every person. Every person has the right to be respected. In this Jesus is an advocate *for* people who are oppressed by the prejudices of society. Second, Jesus stands *with* Bartimaeus and in listening to him he empowers him to come forward despite his rejection by the crowd. The incident significantly ends with the description of holistic healing: "And at once his sight returned and he followed him along the road" (Mark 10:52). No longer is Bartimaeus marginalized by society by being forced to sit at the *side* of the road. Now he is once more part of the community. He has the right to walk again "on the way" (Mark 10:52), his dignity restored.
- Through his actions Jesus illustrates that the healing of poverty must be holistic—social, cultural, economic, spiritual. Charity without the pursuit of justice is not holistic.[7]

Commitment to the Common Good

Response 6: Gospel love impels us to struggle collaboratively for the common good in society, though the cultural obstacles may be at times overwhelming; in so doing we are helping to remove the causes of loneliness in individuals and cultures.

The universal call to love one's neighbor commits us to struggle for the common good. Individualism and individual and corporate greed contradict this imperative (see Chapters 3 and 4). Given the cultural obstacles we face, the task may at times be too daunting. Then we are tempted to give up. But let the advice of Pope Francis be a source of

---

[7] See Gerald A. Arbuckle, *A "Preferential Option for the Poor": Application to Catholic Health and Aged Care Ministries in Australia* (Canberra: Catholic Health Australia, 2007), 32–34.

encouragement: "A single individual is enough for hope to exist, and that individual can be you. And then there will be another 'you,' and another 'you,' and it turns into an 'us.' . . . When there is an 'us' there begins a revolution [of tenderness]."[8]

Of the several lessons in the Good Samaritan parable (Luke 10:25–37), three are particularly relevant here.[9] First, *all creation is a gift of God.* All goods ultimately belong to God, and one must therefore not be exclusively attached to them. In the Good Samaritan story we see an example of Jesus's emphasis on sharing, even one's capital goods, with strangers who lack the necessities. The Samaritan, a trader in oil and wine, shares his capital with a person who has been socially declared a nonperson by both Jewish and Samaritan tradition. The lesson is that *all* economic decisions must be made through the lens of the imperative of an "option for the poor."[10] Careful discernment is required to find the right balance: planning for the future and at the same time risking giving from one's capital to fulfill the "option for the poor."

The second lesson of the parable flows from the first: *We are to use creation as stewards of God,* a truth forcefully spelled out by Pope Francis in *Laudato Si'.* To be a steward is to hold something in trust for another person; that is, to use what has been entrusted to us in ways determined by that person. For us, this means that we are called to co-create with God—to continue God's creation in this world in ways that reflect the dignity of God. This truth contains the core values of justice, mercy, compassion, empathy, excellence, and simplicity. Because all creation comes from God, we must use it as stewards of God.

The value of excellence, for example, flows from the fact that our gifts come from God and are to be used in God's service. *Excellence* in this sense covers all human endeavor, including research, that is at the service of God and humankind. It allows for no selfishness,

---

[8] Pope Francis, "Why the Only Future Worth Building Includes Everyone," address to TED (Technology, Entertainment, and Design), April 20, 2017.

[9] For further explanation, see Gerald A. Arbuckle, *Catholic Identity or Identities? Refounding Ministries in Chaotic Times* (Collegeville, MN: Liturgical Press, 2013), 179–98.

[10] See Arland J. Hultgren, *The Parables of Jesus: A Commentary* (Grand Rapids, MI: Eerdmans, 2000), 130–79.

mediocrity, or laziness in the use of our talents. The Samaritan exercises this value when he uses his experience of human nature in relating to the innkeeper. The inn is a den of thieves, and the head thief was the innkeeper, yet he was prepared to help the victim—for a price. Knowing what to expect from the innkeeper, the Samaritan simply bribed him in order to guarantee that the patient would be looked after and kept alive.[11]

Also note that the value of *simplicity* is not synonymous with ignorance that causes people to act imprudently. On the contrary, people with simplicity act with only the will of God in mind. Out of love God gives creation to us to be used as God wishes, namely, with the single-minded commitment to justice and love in service to others. There is to be no holding back, fuss, pretense, or double dealing in the simple-hearted as stewards of God's gifts. Such is the example of the Samaritan.

The third lesson is this: *Acting as stewards, we are called to collaborate to build communities of justice.* In Jewish tradition people are expected to work together in imitation of God's desire to build community with the Israelites: "I will place my dwelling in your midst, and I shall not abhor you. And I will walk among you, and will be your God, and you will be my people" (Lev 26:11–12). Values of unity, collaboration, dialogue, and mutuality are marks of an authentic community, as is evident in the way the Samaritan acts toward the victim and the innkeeper. *Mutuality* is an integral quality of any true community. The victim's pain of marginalization reminds the Samaritan of his own similar experience and his need for compassion. By first touching the ritually impure victim, the Samaritan heals his inner pain of rejection. The Samaritan gives from his own experience of vulnerability.

Response 7: The common good demands political and individual action to save the planet.

Under President Trump's direction the United States plans to withdraw from international treaties established to save the planet from further ecological disasters. Yet gospel love urgently impels us to

---

[11] See Bruce J. Malina and Richard L. Rohrbaugh, *Social Science Commentary on the Synoptic Gospels* (Minneapolis: Fortress Press, 1992), 346–48.

respond to the ecological crisis. Pope Francis writes in his encyclical *Laudato Si'*: "A sense of deep communion with the rest of nature cannot be real if our hearts lack tenderness, compassion and concern for our fellow human being. . . . Concern for the environment thus needs to be joined to a sincere love for our fellow human beings and an unwavering commitment to resolving the problems of society" (no. 91).

As Francis further observes, "The mindset which leaves no room for sincere concern for the environment is the same mindset which lacks concern for the inclusion of the most vulnerable members of society" (no. 196). From loving there will automatically follow an effective desire to do something—big or small—to relieve our climate crisis. "Love, overflowing with small gestures of mutual care . . . makes itself felt in every action that seeks to build a better world. . . . Social love is the key to authentic development" (no. 231). And, the pope writes, "I wish to insist that love always proves more powerful [than violence]" (no. 149). Pope Francis clearly states the gospel call to Christians to act for the common good of the earth and all of its inhabitants. "A great cultural, spiritual, and educational challenge stands before us, and it will demand we set out the path of renewal" (no. 202). The encyclical challenges us to action at two levels: political and individual.

Political Action

Francis is critical of governments that ignore what is happening. At the same time he recognizes that there is need for a robust role for governments in regulating their economies and protecting the environment according to ethical principles: "A strategy for real change calls for rethinking processes in their entirety, for it is not enough to include a few superficial ecological considerations while failing to question the logic which underlies present-day culture. A healthy politics needs to be able to take up this challenge" (no. 197).

Summarizing what he calls the "weak responses" of global leaders to the environmental crisis, Francis states: "The problem is that we still lack the culture needed to confront the crisis. We lack leadership capable of striking out on new paths and meeting the needs of the present with concern for all and without prejudices towards coming generations" (no. 53). Further, he points out that the strategy of buying and selling "carbon credits" can lead to a new form of speculation which would not help reduce the emission of polluting gases worldwide. This system seems to provide a quick and easy solution under the guise of a certain commitment to the environment, but in no way does it allow for the radical change which present circumstances require. (no. 171)

Francis suggests instead that large payments be advanced to developing countries to assist them in financing clean energy systems, and that richer countries dramatically reduce consumption.

Individual Action

"Not everyone is called to engage directly in political life" (no. 232). What then can we do as individuals? "The ecological crisis is also a summons to profound interior conversion" (no. 217). "An awareness of the gravity of today's cultural and ecological crisis must be translated into new habits" (no. 209). We can all do something—using public transport, car pooling, planting trees, cutting back on air conditioning and heating, turning off the lights, and recycling. "Reusing something instead of immediately discarding it, when done for the right reasons, can be an act of love which expresses our dignity" (no. 210).What do these statements mean for you and me?

Critiquing Prejudice and Discrimination

Response 8: Be alert! We can be blinded by prejudices that isolate people and cultures into loneliness.[12]

"I am," wrote Charles Lamb (1775–1834), "in plainer words, a bundle of prejudices—made up of likings and dislikings." He speaks for all of us. So often we fail to see the virtues of others, the richness of their

---

[12] See Gerald A. Arbuckle, *Earthing the Gospel: An Inculturation Handbook for Pastoral Workers* (Maryknoll, NY: Orbis Books, 1990), 147–66; and idem, *Fundamentalism at Home and Abroad: Analysis and Pastoral Responses* (Collegeville, MN: Liturgical Press, 2017), 164–69.

insights or the sufferings and even joys around us, simply because we are blinded by prejudice. The problem is exacerbated by the fact that as culture is a "silent language" we can absorb unconsciously the insidious prejudices already existing in our cultures. Prejudice, making conclusions without wanting to consider the facts, has two aspects: meaning and feeling.

The *meaning* aspect is commonly referred to as a stereotype, that is, a preformed image or picture that we have of things or people; it is a simple but faulty method of handling or grasping a complex world. By placing things and people into preformed categories we feel we are controlling a world that challenges our sense of order or meaning. The stereotype is a *pre*-judgment. It is the judgment that we make without first checking the facts about things or people. For example, because one Mexican immigrant breaks the law, we conclude that *all* Mexican immigrants are lawbreakers. The whole group is branded as undesirable. Stereotypes of the dangerous, immigrant "other" have serious consequences. Due to these stereotypes immigrants can become implicated in the public acceptance of policies and political decisions that violate their human rights. If that happens, they are further forced into individual and cultural loneliness.

However, prejudices are not just about stereotypes; they are stereotypes motivated by strong impulses. The *feeling* aspect is the blinding power in prejudice; that is, it obstructs objectivity and the openness of dialogue and forces the prejudiced person to see *only* what he or she wants to see, even to see things that are not there at all. Jesus on one occasion spoke about how the people received John the Baptist and himself: "For John came neither eating nor drinking, and they say: 'He has a demon'; the Son of Man came eating and drinking, and they say, 'Look, a glutton and a drunkard, a friend of tax collectors and sinners!'" (Matt 11:18–19). No matter what Jesus does, his enemies will see only evil in him.

Prejudice has many expressions, for example cultural, racial, sexual, religious, and class. Prejudice can quickly lead to discriminatory action. For example, sexism is the *prejudice* that someone is inferior in some way or another as a human person solely because that person belongs to a certain biological category. Sexual *discrimination*, like racism, assumes that members of a particular group, women, are objects to be freely used for the pleasure and the preservation of the dominant position of the other gender.

Actions against prejudice include the following:

- *Self-knowledge:* St. Augustine prayed: "That I may know myself, that I may know thee, O Lord." We can extend this prayer to: "That I may know my prejudices—all that blinds me to seeing you in others, for then I will know you better." Knowledge of oneself is not only the most difficult experience, but it is also inconvenient, for it often demands change in oneself. Those wishing to help others discover their prejudices must first be prepared to examine themselves. The blind cannot lead the blind to light.

- *Stand with others:* Since the vulnerable in society—for example, women, children, people with disabilities, elderly people—are frequently made powerless and stereotyped as useless, be prepared to stand with them. Pope Francis writes: "Doubly poor are those women who endure situations of exclusion, mistreatment and violence, since they are frequently less able to defend their rights. . . . Among the vulnerable . . . are the unborn children. . . . Yet defense of unborn life is closely linked to the defense of each and every other human right" (*Evangelii Gaudium,* nos. 212, 213).

- *Avoid ethnic jokes:* Ethnic jokes are common in all cultures. Are they funny? The object of an ethnic joke is to "put down" members of other cultures. At the same time, one's own group is presented as normal and superior. The practical conclusion is not to tell ethnic jokes. Take the chance to explain to others why such jokes can be unjust and deeply offensive, even if we do not intend them to be so.

- *Avoid offensive and sexist words:* Sexual harassment thrives in an atmosphere where women's rights and those of people belonging to LGBT communities are not respected. Our cultures are filled with words that assume the inferiority of women and people who are LGBT. They must be avoided, because they further reinforce cultures of oppression.

- *Complain about mass-media stereotyping:* Various forms of mass media commonly articulate and reinforce a culture's prejudices about minority groups. If you observe such a bias, complain where this is possible.

***Response 9: Be aware that we—as individuals or cultures—are
all capable of prejudicial fundamentalist behavior.***

Fundamentalism in its multiple different expressions is a
global reality. It is today vigorously and dangerously alive
at home and abroad. Fundamentalists are people who are
outraged when they see the world around them abandoning
the religious values they hold dear. They are fighting back
in the cause of what they consider truth. They are reacting to
threats to their identity in militant ways, whether in the use
of words and ideas or ballots or, in extreme cases, bullets
and bombs. The responses to these threats are simplistic, and
those who question them are intolerantly branded as enemies
of the truth.[13]

Fundamentalism is a reaction to uncertainty, to the "excess
of openness and choice" that accompanies modern life; it is
a way of setting boundaries[14] that claims to end uncertainty
by definitively terminating all arguments over interpretations.
Such interpretations of problems of the world and their solutions admit of no ambiguity. For example, Donald Trump,
when seeking the presidential nomination, repeatedly gave
simplistic solutions to complex political and economic problems facing the future of the United States.[15]

Pope Francis has clearly stated the dangers of fundamentalism, as
when he said in 2015:

Fundamentalism is a sickness that is in all religions. . . . Religious fundamentalism is not religious, because it lacks God.
It is idolatry, like idolatry of money. . . . We Catholics have
some—and not some, many—who believe in the absolute truth

---

[13] Gerald A. Arbuckle, *Fundamentalism at Home and Abroad: Analysis
and Pastoral Responses* (Collegeville, MN: Liturgical Press, 2017), xi.

[14] See Judith Nagata, "Beyond Theology: Toward an Anthropology of
'Fundamentalism,'" *American Anthropologist* 103/2 (2001): 481.

[15] Arbuckle, *Fundamentalism at Home and Abroad*, 9.

and go ahead dirtying the other with calumny, with disinformation, and doing evil.[16]

In 2016, he responded to Donald Trump's talk about a border wall by saying, "A person who thinks only about building walls, wherever they may be, and not building bridges, is not Christian. This is not the gospel."[17]

The fundamentalist pattern of militancy starts as a reaction to what is thought to be the infiltration of the community by secular or religious outsiders.[18] Fundamentalists believe their task is to make history accord with the orthodox principles of their traditional or civic religion. They are absolutely and intolerably certain they are right, demanding submission to "a totalitarian mindset which brooks of no opposition . . . an uncritical adherence to the creed."[19] Their ideological intolerance of dissent is expressed in various forms of physical, verbal, or political violence.[20] For example, verbal violence was evident in the Donald Trump campaign for the presidential nomination and in his presidency; his supporters feel so deeply threatened in their lives by dissenting voices that they encourage Trump to speak harshly of his opponents. Linda Gordon, at the end of her analysis of the militant and powerfully fundamentalist Ku Klux Klan in the 1920s, has this warning:

In the United States these movements and their populist, racist, demagogic, and incitatory orientation are a continuing part of our history, if sometimes dormant. The Klannish spirit—fearful,

---

[16] Pope Francis, comments to journalists on plane returning from Africa, quoted in John Henry-Westen, "Pope Francis Attacks 'Fundamentalist' Catholics, Dismisses Condom Ban as Unimportant" LifeSiteNews (November 30, 2015).

[17] Pope Francis, quoted in Daniel Burke, "Pope Suggests Trump 'Is Not Christian,'" CNN (February 18, 2016).

[18] See R. Scott Appleby, *The Ambivalence of the Sacred: Religion, Violence, and Reconciliation* (Oxford: Rowman and Littlefield, 2000), 87.

[19] Stuart Sim, *Fundamentalist World: The New Dark Age of Dogma* (Cambridge: Icon Books, 2004), 12.

[20] See Henry Olsen and Dante J. Scala, *The Four Faces of the Republican Party* (London: Palgrave Macmillan, 2016), 22–28.

angry, gullible to sensationalist falsehoods, in thrall to demagogic leaders and abusive language, hostile to science and intellectuals, committed to the dream that everyone can be a success
in business if they only try—lives on.[21]

**Response 10: Be alert to the fact that people who seek to hide
the truth by using the expression "fake news" destroy trust and
contribute to the loneliness of individuals and vulnerable people
and cultures.**

The expression "fake news" refers to news that is written and published with the deliberate intention to mislead in order to harm an
institution, cultural group, or individual, in order to gain politically
or financially; frequently the news is sensationally exaggerated in
ways that grab the attention of an audience. Fake or marginally real
news has existed for years, "but never before has it played such a
prominent role in an American [presidential] election [in 2016] and
its aftermath."[22] Another expression that has been briefly used in place
of "fake news" is "alternative facts."[23]

Pope Francis, in his 2018 Message for World Communications
Day, defined fake news as follows:

In general, it refers to the spreading of disinformation on line
or in the traditional media. It has to do with false information based on non-existent or distorted data meant to deceive
and manipulate the reader. Spreading fake news can serve to
advance specific goals, influence political decisions, and serve
economic interests.

The effectiveness of fake news is primarily due to its ability to *mimic* real news, to seem plausible. . . . This false but

---

[21] Linda Gordon, *The Second Coming of the KKK: The Ku Klux Klan of
the 1920s and the American Political Tradition* (New York: W. W. Norton,
2017), 208–9.

[22] Sabrina Tavernise, "As Lies Spread, More Readers Shrug at Truth,"
Times Digest (December 7, 2016), 3.

[23] An expression used by Donald Trump's senior counsellor Kellyanne
Conway in an effort to support Trump's obviously inaccurate statement that
his inauguration had drawn the largest audience in history. See E. J. Dionne,
Norman J. Ornstein, and Thomas E. Mann, *One Nation after Trump* (New
York: St. Martin's Press, 2017), 37–64.

believable news is "captious," inasmuch as it grasps people's attention by appealing to stereotypes and common social prejudices, and exploiting instantaneous emotions like anxiety, contempt, anger and frustration. (no. 1)

Donald Trump has frequently applied the expression "fake news" to many situations that may inconveniently embarrass him or his policies. *The Economist* reports, "There is often more fakery than truth in a tweet from President Donald Trump."[24] This has helped to make him "the leading exponent of 'post-truth' politics—a reliance on assertions that 'feel true' but have no basis in fact."[25] Trump and others repeatedly claim, without proof, that people who create fake news are all part of a massive conspiracy—that people in the media, and even people in highly vulnerable groups such as the poor, immigrants, and refugees, are conspiring to create moral and intellectual corruption at the local and global levels.[26] And these people must be punished! Fundamentalist movements thrive on creating fear—fear of the "other." The sad lesson of history is that fear and contempt are the most predictably powerful promoters for galvanizing one group to move against another in society or even the church.

Fake news, as defined, is deliberate lying, that is, according to the *Catechism of the Catholic Church*, it "consists in saying what is false with the intention of deceiving one's neighbour" (no. 2508). Not only is it an affront to the dignity of the person or groups of people deceived, but it is a violation against God, who is truth itself. Fake news also destroys trust within society. As Sabrina Tavernise comments: "Fake news, and the proliferation of raw opinion that passes for news, is creating confusion, punching holes in what is true, causing a kind of funhouse effect that leaves the reader doubting everything."[27] Moreover, innocent and vulnerable people, such as refugees and migrants, are powerless to contradict fake news published against them. Purveyors of fake news assume that many readers are too busy, unable

---

[24] "Can the Trump Boom Last?" *The Economist* (December 16, 2017), 10.

[25] "Art of the Lie," *The Economist* (September 20, 2016), 11. See also comments by Heidi Schlumpf, "Church Teaching Is Clear: 'Fake News,' Other Untruths are Wrong, Dangerous," *National Catholic Reporter* (December 5, 2017).

[26] See Joshua Green, *Devil's Bargain: Steve Bannon, Donald Trump, and the Storming of the Presidency* (New York: Penguin Press, 2017), 9.

[27] Tavernise, "As Lies Spread, More Readers Shrug at Truth," 3.

or unwilling to check the accuracy of what is published. A commentator writes that there is "an alarming number of people who tend to be credulous and form beliefs based on the latest thing they've read," but the "wider problem is fake news has the effect of getting people not to believe real things."[28]

Individual Gestures: Potential to Influence

Response 11: Remember, a simple greeting to a stranger can relieve his or her loneliness.

Just before Christmas Day last year I made my usual weekly visit to the local supermarket. There were crowds of elderly people struggling to find space to do their holiday shopping. So many looked weary and worried, but this scene changed quite suddenly and in an unexpected way. John, a man with learning disabilities employed by the supermarket to gather used shopping trolleys, appeared. As he spontaneously and smilingly greeted harassed shoppers, I noticed their faces change. People relaxed. In response to his greeting, "Happy Christmas!" they smiled, cheerfully greeting him in return. It was a touching sight. What a Gospel lesson! A simple greeting can alleviate loneliness, even for a brief moment.

Another example of the power of a greeting comes from the Gospel of Luke: One day Jesus "was teaching in one of the synagogues on the Sabbath" (Luke 13:10). He was preoccupied with trying to convince skeptical synagogue officials of the truth of his mission. Then he noticed "a woman with a spirit that had crippled her for eighteen years. She was bent over and was quite unable to stand up straight" (vv. 11–12). Her painful physical complaint had also caused her to be socially marginalized by society, and thus she was lonely. Yet, "when Jesus saw her, he called her over and said, 'Woman, you are set free from your ailment'" (v. 12). He then "laid his hands on her [and] immediately she stood up straight and began praising God" (v. 13). Her socially caused loneliness ceased. At the same time, however, the religious leaders remained unconvinced, isolated within their ideological tribal borders.

---

[28] Michael Lynch, professor of philosophy at the University of Connecticut, cited in ibid.

Response 12: Receive without prejudice migrants and parishioners with cultures different from our own, as Christ would wish.

You shall allot it [land] as an inheritance for yourselves and for the aliens who reside among you. . . . They shall be to you as citizens of Israel. (Ezek 47:22)

The "temptation of exclusivism and cultural fortification" has arisen among Catholics at times in the past, "but the Holy Spirit always helped us to overcome it, guaranteeing a constant opening to the other," the Pope said during a meeting with the directors of migrant and refugee services from the bishops' conferences of Europe.

"I will not hide my concern about the signs of intolerance, discrimination and xenophobia that are seen in different regions of Europe," the Pope said. "These often are motivated by distrust and fear of the other, the different, the stranger."[29]

Many immigrants to Western countries today, particularly Hispanic and Muslim peoples, often encounter xenophobia and discrimination, sometimes made worse by racist politicians and populist speakers.[30] They tend to come from poor, rural areas; most are poorly educated; many are brown. They speak the language of the wider society either poorly or not at all, so they find it difficult to get employment; their children struggle at school. They congregate in poor districts, often in state-owned housing. They desperately need to be welcomed and assisted to integrate into the wider society. This is a lengthy process. It requires not just efforts by immigrant peoples themselves, but the good will of the host society and its willingness to eliminate

---

[29] "Pope Francis Strongly Criticises Catholics Who Refuse to Accept Migrants," *Catholic Herald* (September 22, 2017).

[30] In the days following the successful referendum to exit the European Union, the reports of hate crime increased by 57 percent in Britain, compared with the same period four weeks earlier. Polish and other minorities were targeted. Cardinal Vincent Nichols expressed concern: "This upsurge of racism, of hatred towards others is something we must not tolerate." Liz Dodd, "Cardinal Nichols Condemns Upsurge in Racist Attacks Post Brexit," *The Tablet* (June 29, 2016).

institutional prejudice and discrimination and to guarantee legal and civil rights to immigrants. Where there is identity integration, there is authentic multiculturalism.

In *Evangelii Gaudium* Pope Francis exhorts us:

> Migrants present a particular challenge for me, since I am the pastor of a Church without frontiers. . . . For this reason, I exhort all countries to a generous openness which, rather than fearing the loss of local identity, will prove capable of creating new forms of cultural synthesis. How beautiful are those cities which overcome paralyzing mistrust, integrate those who are different and make this very integration a new factor of development! (no. 210)

Referring particularly to Muslim immigrants, he writes:

> We Christians should embrace with affection and respect Muslim immigrants to our countries [and therefore also in our parishes] in the same way that we hope and ask to be received and respected in countries of Islamic tradition. (no. 253)

Self-Care

Response 13: The role of prophetic ministries, for example, practical theologians, is to critique cultures, including that of the church, according to gospel values. Their task is often a lonely one and to maintain balance they need special gifts.[31]

Advice for self-care:

- Relish times of prayerful solitude: "Be still and know that I am God." (Ps 46:10)
- Choose wise mentors.
- Develop dialogue skills.

---

[31] See Walter Brueggemann, *The Prophetic Imagination* (Philadelphia: Fortress Press, 1978).

- Feed the imagination: In order to remain creative, prophetic gospel people need space to relax and nourish their imagination. Depending on their circumstances, people may be enriched, for example, by reading, walking, listening to music, watching the sun set, meeting friends. Moments of insight may come at the oddest times if we are prepared to create the space for them.

The Humor of Christ

One final piece of advice is to cultivate a sense of humor. This is perhaps the most under-appreciated gift of Jesus Christ.[32] He has a sense of the incongruous, which is at the heart of all true humor. On the one hand, he is the king; yet on the other hand, he lives as one who has nowhere to lay his head. He is charged to do the will of the Father; yet everything appears to end in disaster. Christ accepts the incongruous because of his own inner detachment. He does not take himself too seriously.

So also must it be with devotees of the gospel. All they can do is do their best and let the outcome be in the hands of the Father. The moment gospel ministers become overly anxious about the results of their work, let them sit down and laugh at their stupidity, at their plain forgetfulness of the mystery of God's providential presence. The foundation of a sense of humor is detachment and humility. We simply do not have all the answers. When we think we do, then we are playing God—and that is immensely incongruous! No one has the full truth about anything. There is always something to learn from other disciplines. As Pope Francis says: "Even people who can be considered dubious on account of their errors have something to offer which must not be overlooked" (*Evangelii Gaudium*, no. 236). God can move in ways that are incomprehensible and mysterious to the most skilled of human beings.

---

[32] See Gerald A. Arbuckle, *Laughing with God: Humor, Culture, and Transformation* (Collegeville, MN: Liturgical Press, 2008), 1–18, 32–41, 70–90.

Index